THE COMPTON SHUFFLE

AN INTROSPECTIVE LOOK AT PREVENTING GANG VIOLENCE AND MASS SHOOTINGS IN SCHOOLS

EDWARD GILLIAM

The author may be contacted via the following:
http://www.bolaffirmation.com
edwardgiliamofficial@youtube.com
edwardgilliam71@facebook.com
edwardgilliamofficial@instagram.com
edwardgilliamofficial@tiktok.com

https://www.bookwritingexperts.com/

eBook: 978-1-955901-56-7

Paperback: 978-1-955901-54-3

Hardback: 978-1-955901-55-0

DEDICATION

To my dearest Mom, Maxine,

In the tapestry of my life, you are the most vibrant thread, weaving warmth, love, and unwavering support into every moment. This book stands not only as a testament to my journey but as a tribute to the guiding light you've been in my life.

Your unwavering belief in my dreams has been the cornerstone of my strength. Through your boundless encouragement and unselfish love, you've cultivated the roots from which my aspirations have grown and blossomed.

In your embrace, I found solace, in your wisdom, I found guidance, and in your laughter, I found joy. You've painted the world with colors of empathy, understanding, and resilience, showing me the true essence of compassion and determination.

Your endless sacrifices and unspoken sacrifices have carved a path for my ambitions. With every page of this book, I hope to reflect a fraction of the boundless inspiration you've instilled in me.

This book is as much yours as it is mine. For it's your spirit that dances through its pages, your love that resonates within its words, and your nurturing presence that will forever linger in every chapter.

With all my love and gratitude,

Edward Robin Gilliam Jr.

ACKNOWLEDGMENT

I would like to thank my mother, Maxine Gilliam, and my father, Edward Gilliam, Sr., who have always been in my corner and have been with me through thick and thin. I would also like to thank my daughter, Robin Gilliam, and her mother, Lark Gilliam, who stayed with me through all the ups and downs in dealing with my schools in Compton.

I would also like to thank Superintendent Dr. McKinley Nash for giving me my start in school administration. I thank the Honorable Judge Skiers, Honorable Judge Rudy Diaz, and the Honorable Judge Fruin, who worked endlessly with my students at Centennial High School and Compton High School, participating in the curriculum teaching students about the law and the career opportunities available to them. I thank Dr. Cranford Scott, who helped me to stay alive and attended to my well-being healthwise, allowing me to be an effective principal and to make the necessary changes to stop violence in the schools and to increase student achievement, graduation rates, test scores and increased enrollment of my students into four-year universities and colleges. I thank former Mayor Omar Bradley for his tremendous support and intellectual genius as he tried with great success to turn the city around. I thank the Board of Education's former members, Toi Jackson, LynDynally, Saul Langster, and Aman Rah, for their votes in my support. I thank Harol Cebrun for his support as Superintendent of Schools. I thank Gladys Russel, Karen Mackey, Geoffrey, and T'Wana Gillison, and Felicitas Paredes for being involved parents who supported my programs in Compton and in my career. I also thank Ellery Street, Pat Sneed, Donald Singleton, Maxine Kemp, and Mitch Williams as teachers who went the distance in encouraging me to stay the course and to do the right thing in the face of tremendous odds and to focus on things that supported the students. Thank you all, jointly and severally, for helping me to become successful in implementing methodologies and programs that led to safer schools without violence and school shootings.

TABLE OF CONTENTS

ABOUT THE AUTHOR

Edward Gilliam, a dedicated educator and advocate, served as the principal at two of the most challenging schools in America. With a passion for transforming education and addressing societal issues, Mr. Gilliam's journey has been marked by innovative methodologies aimed at creating safer environments for students, schools, and communities.

As a visionary leader, Mr. Gilliam implemented strategies that extend beyond school walls, offering solutions applicable to schools, districts, parents, students in K-12, colleges, universities, governmental agencies, law enforcement, Congress, local governing bodies, and businesses of all sizes. His work recognizes the pervasive impact of gang violence and mass shootings, affecting every aspect of our lives – from schools and malls to churches, post offices, and workplaces.

In his comprehensive resource guidebook, Mr. Gilliam provides insights from his experiences and research. Recognizing the global nature of gang-related issues, the book serves as a valuable tool for individuals and communities worldwide. It underscores the importance of collective awareness and action to address the root causes and implement effective solutions, fostering a safer and more secure living environment for everyone.

Join Edward Gilliam on this journey towards understanding, prevention, and reduction of the pressing issues of gang violence and mass shootings and contribute to creating a world where safety and well-being are paramount.

Page Blank Intentionally

INTRODUCTION

COMPTON SHUFFLE: A History in Poetry

In Compton's heart, where history resides,
A tale unfolds, with twists and tides.
From Spanish grants to pioneers bold,
A city's story, through ages untold.

Juan Dominguez, in eighteen-four,
Received the land by the ocean's shore.
Rancho San Pedro, a vast domain,
where dreams would sprout like golden grains.

Griffith Compton, a pioneer's name,
Led settlers here, their fortune to claim
From Gibbonsville to Compton's embrace,
A thriving community found its place.

Challenges faced, in harsh weather's grip,
Yet they persevered, with a determined grip.
In search of fuel, they ventured agar,
To mountains near Pasadena, beneath the stars.

Incorporation, in eighteen eighty-eight,
A city's birth, a promising fate.
Five hundred strong, they stood as one.
The journey of Compton had just begun.

Richland Farms, a gift so grand,
A fertile haven on donated land.
Families thrived, with livestock and more,
A place to build, to love, to explore.

The twenties brought change, like wings unfurled,
With an airport, college, and a growing world.
New charter embraced, progress in sight,
Compton's future was shining bright.

Yet shadows loomed, a dark decree,
In nineteen twenty-one, exclusion we'd see.

Racial divide, a painful scar,
A chapter in history, distant and far.

Then in '33, the earth did shake,
Disaster struck, hearts did ache.
Schools crumbled, the city rebuilt,
In unity, its spirit was rebuilt.

The fifties and sixties brought a change,
As segregation laws began to estrange.
Supreme Court's call, justice on display,
Compton's diversity, began to sway.

In Compton's story, highs and lows,
A journey of resilience, the tale it shows.
From its roots in the past to the present so bright,
Compton's spirit shines with enduring light.

Through trials and triumphs, it stands tall,
A city with a history, embracing all.
In unity and hope, let us forever be,
Compton, a place, where dreams roam free.
In Compton's shifting tapestry we find,
A history complex, with layers intertwined.
African Americans once ignored and denied,
Found their place, and their voices amplified.

Centennial High School, a beacon of hope,
For African American students, a way to cope.
City officials' actions, sometimes unclear,
But change was brewing, year by year.

In fifty-eight, men ran for the Council's seat,
African American voices, determined and neat.
By sixty-one, a milestone achieved,
Compton's first Councilman, they proudly received.

Douglas Dollarhyde, then mayor he became,
Breaking barriers, staking his claim.
African Americans and Mexican Americans, too,
Found their roles in leadership, strong and true.

Doris A. Davis, in '73, took the throne,
African American mayor, paving the unknown.
Compton's demographics, a seismic shift,
African Americans' influence, a powerful lift,

But "white flight" came in the mid-fifties tide,
As fear of integration made some decide.
Compton's black population soared high,
A sought-after suburb under the sky.

Spacious houses, streets lined with grace,
African American middle class, finding their place.
But challenges emerged, a downward trend,
Economic struggles, a city to mend.

Unemployment rose, poverty took hold,
Crime surged, neighborhoods turned cold.
Street gangs emerged, an infamous scene,
Compton's struggles, profound and unseen.

The Crips, a name known far and wide,
With youth at the helm, they took their stride.
Raymond Washington, with fists to fight,
Built a gang that would reach a formidable height.

Stanley Williams, a thirst for might,
From New Orleans to LA's city lights.
With Washington's vision, they joined the quest,
To shape the Crips, they did their best.

From "Cribs" to "Crips", the name did shift,
Origins debated, their identity adrift.
With canes or a message to convey,
The Crips emerged in the light of day.

Today, they stand, a formidable force,
With members many they stay on course.
Their influence vast, their actions renowned,
In blue attire, their presence is found.

The Bloods, in red, became their foes,

From Piru Street, their story arose.
A rivalry born, with history intertwined,
In Compton's streets, their paths defined.

Compton's journey, a tale of change and strife,
A city's transformation, a complex life.
From humble beginnings to heights so grand,
Compton's legacy, forever to stand.

In the 1980s, Compton's fame did ignite,
But not for reasons entirely bright.
Gang culture, larger than life, tool hold,
A tale of struggle, and stories untold,

Through the '70s and '80s, a scene did brew,
Innovative music, perspectives anew.
Hip-hop artists, Compton's own, they rose,
Their voices strong, their stories enclosed.

Eazy-E, Ice Cube, Dr. Dre's fame,
In Compton's heart, they staked their claim.
Andre Young, from these streets, emerged,
A music producer, whose talents surged.

Their music spoke of gritty realities,
Challenges faced in tough localities.
Gang culture's weight, they dared to portray,
Through their lyrics, in an unfiltered way.

Extreme hip-hop, in the mid-80s', defined,
A subgenre born from a turbulent mind.
Compton's artists, their voices profound,
In the world of music, their stories resound.

So Compton's legacy, complex and vast,
In the '80s, it make a lasting contrast.
From gang culture's shadow to music's stage,
Compton's story, an ever-evolving page.

WHY DID I CHOOSE TO COME HERE

I served as principal at two of the most challenging schools in America. These educational institutions were inundated with gang-related issues, leaving teachers, staff, and students afraid of both coming to school and pursuing an education. However, I worked tirelessly to transform these environments and thereby leave a proud legacy.

What's critical here is that both the city and the school district experienced high turnover of staff and administrators leading to interrupted systems and lack of continuity throughout both the city and the school district. This book serves as an attempt to share my experiences and insights, a cautionary work where I hope to provide guidance on creating safe environments within schools and communities and, in the process, curb gang violence and mass shootings.

It's been years since the tragedy struck Columbine High School in Colorado. Two gunmen took the lives of 13 people and left a city emotionally scarred. Unfortunately, such incidents remain relevant today, despite steps taken by schools to safeguard student's lives. The core issue lies in the complex root causes of mass shootings and gang violence, which encompass a gamut of factors, including inadequate education, police violence, racism, discrimination, unemployment, fatherless families, female-headed households, social media, music influences, gender identity issues, and feminism. In this book, I will share my thoughts on these matters and propose strategies that will better position schools, local communities, the nation, and global communities to significantly reduce the impact that these issues have on our school systems, and which directly or indirectly contributes to mass shootings and gang violence.

One former student vividly recalls the events of April 20, 1999, at Columbine High School, when an explosion followed by gunfire forever altered the course of his life. The echoes of gunshots reverberated through the hallways as the gunmen closed in, eventually entering the library, and committing barbaric acts. Despite the hope for someone with a firearm to intervene, the epic tragedy unfolded. In the wake of such incidents, many schools in 31 states have authorized teachers and staff to carry weapons on campus. While practical measures like surveillance systems, cameras, lockdown drills, metal detectors, and school police officers have been implemented, there is a glaring component missing from the equation: mental health support and funding for programs catering to young children and students. Furthermore, it is vitally important to inculcate in young minds the belief that they can achieve the American dream without resorting to violence or sacrificing their lives and freedom. A multi-pronged approach that focuses on prevention is necessary in guiding our youth toward making better choices.

We can no longer ignore the shootings and violence that occur daily in urban areas like Harlem, Compton, St. Louis, and Chicago, yet remain unseen due to limited public outcry or media coverage. While these urban ghettos have long grappled with high crime rates, their struggles often go unnoticed. However, regardless of the location, these killings must stop.

The title of this book, "The Compton Shuffle," aptly reflects the situation, as evidenced by a letter from the acting state auditor to California's leadership in October 2022. This letter highlights the ongoing and persistent challenges faced by the city of Compton, a scourge that has spilled over into its schools. "The Compton Shuffle" narrates how I managed to put an end to violence in my schools, with the hope that others will find it a valuable resource for preventing and deterring violence, including mass shootings and gang-related incidents, in their own educational systems and institutions.

The book is divided into four parts to provide a comprehensive perspective:

Part One: I first take a deep dive and describe the initial conditions at Centennial High School and Compton High School in 1991 and 1996, respectively, exploring the current state of school violence and shootings nationwide. This section dissects data, identifies patterns, and critically examines societal and psychological factors contributing to this radical and alarming trend, accompanied by informative charts illustrating the rise of school violence.

Part Two: This section focusses on rap/gangster or drill music and how it affects behavioral patterns among young men and women and its corresponding effects causing gang violence and mass shootings. Also, it focuses on other social factors such as police violence, unemployment factors, legislation that caused the family breakdown in the black community and thus the ability of women to replace fathers with big daddy government particularly in the black community. I outline practical steps for school administrators, educators, parents, and the community at large on how to identify warning signs regarding gang affiliations and mental health issues in order to foster a nurturing and supportive school culture and provide crucial support to at-risk students. The programs I implemented at both schools serve as examples of effective methods to exert control over the school environment, improve graduation rates, and reduce the dropout problem.

Part Three: Here I emphasize the value and importance of mental health support in schools, highlighting the significance of accessible mental health resources and interventions for students facing emotional distress, trauma, or behavioral challenges. Additionally, I address the difficulties faced by both young boys and men in society, advocating for greater support and encouraging those in power to afford opportunities to those in need and the importance of facilitating fathers to remain in the home. Fathers are an important element in the maturation of young boys, and without the leadership of men in the home in turn will result in more mass shootings and gang violence.

Part Four: I felt that it was incumbent to discuss ways to enhance school security measures, as it became clear that there is no one-size-fits-all solution. This portion explores time-tested and proven approaches to improve physical security, crisis response planning, and collaboration with law enforcement, drawing on the programs I set up and executed at Centennial High School and Compton High School as valuable examples. No comprehensive program would be complete without stressing the importance of community engagement and advocacy in fostering safer schools and a more secure future. In this section, I underscore the need for collaborative efforts involving parents, community members, law enforcement, and policymakers to create a safer educational environment.

As a former school principal, I am deeply committed to the physical, emotional, and social well-being of our youth and the preservation of schools as places of growth and learning, this literary work aims to contribute to a national dialogue. Together, we can work towards creating lasting solutions that prevent school violence and shootings in America. By implementing these strategies and joining forces, we can build a safer and more promising future for generations to come. This is my story, an odyssey spanning nearly three decades, and I hope you find it both compelling and informative. It shares the successful strategies I employed to establish peaceful and conducive learning environments, offering a path to counter mass shootings and gang violence in schools. I implore you to take this journey with me, armed with knowledge, compassion, and dedication, as we forge a brighter tomorrow for our children and students.

PART I: HUB CITY AND THE CREATION OF THE CRIPS AND BLOODS IN LOS ANGELES AND COMPTON

Compton, which is located just south of Los Angeles and is sometimes referred to as Hub City because of its central location, has a rich history that is distinguished by its continuous battle against gang and gun violence. Its origins may be found in 1784, when Juan Dominguez was awarded a sizable portion of land in the present-day Compton area, totaling over 75,000 acres, by the Spanish Crown. While serving as soldiers, Dominguez and his family partitioned and sold portions of this land to settlers who were just moving in. The Dominguez family's name endures in the area, and this vast property was afterwards dubbed Rancho San Pedro. Not to mention, the South Compton neighborhood of Dominguez Hills got its name from Dominguez himself. The tree that formerly marked Rancho San Pedro's northern boundary is a painful reminder of this past and may be found at the corner of Poppy Street.

Imagine that in 1867, Griffith Dickinson Compton came to the region with a party of thirty pioneers. From Stockton, California, these families embarked on a wagon train journey in quest of work prospects. After one of the tract donors, the hamlet was first known as Gibbonsville until changing its name to Comptonville. The name was shortened to Compton to avoid

9

confusion with another Comptonville in Yuba County. Attempting to obtain fuel was extremely difficult for these pioneers, and they had to struggle to cultivate the land in inclement weather. To gather firewood, they had to travel to the neighboring mountains near Pasadena for two weeks on end!

The pioneers decided to stay in Compton in spite of these unfavorable circumstances and occurrences. They realized in 1887 that improving municipal government was necessary to ensure the town's continued existence. Town meetings followed, and in January 1888, a petition supporting Compton's incorporation was delivered to the Los Angeles County Board of Supervisors. On May 11th, 1888, the petition was presented to the state assembly, and as a result, the City of Compton—which had a population of only 500— was incorporated. The first meeting of the City Council took place on May 14, 1888.

As the city's population grew, Mr. Compton kindly gave land to the city in 1889, naming it Richland Farms and restricting its use to agriculture. Residents could raise families and care for cattle on the roomy residential lots made available by this land allocation.

Although Compton was not a good place for large-scale farming, the land allowed people to work and support their families.

The terrain of Compton saw a significant transformation in the 1920s. City officials moved City Hall to Alameda Street, the Compton Junior College was founded, and the Compton Airport opened. Voters approved and ratified a new municipal charter during this period. But it's crucial to remember that Compton's population was predominately Caucasian prior to World War II. In 1921, the city enacted extremely restrictive rules to bar African Americans and other people of color from living in the municipality—a regrettable and shameful episode in Compton's history.

Tragic events occurred after a powerful earthquake shook Compton in March 1933. Numerous people lost their lives in this disaster, which also severely damaged the core commercial sector and extensively destroyed schools. The 1950s and 1960s saw a significant change in Compton's racial makeup as a result of the Supreme Court's ruling that housing that was exclusive to one race was unlawful. The first African American families arrived in Compton at this crucial time. However, elected city authorities first disregarded and neglected African Americans despite the shifting demography. The building of Centennial High School, which was intended to serve the expanding African American student body, was one noteworthy exception. Even the replacement of the Compton Police Department with the Los Angeles County Sheriff's Department was debated by the City Council; this was perceived as an attempt to keep African Americans out of law enforcement.

Slowly but surely, things started to shift. African American males began running for City Council in 1958, and the first African American councilman was elected in 1961 as a result. Following the election of two African American men and one Mexican American to the local school board, this momentum was furthered with the election of Douglas Dollarhyde as the first African American mayor. Then, in 1973, Doris A. Davis defeated Dollarhyde and became the first African American woman to hold the position of mayor of a major American city. With more than 90% of the population being black by the early 1970s, Compton was home to one of the highest concentrations of African Americans in the whole nation.

But in the middle of the 1950s, there was a movement called "white flight," in which white families left their areas quickly because of shifting racial demography. Due to their dissemination of anxieties about property prices falling in the face of racial integration, real estate brokers contributed to this migration. As a result, Compton's black population increased dramatically from 5% in 1940 to 40% in 1960. Compton was a sought-after suburb for Los Angeles's African American middle class by the 1970s. Compton's streets are lined with comparatively large and attractive single-family homes, which bear witness to the wealth that once surrounded the area.

Because of this, Compton's history—from its modest origins to its current degree of racial and socioeconomic complexity—is an interesting tapestry of struggles, changes, and resiliency, making it a special and dynamic chapter in American history.

But eventually, the town's illustrious past started to disappear, and unexpected components replaced its regal past. Several factors contributed to this decline's acceleration, including the tax base's slow degradation (which was already declining because there weren't many commercial properties). African Americans started to make progress in their political representation, even while Caucasians continued to dominate both law enforcement and politics. Sadly, the rate of unemployment for African American men rose to 10% at that period, nearly twice the national average.

Consequently, Compton became a notorious hotspot for violent gangs and abandoned areas because of rising unemployment and poverty in the 1970s, which also led to an increase in crime and the formation of street gangs. In 1969, Stanley Williams and Raymond Washington formed the Crips, one of the most well-known and blatantly violent street gangs in Southern Central Los Angeles. The Crips, who were first organized to defend their neighborhood, have grown to become one of the biggest and most infamous gangs in the country.

Imagine a period when the average age of a member of the Crips gang was only seventeen. One of the first members, Raymond Washington, accepted the legitimacy and significance of gang culture but at first avoided using weapons like knives and guns, preferring to fight with his fists. But three years after the Crips were founded, Washington was found guilty of robbery and given a five-year sentence to a dual vocational facility. He aggressively sought out new gang members while incarcerated, which cemented the Crips' expansion.

Stanley Williams, another important character in the history of the Crips, showed an early desire for authority. Williams, who was raised in New Orleans, moved to Los Angeles when his father abandoned him, and his single mother took care of him. When Williams arrived in Los Angeles, he was approached by a youngster of the same age, and the result of the encounter was that the other child had a black eye. Williams maintained this aggressiveness throughout his time in high school, when he founded his own young gang. Afterwards, he teamed up with Washington to drive the Crips' development.

The group's original motivation for organizing was to defend their community. However, when the original 30 members multiplied, the Crips quickly split into two separate groups, and both groups kept growing. They were formerly known as the "Cribs," which was a play on "Avenue Cribs" or just "Cribs." This change from "Cribs" to "Crips" is debatable, though. In his autobiography "Blue Rage Black Redemption," Stanley Williams claims that many people mispronounced "Cribs" as "Crips," which caused them to take on the latter moniker.

Diverse theories exist concerning the etymology of the term "Crips." The word "Crips" is a shorthand for those who claim that members would appear to be disabled by walking with canes or using their weapons as makeshift canes. A few others propose that the term "Crips" stands for "Community Revolution in Progress" and that the Black Panther Party was involved in the gang's founding. Williams, however, refutes this relationship in his writing.

With an estimated membership of between thirty and thirty-five thousand, the Crips are currently among the biggest and most well-known gangs in the country. Their impact is widespread, with multiple sets taking place around the nation. The Crips are well-known for their violent and unrelenting demeanor, their participation in a range of illegal operations, including drug sales, robberies, and murders, as well as their distinctive blue clothing, which makes them easily recognized.

It makes sense that the Bloods, the Crips' opponents, would choose to wear red given that the Crips have made blue their official color. There's an interesting and unexpected parallel between the Bloods and the Crips' past. Sylvester Scott and Vincent Owens started the group, which at first went by the name Piru Street Boys, and they were established on Piru Street in Compton in 1971. City Hall

During a certain period, the Piru Street Boys forged an alliance with the Crips and operated as a faction within the Crips for approximately two years. However, during this time, they faced considerable hostility from rival Crip factions, ultimately leading to inexorable conflict. Feeling outnumbered and under pressure, the Piru Street Boys made a pivotal decision—to completely disassociate themselves from the Crips. This marked the birth of their independent gang, famously known as the Bloods.

The origins of this transformation can be traced back to a tragic movie theater incident. A group of Crips brutally attacked one of their own members over a disputed leather jacket. Shockingly, the individual refused to give up the jacket and paid the ultimate price, succumbing to a fatal beatdown. The Piru Street Boys were outraged by this harrowing incident, prompting them to convene a crucial meeting with neighboring gangs. Together with the Leaders Park Hustlers, the Denver Lanes, and the Bishops, they forged a new entity—the Bloods. This alliance swiftly gained notoriety for offering protection against the dominant Crips.

Identifiable by the vivid red clothing they proudly wear, the Bloods prominently display a five-point star, symbolizing values such as love, truth, peace, freedom, and justice.

Another distinctive element of their attire is a red bandana, usually worn on the right side. Members of the Bloods would often derogatorily refer to Crips as "Crabs." The rivalry between these two formidable groups continues to this very day.

However, it was in the 1980s that Compton garnered widespread attention when the romanticization of gang culture took on "bigger than life" proportions. Throughout the 1970s and 1980s, this culture gave birth to innovative musical expressions. Compton became the home of renowned hip-hop artists like Eazy-E, Ice Cube, Dr. Dre, and The Game. Andre Young, a Compton native, rose to fame as a prominent music producer within the hip-hop industry. From Compton, artists emerged who used their music to convey the gritty realities and challenges of gang culture, ultimately contributing to the emergence of a subgenre known as extreme hip-hop in the mid-1980s.

Piru Blood Gang Originated in Compton in Centennial High School's Attendance Area on Piru Street

Gangster rap, a genre that arguably pioneered this cultural movement, found its pinnacle in the iconic group known as N.W.A. This legendary ensemble boasted prominent members such as Dr. Dre, Ice Cube, Eazy E, MC Green, and the group itself. The inception of N.W.A traces back to 1987 when Eazy E, a high school dropout and former Compton drug dealer, established Ruthless Records. Remarkably, the label was initially funded with illicit drug money, and Eazy E partnered with industry veteran Jerry Heller. Eazy E then recruited Dr. Dre, a former member of the World Class Wrecking Crew, and Ice Cube, who had made his mark in the rap group CIA, to contribute their songwriting talents to the fledgling label.

Their inaugural single, "Panic Zone," dropped on August 13, 1987, featuring all three founding members alongside the new addition, DJ Yella. This track, along with "Boys in the Hood," would become part of their groundbreaking album "Straight Out of Compton." This album also featured revamped versions of "Eight Ball" and "Dope Men." Its release in 1988 propelled gangster rap to national prominence and symbolized the essence of hip-hop culture. However, it also coincided with a disturbing surge in Compton's local crime rate. The city witnessed an alarming murder rate, reaching nearly 91 homicides per 100,000 residents. This dire situation was further exacerbated by the Rodney King rots of 1996.

The catalyst for these riots was the acquittal of four Los Angeles policemen involved in the brutal beating of Rodney King, an African American motorist. This incident, captured by a bystander on video, shocked the nation and the world. The graphic footage led to widespread outrage over the acquittal, culminating in five days of intense riots in Los Angeles. During this tumultuous period, residents set fires, looted, and vandalized liquor stores, grocery shops, retail stores, and fast-food restaurants. These events ignited a national dialogue on racial and economic inequality, as well as the pervasive issue of police use of force.

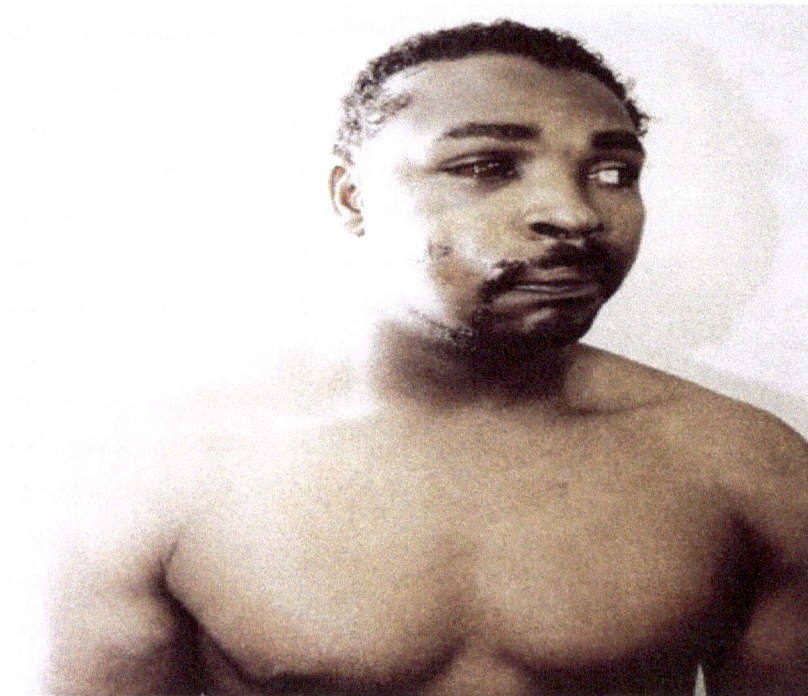

Compton saw escalating tensions. The community had been grappling with increasing problems for years, including a startling and staggering unemployment rate of close to 50% and the devastating impact of widespread illegal drug sale, use, and abuse. These simmering tensions eventually reached a boiling point, and simultaneously, the community's mistrust of the Los Angeles Police Department deepened. African Americans reported unwarranted harassment by law enforcement, which further eroded their sense of security.

Today, Compton has evolved into a diverse and multicultural community, topping out at nearly 100,000 residents. It is strategically located, with easy access to five major freeways, and affordable housing options have attracted new residents. Moreover, developers have shown keen interest in the city, leading to the construction of over 100 new homes and several retail and commercial centers. Gateway Tower Center, a 51-acre mixed-use commercial and residential project on Alameda Blvd, which broke ground in February 2007, holds special promise for Compton's future. At day's end, though, only time will unveil the path that lies ahead for this resilient city.

COMPTON SCHOOL DISTRICT

It's not an exaggeration when I tell you that I had no idea what I was getting into when I first applied to work in the Compton Unified School District (CUSD). And even though I eventually became a principal there, what I encountered at the outset was mind boggling.

During the years spanning from 1991 to 1997, the CUSD grappled with a series of formidable challenges, undergoing demonstrable transformations. Here's a snapshot of the key events and developments that unfolded during that tumultuous era.

MY INAUGURATION

I can still vividly recall the day a letter arrived at my home in Leimert Park, California, a peaceful LA suburb. It was a pivotal moment that marked the significant beginning of my career journey. The letter was from the Compton Unified School District, a name that would soon become synonymous with my professional life.

Several months earlier, I had applied for a principal position that had caught my eye in the California School Administrators newspaper. At that time, I had already spent six years as an assistant principal and served as the Director of At-Risk Programs in the Centinela Valley Union High School District. My wife, Lark, had also forged her own remarkable career path in the health field, earning recognition for her work with prominent politicians at local, statewide, and national levels. Both of us proudly held degrees from the University of Southern California, a testament to our shared commitment to education and excellence.

The longer I stared at the letter's contents, the more my excitement grew. It was an invitation to interview for a high school principalship position within the Compton Unified School District. Lark and I were delirious with joy; it felt like the culmination of years of hard work and dedication. We had always pushed each other to strive for the best versions of ourselves, and this opportunity was no different.

Our educational journeys had taken us through USC, where I earned my master's degree and administrative services credential, while Lark pursued her master's degree in public administration with a background in healthcare. Her undergraduate studies at UCLA had laid a strong foundation for her future endeavors. It was a vision quest marked by determination and a shared commitment to personal growth.

Reflecting on my career, I couldn't help but acknowledge the dramatic influence of my time as a dean of students, assistant principal, and associate principal at Leuzinger High School in Lawndale, California. Under the mentorship of Superintendent McKinley Nash, a remarkable black leader, it was there that I honed my leadership skills. Dr. Nash not only inspired me but also provided opportunities that taught me the true meaning of perseverance and hard work. My experiences at Leuzinger High School also shaped my ability to work with diverse faculty and student populations, instilling in me valuable lessons about leadership and collaboration.

My odyssey began eight years prior as a classroom teacher, with teaching roles at the California Youth Authority, Lynwood School District, and Mountain View Unified School District in El Monte, California. These diverse and enriching experiences had brought me face to face with students and staff from various backgrounds, expanding my perspective on education and leadership.

Upon submitting my application to the Compton Unified School District, I received a letter that revealed two openings for high school principal positions. The uncertainty of whether I would interview for Centennial High School, Compton High School, or Dominguez High School hung in the air. Yet, I was undeterred; the years of dedication had prepared me for any challenge that lay ahead.

Following an interview with a panel comprising teachers, administrators, board members, and the assistant superintendent of personnel, I waited anxiously. It wasn't long before a letter arrived, accompanied by a phone call, bearing the news that I had been selected for a prestigious role as a school principal within the Compton Unified School District. It was a moment of immense pride and anticipation, marking the start of an incredible chapter in my professional journey.

I remember that I reported to the District Administration building on a Monday morning around 8 am in July of 1991. After receiving all my personnel documents involving pay and benefits package, I was told that I was to report to Centennial High School. It was one of the most memorable and auspicious days as I began my tenure as principal of Centennial High School.

CENTENNIAL HIGH "THE APACHES"

Centennial High School was my first stop. The name of the mascot was the Apache, a proud Native American people.

Early Apaches were a nomadic people, ranging over a wide area of the United States, with the Mescalero Apache roaming as far south as Mexico. They were primarily hunter- gatherers, with some bands hunting buffalo and some practicing limited farming.

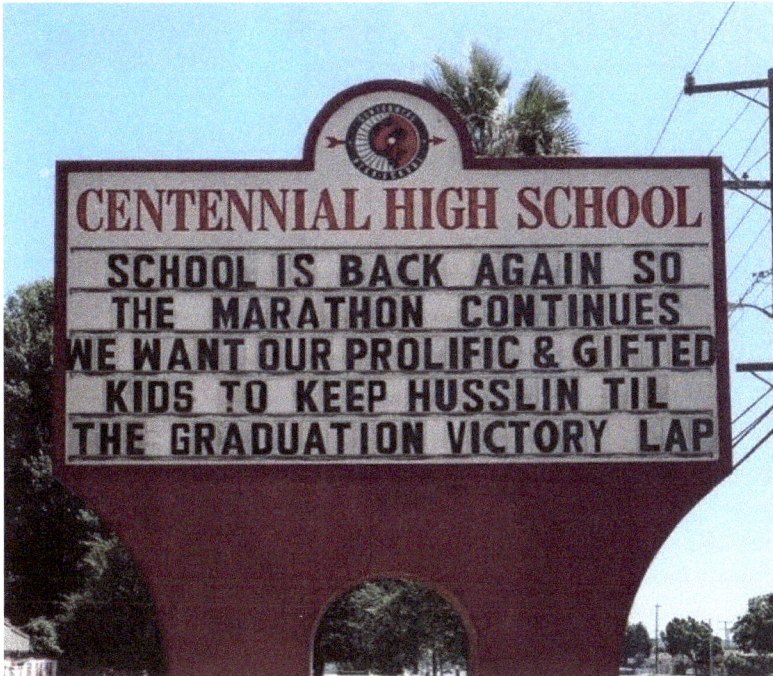

Centennial High

With a sense of anticipation mixed with trepidation, I entered the High School's confines, my new professional home. As I drove into the school's parking lot, an eerie familiarity washed over me, reminiscent of scenes from movies like "Blackboard Jungle," starring Sidney Poitier, or more recent films like "Lean on Me," portraying Joe Clark's turbulent experiences in an inner-city high school. These cinematic stories, especially "Blackboard Jungle," published in 1954 and later adapted into a movie, boldly tackled the issues plaguing public education and unflinchingly depicted student violence.

As I approached the principal's office, I developed a growing sense of unease. I reached out to someone for guidance, as this campus was entirely foreign to me. The signs of graffiti sprawled across the buildings struck me as a lucid portrayal of the challenges faced by this school. The grounds were strewn with litter, and the grass, where it existed, was either nonexistent or overgrown. The overall atmosphere was one of neglect, decay, and despair. The school's fences and gates were riddled with holes, signaling an alarming lack of security.

Centennial High School was in an area that bordered Piru Street and Central Avenue, parts of the city known for affiliations with the Bloods and Crips, respectively. The school drew students from both neighborhoods, setting the stage for a complex and potentially volatile environment.

My encounter with the outgoing principal was nothing short of bewildering. He approached me with the urgency of a jockey riding a champion racehorse, tossing me the keys to the school as if in a relay race. I caught them with the reflexes of an NFL wide receiver, evidence of my athletic background from my days at USC as a running back, defensive back, and wide receiver. Mr. Miller's brief words, "Good Luck. I am Glad to Be Out of Here," left a lasting mark on me, signaling the daunting challenges that lay ahead.

My previous experiences at Leuzinger High School and Inglewood High School had already exposed me to gang-related issues and racial tensions. I had weathered the storms of urban inner-city high schools, and I believed I was prepared for whatever Centennial High School would bring. I now question whether I was as fully prepared as I had originally thought.

As I walked toward the principal's office, my mind was flooded with memories of Centennial High School from my younger days growing up in Compton and South- Central Los Angeles. I recalled the school's rich history and noteworthy alumni, including Dr. Dre and accomplished athletes like Wayne Simpson and Lonnie Smith. The school held a special place in the community, but its current state bore little resemblance to its august past.

Meeting my administrative and clerical staff marked the beginning of my tenure. I was joined by Mrs. Cheryl Highland, assistant principal of master schedules, and Mrs. Dessie Kelley, assistant principal of student services and attendance. My secretary, Bridgett Brown, greeted me with warmth. The clerical staff appeared friendly and professional, setting an overall positive tone.

With only two weeks to prepare for the upcoming school year, I set out on a campus tour, determined to assess the entire staff. My first stop was the security personnel's office, where I discovered a lack of visibility and engagement with students. From there, already a bit non-plussed, I moved on to various classrooms. Some teachers had inconsistent attendance, while others seemed to have been placed at Centennial due to past performance issues at other schools in the district. The physical state of the campus mirrored the challenges it faced, with graffiti defacing the surroundings, a reflection of the neighborhood's struggles.

My mission was clear: to revitalize Centennial High School, address gang violence, and restore safety. It was a daunting task, but one I was ready to tackle head-on.

The situation in Compton is complex and multifaceted, with a variety of factors contributing to the entrenched gang culture and recent spikes in violence. Let's break down some of the key points:

• **The Release of Hard-Core Gang Members**: The recent release of seasoned gang members from prison raises concerns. These individuals, with their criminal expertise, often reintegrate into the community, potentially triggering gang-related criminal activities and intensifying the cycle of violence.

• **Racial Tensions** Among Gangs: Strained relations between various gangs, particularly those divided along racial lines, can be fodder for more conflict and violence. Factors like territorial disputes, resource competition, and power struggles within the criminal underworld can exacerbate these tensions.

• **Law Enforcement Hurdles**: The efficacy of law enforcement, specifically the L.A. County Sheriff's Department, in combatting gang violence faces scrutiny. Frequent rotations of officers across the county tend to hinder their ability to build crucial community relationships and gather intelligence needed to effectively counter gang activity.

• **Transition from Compton Police to Sheriff's Department:** The transition from the Compton Police Department to the Sheriff's Department may have created a gap in understanding the intricacies of the city's gang landscape. Some argue that Sheriff's deputies lack the local insights necessary to address gang-related issues optimally.

• **Economic Struggles:** Limited economic opportunities can and does readily perpetuate gang involvement. For some, the absence of legitimate job prospects can drive them towards gang activities, despite their illegal and perilous nature. Employment opportunities are central to breaking the cycle of gang violence.

• **Neighborhood Identity and Gangs:** The association of specific city blocks with different gangs underscores the deep-rooted nature of these affiliations. Gangs often form around a shared sense of identity, belonging, and protection within a particular neighborhood.

• **Cultural and Media Impact**: The influence of hip-hop culture and music, particularly gangster rap, has significantly shaped Compton's reputation. The legacy of N.W.A. and similar groups has contributed to the city's image as a hub for gang-related activities.

• **Intergenerational Inheritance:** The fact that Eazy-E's son is following in his footsteps highlights the intergenerational nature of gang culture. These behaviors and affiliations can and often do become deeply ingrained within families and communities, perpetuating a cycle that is hard to break.

Addressing the complex issues surrounding gang violence in Compton requires a multi- pronged approach that includes community engagement, targeted law enforcement strategies, educational and economic opportunities, and efforts to de-escalate racial tensions. It's important to consider the broader social, economic, and cultural context that contributes to the perpetuation of gang activity.

The restrooms bore the scars of rampant graffiti, with profanity-laden messages and menacing gang-related threats covering virtually every surface; there was scarcely a trace of the original paint. I witnessed an alarming sight while exploring the campus – the trees in the quad area, where students gathered during breaks, had succumbed to fire and had been reduced to charred remnants. It was hard to comprehend how several trees at the heart of the school had been allowed to burn down. Evidence of neglect was pervasive.

As I continued my inspection, I meticulously counted every window on the premises, and the tally exceeded 200 shattered panes. From the cafeteria to the classrooms, the main administration building to the gymnasium, every structure on the campus resembled the most forsaken areas of downtown Los Angeles or a city's skid row. It was evident that many students had lost all interest, and the environment was far from conducive to learning.

The bleachers at the football and athletic field were either reduced to either cinders or disjointed fragments, rendering them unusable for spectators or anyone attending the school's sporting events. Trash littered the area as if a large crowd had just left the Staples Center or the Coliseum, leaving behind empty cups, hot dog wrappers, beer bottles, and an assortment of garbage. I was disheartened, left to wonder how the school had deteriorated to such an extent, with no intervention from the adults.

Meanwhile, some teachers began preparing for the upcoming school year. They visited my office to introduce themselves, offering me a glimpse of my staff before the first day of school, only a few weeks away. As I met each educator and staff member, I made it clear that I wouldn't dwell on their previous evaluations or work history. Instead, I pledged to assess them based on their current productivity, enthusiasm, creativity, and professionalism. Past judgments would hold no sway under my leadership; everyone would start with a clean slate.

In the initial weeks of my tenure at Centennial High School, I undertook an exhaustive review of every student's transcript. What emerged was troubling – over 60% of our students exhibited poor attendance, accumulating more than 15 unexcused absences per school year. Even more concerning was the discovery that over 70% of our students were dropouts. Examining the attendance records, I found a disturbing trend: students weren't completing their education and weren't graduating within four years. Equally concerning was the fact that 50% of the 9th-grade population consisted of 18, 19, and 20-year-olds. This was a stark indicator of the high crime rate on campus, with students either skipping school entirely or aimlessly causing disruptions. It was clear to me that there was little regard for the educational environment, and it was no surprise that the school was both physically and academically in disarray.

Centennial V. Compton Football Game

Centennial was a school that was adjacent to Piru Street, a place where one of the most notorious gangs representing the Bloods in Los Angeles at that time claimed as its own. It was less than a mile from Jordan Downs, a hot bed for the notorious Crip Gang called the Jordon Down Crips. Both groups were represented at the school. The district, for whatever reason, did not bother to redraw the attendance area to prevent such a clash of the different rival gangs attending the same school. This indeed was a problem.

Teachers recounted harrowing tales of a day when more than thirty cars converged at the front of the school on Central Avenue. Gunfire erupted from the vehicles, turning the school into a battlefield of flying bullets. In the chaos that ensued, students and staff sought refuge beneath their desks and any available cover. The teachers' stories were filled with panic and dread, and many of them admitted to harboring deep fears about returning to teach at the school after that traumatic experience.

The climate of fear was not limited to the staff; it had permeated the student body as well. Enrollment had plummeted to just 1300 students, even though the school had the capacity to accommodate well over 2500. Many students who would typically have attended Centennial High School had opted for schools in other districts due to the subpar educational standards and the prevailing violence on campus. It became abundantly clear to me that I had a monumental task ahead of me. I needed to go above and beyond to not only bring students back to Centennial High School but also to restore a productive and safe educational environment that would make everyone feel more comfortable and secure.

COMPTON HIGH "BABY TARTARS"

Blue and white were Compton High's colors. Naturally, Crips attended Compton High; however, there were no known Bloods attending Compton High, unlike Centennial High, which featured many of these rival gang members. The school's `official name was the "Tarbabes" or, in other words, Baby Tartars. This tag was adapted from the name given by Compton Junior College - Tartars. Compton Junior College at one time was on the same campus as Compton High School, so the name became Tarbabes or Baby Tartars.

This old 127-year-old building was torn down to build a brand new school

TATARS IN HISTORY

The name Tatar (often spelled Tartar) is said to have first appeared around the beginning of the 5th century AD amongst the nomadic Turkic peoples of northeastern Mongolia in the region of Lake Baikal. The Chinese term, 'Ta-Ta,' is said to mean 'dirty' or 'barbarian.' Although the Tatars were already in contact with the Chinese during the early part of their history, their encounters with Europeans came much later. During the early part of the 13th century, Genghis Khan united the various nomadic tribes of the Mongolian steppes and set out to conquer the world. Batu Khan, one of Genghis Khan's grandsons, led the Mongol invasion of Eastern Europe.

Old Compton High Auditorium

Upon assuming the role of principal at Compton High School in 1996, I was confronted with a slew of pressing issues that demanded immediate attention. One of the most glaring problems was the teachers' long-standing complaint about not receiving their summer school pay and compensation for extra duties. This situation has persisted for two years, unsettling me and striking me as unprofessional and detrimental to the motivation and enthusiasm of our teaching staff. Teachers, already among the most modestly compensated professionals, deserved fair remuneration for their hard work.

Failing to pay them for their dedication was a recipe for disaster, and addressing this became my top priority.

Another alarming concern revolved around a California state mandate requiring all ninth- grade students to complete a computer literacy course. I was shocked to learn from the teachers that the computers required for this course had been gathering dust in storage at the district office for over two years. The district had ordered enough computers for all ninth graders but had failed to deliver them to the school. Consequently, teachers were left with no choice but to show pictures of computers and rely on books to teach computer literacy, depriving students of the hands-on learning experience they needed. It was disheartening to witness such a stark example of the district's negligence in ensuring that students and staff received the resources necessary to meet state graduation requirements. The widespread incompetence and indifference of district officials was deeply troubling.

The band program at Compton High School presented yet another mountain that needed to be scaled and conquered. For over 25 years, it had gone without new uniforms and band instruments. It's common knowledge that motivating students to learn involves providing extracurricular activities they can enjoy, and a band program without instruments and uniforms is virtually nonexistent. To address this issue, I collaborated with a committee of teachers to secure funding for new uniforms and instruments as well as computers for every ninth-grade student. We buckled down, wrote grants, and successfully secured a five-million-dollar win, which may sound large, but was really only a small victory in the face of the school's plethora of challenges.

Compton High School had reached a major milestone, celebrating its centennial year upon my arrival. However, the preceding year had been marred by a tragic on-campus shooting that left a student injured. Once again, I found myself tasked with rectifying a deeply troubling situation. Ongoing gang violence, accompanied by abysmal test scores, poor attendance, a high dropout rate, resource deficiencies, and dismal overall facilities gave rise to a campus attitude suffused with hopelessness, misery, discouragement, anguish, agony, and distress, afflicting faculty, staff, and students alike. Life for many seemed devoid of meaning. It was no surprise that, in the face of such despair, students made choices driven by desperation, some of which were severe and perilous.

Compton High Football

Compton High School's main building harbored a basement that, before my tenure, had housed classes. My initial encounter with that basement, however, was nothing short of appalling. The walls were inundated with graffiti, and the presence of rat feces pervaded the air, making my stomach churn with disgust. The basement had become a dumping ground for old, broken furniture, strewn haphazardly across the floor. Water damage on the ceiling hinted at a significant issue, and I learned that homeless individuals would occupy this space at night and on weekends, engaging in various illicit activities. This nauseating discovery cast a shadow over the entire campus, but my inspection of the school grounds revealed a situation no less dire.

The campus was riddled with glaring problems reminiscent of those I had encountered at Centennial High School. Holes in the fences offered easy access for outsiders, raising concerns about security. Several buildings bore the scars of fire damage, rendering them unsafe and unusable. The schoolyard sported overgrown grass, and the overall appearance was revolting and repugnant. What struck me most was the palpable sense that the environment was not only unsightly and unpleasant but also fundamentally unhealthy for both students and staff.

In January 1997, Bill Boyarsky, a writer for the LA Times, conducted a revealing investigation of Compton High School's deplorable conditions. He reported on the sorry state of the school, which had languished for three years under state control, following a history of local mismanagement, corruption, and neglect. The dire situation included exit doors sealed shut, rainwater pooling on the floors, bare bathrooms without basic amenities, graffiti-covered walls, and a shocking absence of textbooks in some classes. Boyarsky's visit unveiled an educational nightmare and posed a perplexing question: If the state Department of Education couldn't manage one small school district, how could it offer guidance to the entire state?

The deteriorated state of Compton High School was underscored by Boyarsky's account. The basement, once used for classrooms and student activities, had become a weekend haunt for a gang, its graffiti obscuring a mural painted by long-forgotten student activists. The theater was in shambles, its dressing room vandalized, and its seats broken. Puddles of water dotted the muddy courtyard and electrical hazards loomed. The classrooms were plagued by leaks, and critical exit doors were locked or obstructed. Boyarsky's report echoed my own grim encounters.

Despite these alarming conditions, the state administrator, Randy Ward, who had taken charge just two months before, acknowledged the severity of the issues but vowed to work towards improvement. Yet, the daunting task seemed insurmountable. Ward needed substantial support to tackle the overwhelming challenges that plagued Compton High School. In the face of abysmal facilities, poor student achievement, low test scores, and a high dropout rate, the enormity of the mission weighed heavily on me. Only a fool, I thought at the time, would willingly accept the responsibility of resurrecting such a disastrous situation. Compton High School is in the process of a much-needed revitalization, thanks in part to a generous commitment of $10 million from Dr. Dre, an alumnus of Centennial High School. This remarkable contribution is a testament to the strong bond former alumni maintain with the Compton community, as they willingly return to provide valuable resources, financial support, and their time to benefit the students in Compton's schools. A high school in Compton can thank Dr. Dre for financially assisting in its development. The Los Angeles Times reported the Hip-Hop mogul provided $10 million in funding toward a new $200-million campus for Compton High School. The school's new performing arts center will be named the "Andre 'Dr. Dre' Young Performing Arts Center" in his honor. The full project is funded through the school district's bond measure, which was passed in 2015. "I was an artistic kid in school with no outlet for it," remarked Dre at Saturday's groundbreaking ceremony according to the newspaper. "I knew I had something special to offer to the world, but with nothing to support my gift, schools left me feeling unseen." He continued, "This city is special, and [the] young people living in it are special."

According to a press release, the unanimous decision was made to name the performing arts center after the Grammy Award-winning musician back in November of 2017.

"I am looking forward to seeing this tremendous vision break ground and am so thankful to Mr. Young, who has done Compton proud," expressed Compton Unified Board President Satra Zurita in a statement at the time. "He is firmly planting a legacy of opportunity for our students!"

Superintendent Darin Brawley added, "I am grateful to Mr. Young, not only for making such [a] contribution to our District and its students, but also for seeing our students as valuable… as having potential and deserving of opportunity."

The LA Times reported the facility seats over 900 guests and the new campus for the 126-year-old school will serve up to 1800 students. Upgrades include a new gym, an aquatics center, a football stadium, and a track. The new campus is set to open in early 2025. This certainly will be a far cry from what Compton High School was in the 1990's when I was principal.

PART II: EAST COAST VERSUS WEST COAST

The gang situation took a dramatic turn on July 17, 1996, when Las Vegas police conducted a raid on the residence of Duane "Keefe D" Davis. The goal was to uncover any possible connections to the 1996 murder of Tupac Shakur. However, the mysteries surrounding the deaths of both Tupac Shakur and The Notorious B.I.G., six months later, extend far beyond the realm of hip-hop. These stories encompass various facets of American celebrity culture: the rise of young and charismatic stars, the distortion of miscommunication for entertainment, manipulation within the music industry, a friendship shattered into violence, and decades of conspiracy theories attempting to make sense of it all. It is essential to note that no one has been charged, let alone convicted, in either man's murder. Therefore, when exploring these stories, whether through the perspective of a gang member, journalist, or detective, one must always distinguish between factual evidence and speculative (conspiracy) theories.

Russell Poole, the initial investigator for the Los Angeles Police Department assigned to The Notorious B.I.G.'s case, developed a theory implicating Death Row Records founder and CEO Suge Knight in both Shakur's and The Notorious B.I.G.'s homicides. He also suggested that Los Angeles Police Department officers were involved in off-duty work for Knight. Poole retired in 1999, under circumstances he deemed involuntary, while the department cited it as a mutual decision. Nonetheless, he remained connected to both cases until his passing in August 2015. Poole's investigative work and subsequent book served as the foundation for the 2018 film City of Lies, featuring Johnny Depp portraying Poole.

Another investigator from the Los Angeles Police Department, Greg Kading, led a special task force dedicated to The Notorious B.I.G.'s case from 2006 to 2009. However, before his team could present their findings, Kading faced an internal affairs investigation related to alleged false statements in an unrelated case. Although he was later exonerated, Kading retired from the department, and the task force was disbanded. It's worth noting that Kading, too, has become a somewhat minor celebrity due to his claims, whether intentionally or not.

Tupac

Kading concluded that both slayings were a result of a murder-for-hire. In Shakur's case, he argues, Sean "P. Diddy" Combs allegedly paid a bounty for the slaying of either Shakur or Knight stemming from the bitter feud between Knight's Death Row Records and Combs' Bad Boy Records. He bases that conclusion on a confession by Davis, who has repeated the same story in several interviews. Combs repeatedly denied the claims and was never charged.

'Hip Hop Uncovered' tells the story of the feared 'Haitian Jack'

"Regardless of any planning," said Kading, "Shakur's shooting appears to have resulted from mere happenstance." Had Shakur and Knight never ambushed Orlando Anderson, Davis' nephew, on that trip to Nevada, there's a good chance Shakur would be alive today — or, at least, he wouldn't have been shot in Las Vegas. Davis admitted he was in the car that pulled alongside Knight's BMW and Anderson opened fire. (Anderson was slain in a Compton car wash shooting in 1998.) Shakur involved himself in gang-related politics by jumping Anderson, who was involved in a brawl at a Los Angeles mall months earlier.

"The gangbanging from the hood, and touching Orlando — he shouldn't have done that," said former Death Row Records muscle Mob James. "It was people from Compton there that knew who Orlando was. If they wanted to take off on him, that's what they should've did. Not Tupac."

The Notorious B.I.G. was allegedly killed by a man named Wardell "Poochie" Fouse, one of Knight's well-known hitmen. The plan was reportedly concocted by an incarcerated Knight (for his role in the Anderson assault months earlier), "Theresa Swann," a former girlfriend and mother of one of Knight's children (her government name was withheld as part of her deal with investigators) and Fouse for $25,000 — to be split between him and Swann. Fouse was killed in a drive-by shooting in July 2003. As for Kadin's findings and the Unsolved series, Voletta Wallace, The Notorious B.I.G.'s mother, gave her perspective in a 2020 interview with The Breakfast Club. "To be honest with you, I watched it. There's some things that went on [and] I knew about it," she said, sitting beside Wayne Barrow, manager of The Notorious B.I.G.'s estate. "But I watched it and I'm glad it was out. I'm glad because 98% of it is the truth."

Notorious BIG

All the preceding events culminated in what was tantamount to gang warfare between the East Coast Rappers and West Coast Rappers. From then and onward, Compton rivalries only increased.

The involvement of Compton gangs in the Tupac Shakur case, particularly Orlando Anderson, a Southside Crip member, created a ripple effect that reached into the local schools. Reports surfaced of Little Half Dead, a Crip and close friend of Tupac Shakur, being brutally assaulted in Las Vegas. To complicate matters, the Compton Police Department and several other local police officers were providing security for Death Row Records. This incident became the talk of the town in Compton.

I have strong memories of helicopters hovering over Compton High School and the surrounding community just a day after Tupac's tragic murder. The entire campus was buzzing with tension and unease. This chilling event had a profound impact, not only on students but also on teachers, staff, and the entire Compton community. It was a somber period when conversations about Tupac and Biggie dominated, overshadowing the importance of education and learning.

Growing up, one constant in my life was the expectation of being stopped by the police while out on the streets. Even as a principal, I found myself being pulled over by the police for no apparent reason every time I got into my car. This experience is shared by famous black athletes, movie stars, and artists alike. Regardless of a black man's accomplishments or contributions to society, there persists a lingering stigma that necessitates constant surveillance of black boys and men. This ongoing issue continues to breed animosity within the black community to this day.

I posit that the root of the issues we grapple with concerning mass shootings and gang violence is a multi-pronged challenge encompassing inadequate education, police misconduct, racial disparities, discrimination, job shortages for men, single-parent households led by women, the influence of social media, gangster rap music, negative and harmful musical content, and feminism. In the following sections, I will delve into each of these facets, discussing the current situation and proposing strategies for addressing these problems at the levels of schools, local communities, the nation, and global communities.

A disheartening trend has emerged from decades of data: the unequal treatment of black boys begins at a young age. From their early years through adolescence, black boys are subjected to an excessive level of surveillance by law enforcement. This pervasive scrutiny occurs in various settings, including streets, schools, shopping centers, homes, and even on social media platforms. The methods used to police black boys have wide- reaching implications, influencing not only their perceptions of law enforcement but also their attitudes towards authority and the justice system. In this section, I will explore the disproportionate targeting of black boys by the police, examine the detrimental consequences of such experiences on their development, and propose potential avenues for reform.

In their daily lives, a troubling reality unfolds for black boys—one where they face disproportionate encounters with law enforcement based on the flimsiest of pretexts. Often, they become targets based only on their appearance, reduced to labels like "black boys on the move" or "two black males in jeans, one wearing a gray hoodie." These encounters are not limited to unfamiliar, predominantly white, middle-class neighborhoods; they unfold in their own communities, even on their front porches. Such relentless surveillance leaves them with a haunting feeling of being perpetually "out of place," engendering emotions of mistrust, fear, and hostility towards the very authorities meant to protect them.

Adolescence marks a critical phase where young individuals shape their attitudes and perceptions of the law and legal institutions. Negative experiences with law enforcement during childhood and adolescence exert lasting influence, steering their behavior and outlook as they transition into adulthood. The historical backdrop of biased and confrontational encounters with the police, whether real or perceived, has culminated in the socialization of an entire generation of black boys. This socialization promotes cautious avoidance of police interactions and, when inevitable, fosters a disposition towards hostility and confrontation.

Even when black boys congregate in public spaces, such as street corners, they tend to attract the attention of law enforcement, irrespective of the time of day. Factors like dressing well or owning nice vehicles offer no shield against police scrutiny. Regrettably, symbols of prosperity among black youth are often misconstrued as indicators of illicit involvement. This stereotype-driven policing serves only to further marginalize these individuals, exacerbating the racial disparities in their encounters with the police.

Interactions between black youth and the police frequently take on a negative hue, significantly shaping their perceptions and attitudes. Accounts of aggressive, antagonistic behavior, racial slurs, and even physical force during stops abound. This hostile treatment not only breeds resentment but also perpetuates a cycle of fear and distrust.

Consequently, black boys become conditioned to anticipate hostility and violence from law enforcement.

Studies have shed light on the age bias harbored by police officers when perceiving the innocence of black adolescent felony suspects. Officers consistently overestimate the age of these young individuals by a substantial margin. This age bias results in black boys being treated as adults much earlier than their counterparts from other racial backgrounds. The implications are profound, leading to arrests, harassment, and assault for behaviors that would be considered normal adolescent conduct for others.

To confront the deeply ingrained issues of racial disparities in policing and their profound impact on black boys, a call for transformative reform resonates. Initiating this change at an early stage is paramount. Here are some proposed reforms:

Police Training: Officers should undergo comprehensive training encompassing adolescent development and implicit bias. This knowledge equips them to better comprehend and engage with young black boys.

Reducing Police Presence in Schools: A critical review of police officers' presence in schools is imperative. The aim is to cultivate environments that nurture positive relationships, rather than perpetuating feelings of surveillance and intimidation.

Policy and Procedure Overhauls: The revamping of police policies and procedures is essential. These revisions should encourage and facilitate positive interactions between black youth and law enforcement, dismantling the reinforcement of negative stereotypes. The widespread and prejudiced policing of black boys leaves unmistakable imprints on their perception of law enforcement and overall growth. To forge a path toward genuine change in the relationship between black men and the police, the reformation journey must commence early, focusing on nurturing trust and eradicating biases. By addressing the systemic underpinnings of these disparities and championing constructive interactions, we move closer to a society that embodies justice and equity for all.

REDUCING POLICE VIOLENCE

Recording video, using offensive language, failing to comply with an officer's commands, and attempting to flee can all contribute to heightened tension, diminished respect, and often result in the application of physical force by law enforcement. It's not surprising that black youths are more likely to experience the use of force compared to their white counterparts.

These young black individuals aren't just angered by the frequency of stops; they're also deeply troubled by the way these encounters unfold. They describe police officers as confrontational and hostile, expressing their outrage at the use of racial slurs, offensive language, and derogatory terms like "punk" and "sissy." They voice their dissatisfaction with encounters that frequently commence with physical contact, such as grabbing, pushing, shoving, pulling, or even forcibly bringing them to the ground.

Once on the ground, multiple officers might employ methods like sitting or lying on black youths, while others resort to actions such as kicking, punching, or deploying pepper spray. More severe confrontations involve the use of clubs or chokeholds, as tragically exemplified in cases like Eric Garner's death in New York. The victims of police violence encompass young black individuals like La Quan McDonald, Tyre King, and, more recently, Jordan Edwards. The fear of encountering police violence has regrettably become a commonplace experience for young black individuals.

In a recent study probing police perceptions of childhood innocence, researchers presented police officers with images of young white, black, and Latino males involved in assumed criminal activities and requested them to estimate each child's age. The outcomes revealed that officers consistently overestimated the age of black adolescent suspects by an average of 4.59 years, while underestimating the age of white adolescent felony suspects by a year. Due to these distorted perceptions, black boys are predisposed to premature treatment as adults, facing elevated risks of arrest, harassment, and aggression for behaviors that align with their age group. They are also more prone to being viewed as accountable and deserving of punishment, or even death.

Consider the case of Tamir Rice, a 12-year-old boy from Cleveland fatally shot by the police on November 22, 2014. The police were responding to a 911 call reporting "a person with a gun," which was nothing other than a toy. The officers' portrayal of Tamir as "older," larger, and more menacing than he truly was echoes findings from research on implicit racial bias among law enforcement, where young black boys are frequently perceived as older and more menacing than their actual age. For any substantial change in the relationship between black men and the police to occur, intervention must start early. Efforts should be made to challenge the distorted perceptions that portray black youth as aggressive and dangerous, and to foster trust between black boys and law enforcement.

This can involve reevaluating the reliance on police presence in schools, ensuring officers are trained in adolescent development and implicit bias, and implementing significant changes in police protocols to create opportunities for positive interactions between black youth and the police.

List of Unarmed African Americans Killed by Law Enforcement Officers in the United States

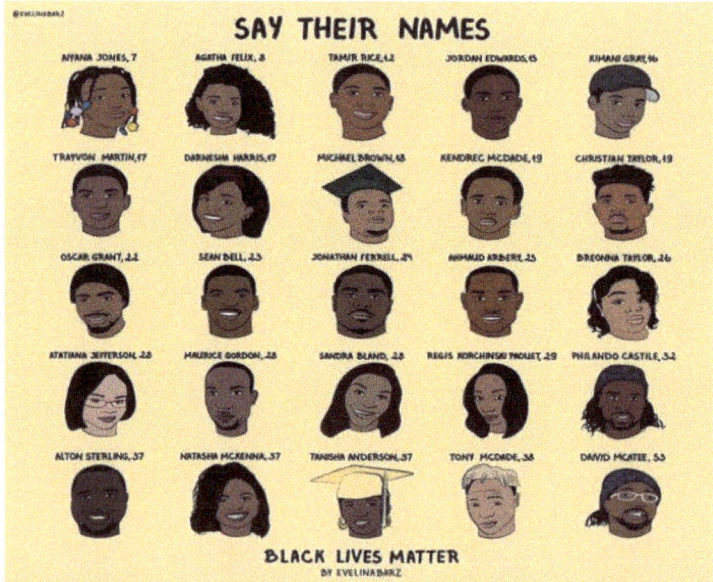

Many of the names are of African Americans who were unarmed when they were killed by law enforcement officers

- **2016 shooting of Dallas police officers:** A mass shooting that was motived by the suspect's anger over the shootings of unarmed black people by police.
- **2016 shooting of Baton Rouge police officers:** A mass shooting that was motived by the shootings of unarmed black people by police.
- **2014 killings of NYPD officers:** A shooting that was motived by the killings of Eric Garner and Michael Brown.
- **Mark Essex:** A man who's killing spree was partially motivated by the police shooting deaths of Leonard Brown and Denver Smith.

No longer an anonymous Black man: a George Floyd mural in Houston, Texas

In the absence of such reforms, the unjust treatment of black boys — and black men — by law enforcement will persist. I believe that substantial improvement is possible in this area, and that black males must be encouraged to trust law enforcement which, in turn, will likely lead to a reduction in gang violence.

SOCIAL MEDIA AND GANGS

A gang transcends mere companionship among young individuals. Virtually every state in the nation has enacted laws addressing gangs and their recruitment, many of which provide a precise delineation of what constitutes a gang. Although there are shared characteristics across states, it's advisable to refer to local regulations, particularly when dealing with legal matters in this domain.

In essence, a gang comprises three or more members, with street gangs primarily consisting of individuals between the ages of 12 and 24. These members share a collective identity often tied to a specific gang name or recognizable symbols. This identity carries an element of fear and intimidation that significantly impacts communities. Gang members typically embrace their affiliation, adopting gang-related monikers, which are also recognized by other gangs and members of the community. The critical aspect in this definition is that the group's core revolves around engaging in criminal activities, typically involving a higher level of criminal behavior, often extending to acts of violence.

Insights gleaned from studies conducted over the past decade reveal that there are over 33,000 gangs in the United States, comprising approximately 1.4 million gang members. Their criminal activities encompass traditional offenses such as drug-related activities, robberies, and thefts. However, gangs have also expanded their involvement to encompass emerging criminal activities like human trafficking, fraud, and identity theft.

Another substantial impact of gangs is their involvement in violent crimes. In 2011, the National Gang Threat Assessment study gathered responses from law enforcement agencies across the nation. The findings indicated that, on average, gangs or activities related to gangs accounted for about 48% of violent crimes in the participating jurisdictions. This represents a significant portion of violent crime associated with gangs throughout the country. In some areas, the reported figure climbed to as high as 90% of violent crime incidents being attributed to gangs. Additionally, gangs create an intangible but deeply felt atmosphere of fear and intimidation within communities, which can severely disrupt these areas—a phenomenon I've personally witnessed.

Shifting our focus to indicators of gang involvement a list of well-known gang names like Bloods, Crips, 18th Street, Vice Lords, and more comes into view. It's important to note that these names may vary by region. Furthermore, numerous other names are linked to gangs. Some gangs incorporate localized identifiers, such as "Athens Park Bloods," which may not necessarily have a direct connection to the national organization but seek the notoriety associated with such names. Moreover, gangs often adopt street names or directional terms like "West Side" or "North Side" in conjunction with words like "Boys" or "Gang." However, these naming conventions are by no means exhaustive, as gangs employ a wide array of names, including those derived from park or school district affiliations to convey their identity.

While these names may not overtly feature the term "gang," their criminal activities remain in line with the legal definition of gangs.

Now, let's explore the signs, symbols, and graffiti associated with gangs. Graffiti serves as a means for gangs to assert their territory, display their reputation, pay tribute to fallen members, and challenge rival factions. In many ways, this graffiti operates as a street- level form of social media. You might observe young individuals carrying spray paint, markers, or sketchbooks, with potential paint residues on their attire or backpacks from overspray. It's crucial, however, to acknowledge that there are individuals unrelated to gangs, commonly known as graffiti artists or taggers, who partake in similar practices.

Thus, it's essential not to rush to conclusions based solely on the presence of graffiti. Symbols, numbers, and marks hold particular significance within gang culture. Typical symbols encompass stars, often with five or six points, crowns, downward-pointing pitchforks, and various dot configurations. Numeric values like "18" carry specific meanings, often linked to a particular gang, such as the 18th Street gang. These symbols may appear on notebooks, where they convey a gang's clandestine codes, regulations, anthems, and communication methods. Detecting such symbols, particularly when combined with other indicators, can raise concerns regarding gang affiliation.

Gangs also use gang-specific, unique hand signals or signs. These signs might spell out the gang's name or involve distinct hand gestures. These signals frequently find their way into social media posts, reinforcing the individual's affiliation. Keep in mind that the interpretation of these signals can be context-dependent and might differ from one region to another. Local law enforcement, particularly those specializing in gang activity, can offer valuable insights into deciphering these signals.

Colors and clothing are essential elements that gangs use to signify their identity. Gang members often wear specific colors in a distinct manner to differentiate themselves and communicate their affiliation. This might include bandanas, sports jerseys, or even a preference for a single color. While wearing a certain color isn't indicative of gang involvement on its own, a consistent pattern of wearing the same color across social media posts, coupled with other indicators, can raise eyebrows and warrant attention.

Tattoos are another crucial aspect of gang culture, often featuring symbols, abbreviations, or even depictions of committed crimes. Recognizable symbols like crowns, diamonds, and pitchforks might be tattooed to signify affiliation. Certain initials, like "MS13," indicate membership in dangerous gangs. Interpreting tattoos can be complex, but common gang-related symbols are usually straightforward. If you encounter such tattoos, especially in conjunction with other indicators, it's wise to exercise caution.

Gangs are actively present on social media platforms. The misconception that gangs lack sophistication or access to technology has been dispelled. Recent research shows that approximately 82% of gang members use the Internet, with around 71% actively engaging on social media. About a fifth of gang members even admit to operating websites or dedicated social media pages. These numbers are comparable to the online activity of non-gang members, including youths. Thus, the notion that gangs are technologically lagging is sorely inaccurate and misleading.

Gangs employ social media for member recruitment, internal communication, rival targeting, criminal activities, and evading law enforcement, often relying on cryptic codes they assume are beyond deciphering.

Now, let's delve into the subject of gang recruitment through social media. There are two distinct methods at play. One involves direct recruitment where a non-gang individual might be approached with an invitation to join a gang, or the reverse scenario where a non-gang member expresses interest in affiliating with a gang. Examples even include instances where text messages outline a $150 fee for gang membership. However, it's worth noting that most recruitment endeavors are not as overt. You won't commonly find gangs posting "members wanted" ads on platforms like Facebook or Instagram. Gang members recognize that such public recruitment could result in criminal charges, and many jurisdictions categorize this as a felony offense. Thus, indirect methods tend to dominate. Gangs employ videos, images, and posts to glorify their lifestyle, emphasizing power, wealth, and the camaraderie that appeals to vulnerable youth, making this approach the most effective recruitment strategy.

NAVIGATING THE DIGITAL LANDSCAPE

Shifting focus to criminal activities, there's a recurring pattern of gangs exploiting social media platforms to orchestrate crimes. These platforms serve as tools for identifying rival groups, showcasing illicit exploits, evading law enforcement, and more recently, engaging in human and sex trafficking. A tragic case illustrates this trend, involving victims Neeson, Mickens, and Kayla, who fell prey to the MS13 gang after online provocations, highlighting the substantial dangers tied to online confrontations.

Specific platforms come into play, with one of the earliest and most notable being Facebook back in 2015, boasting a staggering 2.6 billion monthly users and reigning as the top choice among gang members. However, perceptions have since changed, with gangs now viewing Facebook as a conduit for law enforcement surveillance. This shift has transformed Facebook into a gateway, redirecting users toward alternative platforms for secure communication.

Despite this shift, a gang presence remains on Facebook, exemplified by pages like that of "The Blood," which has amassed a significant following and even provides a telephone number for contact. However, most gangs have migrated to YouTube, an American video-sharing platform, to broadcast gang-related content. This shift is noteworthy since YouTube ranked second in popularity among gang members in 2015. Gang-related videos on YouTube can garner millions of views, often featuring violent content or rap music that glorifies gang activities. These online platforms remain a hotspot for gang-related content, even as time passes. Recent events underscore this reality, as arrests in Boston revealed gang members using YouTube to flaunt their criminal deeds and attract followers. They posted rap videos boasting about shootings, murders, and criminal activities, often wearing ankle monitors for previous charges.

It's evident that YouTube continues to serve as a repository for gang-related content. While many of these videos exalt gang life and act as recruitment tools, their popularity among youth and aspiring gang members poses significant concerns. Thus, ongoing vigilance is essential to monitor these platforms, as they remain vital to contemporary gang activities.

In conclusion, gangs' utilization of social media has evolved over time, encompassing recruitment, communication, criminal endeavors, and evasion tactics. Authorities, educators, and caregivers must remain attuned to these trends and the platforms where they unfold, as these digital spaces continue to shape gang dynamics and pose risks to vulnerable youth.

Transitioning to another aspect, YouTube provides an option in the video settings to activate subtitles, automatically generating English lyrics or captions in the chosen language. However, as the captioning is automated, it might require human review for accuracy. This feature can still offer insights into the video's content.

Moving to a different social media platform, let's examine Instagram, which functions as a photo-sharing network. Sharing statistics, it was the third most favored platform by gang members in 2015 and continues to be highly popular today, displaying more engagement than both Snapchat and Facebook. With a substantial user base of 1 billion monthly active users, Instagram plays a significant role in digital interactions.

When tracking an app or a person, including children, it's vital to recognize that the content they post, including stories, can often be saved in their device's album section. Even if content disappears or gets deleted, it could have been downloaded and stored locally. This is crucial to consider for potential exploitation or criminal activity assessment. Notably, incidents have been linked to single Instagram posts leading to violent acts.

Snapchat, on the other hand, introduced the concept of ephemeral content, where photos and videos are designed to vanish after a brief viewing. Stories, a popular feature on Instagram as well, can be posted and disappear within 24 hours unless saved as a highlight. Familiarity with this tool is essential when tracking individuals or assessing their online activities.

Additionally, Instagram introduced Instagram TV (IGTV), a standalone app for short video content. Videos under 60 seconds can be directly uploaded to Instagram, while longer ones, up to 10 minutes, typically find their place on IGTV. This platform's popularity among youth remains high, particularly among those who aim to achieve viral status.

Tragically, Instagram has also been linked to darker activities, including human trafficking. Instances have emerged where individuals exploit their social media presence for illegal endeavors. An Instagram star and Colombian model ran an international sex trafficking ring, luring hundreds of underage girls with promises of becoming models, only to subject them to exploitation.

Concerning safety tips, Instagram provides options to enable post and story notifications for specific users. This helps to keep track of their online activities and well-being.

Additionally, the presence of a green dot next to a user's name indicates that they're currently online. While it could indicate someone else using their device, it's worth noting for potential situations involving at-risk individuals.

A few open-source tools are available, though it's essential to be cautious as their functionality can change. "Graham Find," previously known as "Grammy User," is a search engine specific to Instagram that aids in user analysis. Various browser extensions can simplify desktop interactions, making it easier to view, download, and manage content. Moreover, if an individual has linked their Facebook account to Instagram, this can provide insight into potential usernames across different platforms.

Twitter, a long-standing platform, maintains relevance, especially in terms of news dissemination and engagement. It was the fourth most used platform by gang members in 2015. It introduced hashtags to digital discourse, allowing users to attach photos and short videos. Gangs use Twitter to threaten rivals, carry out violence, and establish their presence.

"Search Twitter" is a useful tool to monitor discussions involving certain topics or usernames. This can provide insights into community conversations, current trends, and relevant content. Various analytics tools offer further insights into user behavior and interactions.

Social media platforms like YouTube, Instagram, Snapchat, and Twitter play significant roles in gang-related activities, recruitment, and communication. Awareness of the dynamics on these platforms, the tools available for monitoring, and the potential for exploitation is crucial for promoting safety and addressing potential risks.

DRILL MUSIC

In today's context, it's evident that social media hasn't served as a catalyst for diffusing disputes among gangs. Additionally, there's a noteworthy rise in mass shootings, often appearing as copycat incidents, which can be partly attributed to the influence of social media.

Another factor to consider is the impact of Drill music or 'gangsta' rap on street violence. Drill music, a subgenre of hip-hop characterized by its gritty lyrics and aggressive beats, has played a role in various social and cultural aspects, particularly within urban communities. While it's not the sole cause of violence, drill music has faced criticism for its potential to amplify existing issues related to crime and violence, especially in marginalized neighborhoods. It's important to recognize that drill music isn't the primary instigator of violence but rather a reflection and amplification of preexisting social, economic, and cultural factors.

Lyrics and Themes: Drill music frequently incorporates lyrics that celebrate violence, criminal activities, and the street lifestyle. Its themes often center around gang rivalries, drug trade, gun violence, and defiance of authority. These lyrics have the potential to desensitize violence, particularly among impressionable young listeners.

Normalization of Violence: Repeated exposure to violent content in drill music can lead listeners to become desensitized to the real-world consequences of violence. This normalization can influence attitudes and behaviors, blurring the lines between the severity of violent actions and their impact on communities.

Fueling Real-Life Conflicts: Many drill artists have affiliations with local gangs or groups, and their music frequently references ongoing street disputes and rivalries. This music can serve as a platform that escalates these tensions, turning virtual conflicts into real-life confrontations.

Reinforcing Gang Culture and Identity: Drill music can contribute to the reinforcement of gang identity and culture. Young individuals may see gang affiliations as a means to gain respect, power, and protection, thereby perpetuating cycles of violence and criminal behavior.

Peer Pressure and Social Influence: Young listeners who aspire to emulate the lifestyle depicted in drill music might succumb to peer pressure, engaging in risky behaviors to fit in or gain acceptance. This, in turn, can perpetuate a cycle of violence and criminality.

Coping with Socioeconomic Challenges: For some artists, drill music offers a platform for self-expression and potentially a way out of poverty and adversity. However, it can also foster the belief that engaging in illegal activities is the sole path to escaping poverty, reinforcing cycles of violence and crime.

Impact on Mental Health: The pervasive themes of violence and aggression in drill music can have detrimental effects on the mental health of listeners, potentially leading to increased anxiety, heightened aggression, and reduced empathy.

Public Perception and Stigmatization: The association of drill music with violence can result in the stigmatization of the entire genre and its audience. This can affect how individuals from these communities are perceived by society, potentially deepening divisions and stereotypes.

Drill music is a form of artistic expression, and not all artists within the genre promote violence or negative behaviors. Additionally, factors contributing to violence and crime are complex and multifaceted, including socioeconomic disparities, lack of opportunities, systemic racism, and inadequate community resources. Addressing the issue requires a holistic approach that includes community engagement, youth programs, improved education, and addressing the root causes of violence.

DECODING ALLEGED DEMONIC INFLUENCES IN THE MUSIC INDUSTRY AND THE CHRISTIAN RESPONSE

The music industry has always been a subject of scrutiny, and it's not uncommon for controversies and conspiracy theories to surround its practices. One such theory revolves around the idea that certain elements within the industry are involved in or promoting occultism, satanic rituals, and demonic influences. I will discuss these allegations and the claims that suggest the entertainment world, particularly events like the Grammys, are mocking Christianity and promoting dark forces. Additionally, we'll delve into the Christian perspective on these claims, considering the balance between entertainment, artistic expression, and spirituality.

THE ALLEGATIONS: DEMONIC INFLUENCES IN THE MUSIC WORLD

A particular narrative claims that the music industry, including events like the Grammys, is intentionally promoting rituals and symbols associated with demonic entities. Artists like Taylor Swift, Doja Cat, and Beyoncé have been singled out for their alleged involvement in occult practices, as inferred from their music videos, performances, and statements. This theory contends that these artists are willingly collaborating with malevolent forces to achieve fame and success.

The Taylor Swift Example

One example often cited is Taylor Swift, with claims that her performances and statements carry hidden messages of witchcraft. Allegedly, she hinted at her engagement with dark forces during her shows, with references to circles, signals, and demonic imagery. This has led to concerns that her influence could be negatively affecting her audience, particularly those who are more impressionable, including children.

Similar allegations surround artists like Doja Cat and Beyoncé. Their music videos, stage performances, and lyrics are said to contain symbols and themes associated with witchcraft and the occult. The "vagina portal" reference in Beyoncé's performance and Travis Scott's astral portal stage design are cited as evidence of these supposed connections. The audience is immersed in Beyoncé's inner world, and evidently, it is a highly nuanced and suggestive environment in which they find themselves.

As the tunnel journey concludes, Beyoncé-bot makes an appearance (possibly within her own essence) and emulates horn-like structures atop her head. It's a way of revealing the minds behind her creation. Subsequently,

Beyoncé emerges once more before the audience, now adorned in a completely fresh ensemble.

Beyoncé is positioned beneath a radiant sun/star, clad in a glossy android attire, serving as a direct homage to the character Maria from the 1929 film Metropolis.

In Metropolis, the android stands beneath an inverted pentagram, a symbol of significance. The Metropolis film holds immense importance for the occult elite, particularly within the entertainment industry. Over the years, many female artists, including Beyoncé herself on multiple occasions, have drawn inspiration from the character Maria in their performances.

Beyoncé, much like thirteen years ago, has a specific reason for choosing this form of resurgence. The recurring presence of this character from an obscure German film in contemporary pop culture holds great significance today.

In Metropolis, Maria emerges as a charismatic leader deeply cherished and relied upon by the working class. However, an elite scientist abducts her and crafts an android in her likeness. This android is then dispatched to the workers, where it is employed to corrupt their values and manipulate them into working against their own interests. The movie reaches its climax with the robotic Maria performing a provocative dance, embodying the persona of Babylon, the Great Harlot of the Apocalypse.

In summary, Maria serves as the ideal representation of the role played by pop stars in today's popular culture.

During the performance, several video segments depict Beyoncé immersed in water, resembling an unborn child, and connected to various tubes and apparatus. This imagery symbolizes her being shaped and controlled by those overseeing her career.

This image encapsulates the entire performance. The visual symbolism in this picture is rich with meaning. Beyoncé's entire physique is composed of circuits, affirming the absence of her human essence. Most notably, one of her eyes is concealed by a technological component, symbolically illustrating her position as a captive of the industry. In the center of the screen, a digitally rendered rendition of Beyoncé's face is encircled by phases of the moon, suggesting the involvement of mystical practices in the formation of this android, akin to the narrative in Metropolis.

This specific image speaks volumes as well. Beyoncé is visibly bound, simultaneously grasping a microphone. It serves as a powerful representation of someone ensnared within the clutches of the entertainment industry.

Like Maria in Metropolis, Beyoncé-bot has messages to convey to her audience.

As the show nears its conclusion, the audience is exposed to a mesmerizing, swirling pattern, accompanied by eerie sounds in the background. Subsequently, an extremely ironic message is presented to the viewers.

The screen showcases the quotation, "The one who wields power over the media wields power over the mind," attributed to Jim Morrison.

The inclusion of this quote in the show carries a significant dose of irony. Beyoncé, as a product, is essentially under the ownership and influence of those who control the media. Every facet of her career is orchestrated by the most prominent figures in the media industry. In essence, those in control of the media are effectively conveying to the viewers that they are directing their thoughts.

Subsequently, the presentation becomes even more overt.

During a disturbing section of the show, the phrase "MIND CONTROL" is presented to the audience. Furthermore, within the word "CONTROL," a figure is prominently featured in a position suggesting submission, which alludes to themes associated with Beta kitten programming. After telling us that media controls the mind, Beyoncé re-emerges as ... a media personality.

In the song "America Has a Problem," Beyoncé assumes the character of a robotic news presenter, coincidentally adorned with horns reminiscent of Baphomet. Like Maria in Metropolis, Beyoncé is used by the elite to communicate specific messages to the masses. Then, the show ends in the most Beyoncé way possible. Beyoncé ascends into the air and suspends herself over the audience, creating the impression that she is embodying a certain form of a "deity" or "god."

While the music industry often portrays Beyoncé as the queen of music, the Renaissance World Tour, upon closer examination, paints a contrasting narrative. It unfolds Beyoncé's metamorphosis from a soulful R&B singer into a tool of the elite, ensnared through a fusion of science and occultism, akin to Monarch programming. As the show progresses, the theme of mind control becomes increasingly conspicuous, culminating in the stark display of the words "MIND CONTROL." In essence, the Renaissance World Tour narrates Beyoncé's conversion from an artist to an instrument of the elite, all while the audience watches with reverence and awe.

Conspiracy theories about either satanic rituals, or rituals that use imagery or themes Satan-related, follow the history of the "Satanic Panic" in the US when people began circulating false claims about children being abused in mass satanic rituals. Many people were convicted of crimes related to the panic, but some of them were later released, as reported by The New York Times. In earlier performances, Lil Nas X ignited a similar uproar from religious folks and conservative politicians when he released a music video that depicted him giving a lap dance to Satan. In Travis Scott's Astroworld Travis Scott performs on day one of the Astroworld Music Festival at NRG Park on Friday, Nov. 5, 2021, in Houston. One of the most popular conspiracy theory clips spreading online shows someone purporting to be an Astroworld attendee claiming that Scott was doing "some demonic shit" after "he just kept going" and performing despite people "screaming help."

Several conspiracy theories related to Travis Scott's Astro world concert being labeled as a "satanic ritual" had the following effects and implications:

- **Navigating Misinformation in the Age of Fact-Checking**: This statement underscores the persistent challenge of misinformation in the digital era, despite social media platforms' efforts to fact-check and moderate content. It raises questions about the effectiveness of these measures and their ability to combat the spread of false information that can sway public perception.
- **Drawing Parallels with History - The Satanic Panic**: A historical comparison emerges, reminiscent of the "Satanic Panic" phenomenon in the United States. This reference serves as a stark reminder of the tangible, real-world consequences that unfounded conspiracy theories can have. The Satanic Panic era saw innocent individuals wrongly accused and convicted, leaving lasting scars on both individuals and communities.
- **Pop Culture's Role in Shaping Narratives**: Lil Nas X's controversial music video, featuring satanic imagery, highlights the power of pop culture to fuel and perpetuate conspiracy theories. It sheds light on how creative expression,

while provocative, can ignite discussions and controversies that, in turn, facilitate the spread of baseless claims and unfounded theories.

- **Social Media's Amplification Effect**: The passage vividly illustrates a widely circulated clip where an alleged Astro world attendee accuses Travis Scott of "demonic" behavior amidst the concert chaos. This snapshot exemplifies how personal accounts and narratives can quickly gain viral traction on social media, even in the absence of concrete evidence. Such instances wield significant influence in molding public opinion.
- **The Sway of Online Influencers:** The involvement of YouTube influencers like Rich Lux and NiTris Tv in endorsing these conspiracy theories underscores the substantial impact that social media influencers can wield. Their vast viewership and extensive reach further contribute to the dissemination and legitimization of these unfounded narratives.

In summary, the effects of these conspiracy theories are multifaceted. They demonstrate the challenges social media platforms face in curbing misinformation, emphasize the historical precedents of false allegations, and highlight the role of pop culture, individual accounts, and online influencers in perpetuating and popularizing unfounded claims.

Christian Response and Perspective

From a Christian vantage point, these allegations stir deep concerns regarding the potential spiritual consequences associated with the consumption of such content. Many contend that music and entertainment wield considerable influence in shaping cultural norms and values. Consequently, the proliferation of occult symbolism and themes could be perceived as detrimental to the spiritual well-being of society. However, it's worth noting that not all Christians share this perspective.

Harmonizing Entertainment and Spirituality

While some Christians hold fast to the notion of demonic influences within the music industry, others advocate for a more nuanced stance. They posit that artistic expression and entertainment can exist independently of spirituality. It is possible to derive enjoyment from music and performance art without necessarily endorsing or participating in any perceived occult practices.

Exercising Critical Thought and Discernment

The ongoing debates surrounding these allegations underscore the paramount importance of critical thinking and discernment. In an age where information can be readily distorted or taken out of context in the digital realm, it becomes imperative to approach such claims with a judicious and discerning mindset. Additionally, it is crucial to differentiate between artistic symbolism, metaphorical expression, and the literal endorsement of certain entrenched albeit questionable beliefs.

Travis Scott

THE CHANGING LANDSCAPE OF HIP HOP AND ITS SHIFTING POPULARITY: A DEEPER ANALYSIS

The realm of hip-hop, a genre that has long dominated the music industry and popular culture, is experiencing a notable shift in its popularity and reception. Traditionally a powerhouse in mainstream music, hip hop is now grappling with challenges that are reshaping its standing on the charts and within the cultural zeitgeist. The evolving landscape of hip-hop and the factors contributing to its growing unpopularity in the mainstream still plays an abiding role in homicides occurring in big cities.

In recent times, the Billboard charts have reflected a decline in hip hop's customary domination. Historically accustomed to ruling the charts with its infectious beats and lyrical prowess, hip hop's ascent to the number one spot has slowed down. While this decline might appear as a mere ebb and flow in the industry, a closer examination reveals a more complex narrative.

The music industry's terrain is inherently entwined with business strategies and prevailing trends. As the adage goes, "music is fundamentally a business." When sales fluctuate and market dynamics undergo transformation, adaptability becomes paramount. A notable tweet from a prominent radio host succinctly captures this paradigm shift in the industry's priorities. Major record labels, often at the forefront of shaping musical trends, are shifting their focus away from signing rap artists in favor of African and Latin music.

This development sparks pertinent questions about the changing tastes of music consumers and the industry's pivot toward genres that have successfully embraced new cultural influences.

Amid this ever-evolving musical landscape, discussions concerning mental health and the repercussions of media consumption have risen to prominence. Music enthusiasts are increasingly mindful of the messages they absorb and the potential impact on their mental well-being. As these conversations gain traction, there emerges a yearning to filter the content that enters one's mind. This phenomenon manifests in the music choices people make, with a preference for uplifting and positively charged tunes. Consequently, this choice influences purchasing decisions related to merchandise and products associated with artists and their music.

The changing face of hip-hop is also evidenced by its apparent struggle to maintain its position atop the charts. The article's observation that there has not been a #1 hip-hop song on the Billboard charts underscores this shift. While hip-hop has made strides in both the underground and mainstream, its traditional dominance is being challenged by other genres that have embraced new cultural and sonic influences.

An intriguing aspect to consider is the prioritization of Afrobeats and Latin music over rap by major record labels. A cursory glance at the Billboard charts reveals the ascendancy of artists like Bad Bunny and Wiz Kid. These artists have successfully tapped into a post-genre landscape, combining musical influences from different corners of the world. This success highlights the allure of genres that can transcend linguistic and cultural barriers.

However, the challenges facing hip-hop extend far beyond market dynamics. A case in point is Lantana Easy, an artist hailing from Cincinnati, OH, who represents and encapsulates a growing sentiment within the hip-hop community. He eloquently articulates the concern that certain hip-hop music, saturated with themes of violence and aggression, might be casting a shadow over the mental well-being of its listeners. As conversations surrounding mental health continue to gather momentum, music enthusiasts are reevaluating the impact of the content they consume and its profound implications for their emotional states.

From a business vantage point, record labels are not merely gravitating towards Afrobeat's and Latin music due to prevailing market trends; they are also assessing the sustainability of their investments. Hip-hop, especially within specific sub-genres, can carry inherent risks, including legal entanglements and the potential for fleeting careers. With a paramount emphasis on financial returns, record labels find themselves compelled to redirect their focus toward genres that offer greater stability and fewer vicissitudes. It would indeed be beneficial if record labels encouraged their artists to produce uplifting records that inspire and motivate young individuals to make positive contributions to society, steering them away from themes of violence and non-productivity. Perhaps the public is effectively conveying to record labels that they are no longer receptive to music centered around themes of death, destruction, and murder.

JOBLESSNESS DUE TO OFFSHORING AND OUTSOURCING

Many of the opportunities formerly available to young men 50 years ago no longer exist. Young men in high school and between the ages of 15-34 see no future; this is a problem that will affect society in many ways in the future. We must solve this issue because young boys and men will find ways to utilize their energies in negative and often brutal fashion if not otherwise constructively directed.

The loss of factories and manufacturing jobs to countries like China and other Asian countries can have significant effects on employment opportunities for all men in America. This phenomenon is often referred to as "offshoring" or "outsourcing," where companies move their manufacturing operations to countries with lower labor costs and different regulatory environments. Here are some ways in which this can impact jobs for men in America:

Job Displacement: The most immediate and profound impact is the displacement of jobs within the manufacturing sector itself. As factories shut their doors or relocate to foreign shores, the consequences reverberate through the workforce. Workers, including a significant number of men, who once relied on these industries find themselves facing layoffs and unemployment. The ramifications are far-reaching, encompassing reduced incomes, job insecurity, and the daunting challenge of seeking new employment, especially when their skills may not easily translate to other fields.

Decline in Blue-Collar Opportunities: Many manufacturing roles have long been synonymous with blue-collar employment, demanding a blend of physical labor and technical proficiency. The decline of manufacturing inevitably leads to a shrinking pool of such opportunities. This shift disproportionately affects men, who have traditionally dominated these fields and now confront a dwindling landscape for their skillset.

Deepening Income Inequality: Historically, manufacturing positions have offered relatively stable wages and comprehensive benefits, often without the requirement of advanced degrees. The erosion of these jobs can exacerbate income inequality. Men who previously held secure manufacturing positions may grapple with the challenge of securing comparable employment in other sectors, resulting in a widening chasm between skilled and unskilled labor.

Evolution of Skill Demands: As manufacturing roles are outsourced, the employment landscape can undergo a transformative shift. Emerging industries demand distinct skillsets, emphasizing technology, services, and knowledge-based professions. Men transitioning from manufacturing may face the imperative to retrain or acquire new competencies to remain competitive in this changing job market.

Local Economic Fallout: Factory closures send shockwaves through local economies. The disappearance of manufacturing jobs precipitates reduced demand for goods and services within the community. The ripple effects extend to related sectors such as retail, transportation, and hospitality, amplifying job losses and economic strain in these areas.

Erosion of Expertise: The exodus of factories to foreign shores carries a hidden cost— the loss of specialized expertise and knowledge associated with certain industries. This erosion hinders a country's capacity to innovate, manufacture unique products, and compete on a global scale.

Diminished Economic Resilience: A heavy reliance on outsourced manufacturing can render a nation's economy susceptible to disruptions in global supply chains. The vulnerabilities exposed by events like the COVID-19 pandemic underscore the importance of maintaining a diverse and robust domestic manufacturing base. Such resilience is paramount to weathering economic challenges and ensuring a nation's stability in an ever-changing world.

It's crucial to recognize that offshoring, although a substantial contributor, represents just one facet of the intricate forces shaping employment dynamics. Automation, relentless technological progress, evolving consumer tastes, and the ebb and flow of the global economy all wield considerable influence over the employment landscape for both men and the broader American workforce.

In response to the formidable challenges posed by the erosion of manufacturing employment, policy interventions come into focus. These encompass strategic investments in education, robust workforce development initiatives, targeted retraining programs, and bolstering emerging industries. Such measures are advanced as essential means to facilitate the transition of affected workers toward fresh opportunities and sectors.

Technology has had a profound impact on employment opportunities for men, shaping the job landscape in various ways. While technology has brought about new opportunities and efficiencies, it has also led to challenges and disruptions in certain industries. Here are some ways in which technology is affecting employment opportunities for men:

- **Automation and Employment Shifts**: Undoubtedly, technology's transformative force lies in automation, the process of harnessing machinery and technology to take over tasks once carried out by humans. This often results in the displacement of roles, particularly those tethered to repetitive and routine functions. For men employed in fields like manufacturing and specific service sectors, heavily automated processes may spell job loss.

- **Rise of Novel Job Opportunities**: However, the advent of automation doesn't only spell gloom; it also ushers in fresh employment vistas. New positions emerge, centered on the development, operation, and maintenance of technology. Men skilled in realms like software development, data analysis, cybersecurity, and artificial intelligence find promising prospects, both within the tech sector and beyond.

- **Flexible Work and Remote Horizons**: The technological surge facilitates remote work arrangements and flexible job structures, liberating men to operate from the comfort of their homes or other locales. This dynamic

69

promotes superior work-life equilibrium and offers avenues for pursuing careers that might have previously been geographically implausible.

- **Impacting Traditional Male-Dominated Arenas**: Industries historically dominated by men, such as manufacturing and construction, stand witness to profound alterations under technology's influence. The advent of automation and fresh technologies reshapes the requisite skill sets, fundamentally altering employment dynamics in these sectors.

- **Skill Set and Education Imperatives**: Adapting to the contemporary job market, men must acquire technological proficiencies. Digital literacy, coding prowess, and adeptness in utilizing technology tools position individuals more competitively in the workforce.

- **Freelancing and the Gig Economy**: The technological realm fuels the gig economy's ascent, empowering men to undertake short-term projects and freelance labor. Although this offers heightened flexibility, it may concurrently introduce income volatility and a diminishment in benefits compared to conventional full-time employment.

- **Data-Driven Decision Craft**: Across multiple sectors, the collection and scrutiny of data through technology assume paramount importance. Men equipped with data analytics expertise and the capacity to decipher complex information contribute substantially to informed decision-making and strategic planning.

- **Continuous Learning Through Reskilling and Upskilling**: Given technology's rapid evolution, men must engage in continual skill refinement to preserve market relevance. Initiatives for reskilling and upskilling prove indispensable for adapting to shifting technological demands.

- **Influence of Artificial Intelligence and Machine Learning**: AI and machine learning increasingly permeate diverse industries, leaving their imprint on functions like customer service, data analysis, and even creative tasks. Men well- versed in these technologies discover opportunities to enhance efficiency and foster innovation.

- **Navigating Disruption and Transition**: The advent of novel technologies often ushers in disruption across industries and sectors. Men may find themselves compelled to transition from dwindling domains to burgeoning sectors, necessitating adaptability and a readiness to acquire fresh proficiencies.

In summary, technology is reshaping the employment landscape for men in profound and often unforeseen ways. While it presents both challenges and opportunities, staying adaptable, acquiring relevant skills, and embracing new technological advancements are crucial for men to navigate the evolving job market successfully.

THE CHANGING LANDSCAPE OF WORK AND THE STRUGGLES OF MEN: INSIGHTS FROM "OF BOYS AND MEN"

The dynamics of work and its association with gender roles have been undergoing a profound transformation in recent decades. Richard V. Reeves' thought-provoking book, "Of Boys and Men," brings to light the challenges faced by men in an evolving economy and society. I will delve into the key arguments presented in the book, highlighting the changing nature of work, the implications for men, and the proposed strategies for addressing these challenges.

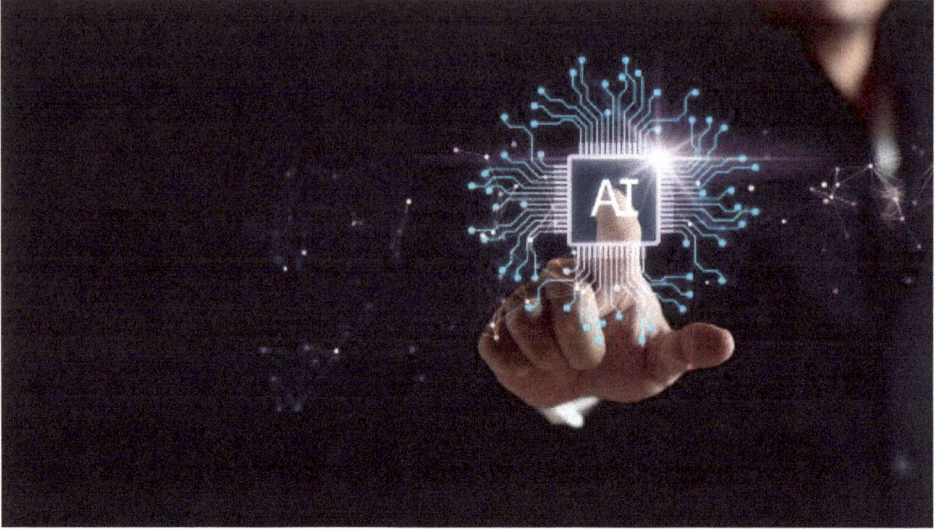

Reeves' book draws special attention to the declining participation of men in the workforce, particularly among those in the prime working age bracket of 25 to 54. Over the past sixty years, the percentage of men in this age group working or seeking employment has steadily decreased. This downward trend raises concerns about the well- being of families and exacerbates economic inequality. Reeves argues that these challenges cannot be ignored, and it is possible to address both gender inequalities simultaneously, without undermining the progress made for women.

RACISM ~ DISCRIMINATION ~ PREJUDICE

The author emphasizes that the economic landscape has shifted dramatically, with women entering the workforce in substantial numbers. As a result, the traditional role of men as sole breadwinners has been disrupted. This transformation, while advancing the goal of economic independence for women, has not been fully absorbed by society's cultural norms. The rapid pace of change in economic dynamics has outstripped the corresponding changes in societal perceptions of masculinity, femininity, and family roles.

One of the key insights of the book is that the gender pay gap is not a one-sided issue. While women's wages have risen, particularly at the higher end of the pay scale, men's wages have stagnated or even declined, particularly in the middle-and lower-income brackets. This has led to a paradoxical narrowing of the gender pay gap but has also resulted in economic challenges for a significant portion of the male population.

The evolving labor landscape has ushered in a decline in occupations traditionally associated with physical prowess and minimal educational prerequisites. Fields like manufacturing have borne the brunt of this transformation, disproportionately affecting men. Reeves posits that the solution doesn't entail reversing these largely irreversible economic shifts but rather fostering men's adaptability to new professional domains.

Enter the concept of "HEAL" sectors, championed by Reeves, encompassing health, education, administration, and literacy. These sectors brim with abundant opportunities, offering men a promising avenue to transition into vocations that prize verbal and written acumen over sheer physical strength.

However, venturing into HEAL sectors isn't without its challenges. Many of these domains have progressively tilted towards female predominance, perpetuating gender disparities in the job market. Reeves underscores that men encounter stereotypes and stigmatization when entering professions like teaching, nursing, and social work. In response, the author advocates for the establishment of scholarships aimed at incentivizing men to embrace these fields, mirroring efforts to bolster women's participation in STEM disciplines.

Additionally, Reeves emphasizes the societal dividends reaped from having more men engaged in roles such as teaching and counseling. Male role models in education can wield particular significance for male students, offering guidance and inspiration. Furthermore, in arenas like mental health counseling and substance abuse counseling, the gender of the provider can profoundly influence the comfort and rapport experienced by recipients of these services.

In conclusion, Richard V. Reeves' book "Of Boys and Men" sheds light on the challenges faced by men in an evolving economic and societal landscape. The decline of traditional male-dominated sectors and the rise of new industries present both opportunities and obstacles. Reeves argues for an approach that encourages men to adapt to changing job markets, particularly in the HEAL sectors, and advocates for breaking down the stereotypes that discourage men from entering these fields. Ultimately, the book urges policymakers and society to acknowledge the struggles faced by men and work towards fostering a more inclusive and adaptive workforce that benefits everyone.

OCCUPATIONAL SEGREGATION: A COMPLEX ISSUE IMPACTING ECONOMIC EQUALITY

Occupational segregation, the persistent phenomenon where specific demographic groups find themselves overrepresented in certain job categories, casts a long shadow over the American labor landscape. This issue reverberates beyond individual employment prospects, rippling through society with dire implications. The consequences include wage stagnation, substandard working conditions for marginalized populations, the exacerbation of wage disparities rooted in inherent traits, and a dampening effect on overall economic growth. In the following exploration, I will dissect the causes and ramifications of occupational segregation, with a focus on race, ethnicity, and gender, while also offering potential policy remedies.

Unearthing the Underpinnings of Occupational Segregation

Occupational segregation finds its genesis in deeply ingrained societal biases and historical policy decisions. Discriminatory practices, pervasive stereotyping, and systemic prejudices have conspired throughout history to corral certain groups into narrow job pathways. The historical roots run deep, with race-based occupational segregation tracing back to the harrowing era of slavery. Legislative acts, notably the New Deal, fortified these disparities by withholding workplace safeguards from specific groups, perpetuating the cycle of low-quality employment for marginalized individuals. Occupational segregation finds reinforcement in discrimination and stereotypes. Women, for instance, have traditionally been corralled into predefined roles, shackled by gender- based misconceptions about their capabilities and societal roles. The devaluation of work anchored in the demographics of the labor force further fuels this divisive issue. Despite legislative milestones such as the Equal Pay Act and the Civil Rights Act, the persistence of discriminatory practices and biases in workplaces has stymied meaningful progress in combatting occupational segregation.

The Far-Reaching Impact on Wages and Economic Equity

The ripples of occupational segregation extend far and wide, making a palpable mark on wages and economic equity. It casts a long shadow, giving rise to glaring gender and racial wage disparities. Women, especially women of color, find themselves grappling with significantly lower earnings compared to their white male counterparts. What's more, even when women and individuals from diverse backgrounds access higher education, they often confront the stark reality of being funneled into lower-paying roles that don't align with their educational achievements. This pervasive injustice results in across-the-board wage suppression and constrained economic mobility.

The grip of occupational segregation isn't limited to individual workers; its impact reverberates throughout the employment landscape and the economy. The overconcentration of specific demographic groups within select job sectors can lead to an oversupply of labor, inevitably driving down wages within those fields. Additionally, the glaring lack of diversity in certain industries stifles innovation and hampers productivity, thus placing a stranglehold on overall economic growth.

Charting a Course Toward Solutions

Effecting change on the frontlines of occupational segregation necessitates a multifaceted strategy that combats both the prevalence of low-quality jobs and the persistent barriers hindering access to high-quality ones. Policy solutions must zero in on elevating the minimum wage, expunging subminimum wages and discriminatory practices, bolstering collective bargaining, and expanding access to paid leave. Furthermore, equitable access to education, workforce development initiatives, and apprenticeship programs can inject diversity into high-quality professions, opening pathways of advancement for underrepresented groups.

Anti-discrimination measures and enforcement are also vital in combating occupational segregation. Paycheck fairness laws and incentives for equitable hiring can promote diversity and reduce the concentration of groups in specific occupations. By tackling both the root causes and the immediate consequences of occupational segregation, policymakers can foster a more inclusive and economically prosperous labor market.

Occupational segregation continues to perpetuate inequality in the American labor market. Its origins in societal biases, discriminatory practices, and historical policies have led to persistent wage gaps and limited economic growth. To address this issue, policymakers must implement a range of solutions that target both low-quality jobs and barriers to entry in high-quality jobs. By taking decisive action to combat occupational segregation, society can pave the way for a more equitable and prosperous future for all workers, regardless of their demographic characteristics.

The origins of race-based occupational segregation can be traced back to the dark era of slavery. When emancipation finally arrived in 1865, a staggering two-thirds of enslaved individuals toiled in forced labor on farms, while others served in domestic capacities. However, with the abolition of slavery, legislative barriers and limited access to alternative employment opportunities often left Black workers with little choice but to persist in agricultural or domestic roles. An illustrative example can be found in South Carolina, where Black residents could only pursue careers as farmers or servants if they obtained a license from a judge.

The introduction of the New Deal, which laid the foundation for job protections in the United States, notably and regrettably excluded farmworkers, as well as domestic and agricultural laborers from fundamental safeguards such as minimum wage, Social Security, and overtime benefits. This deliberate omission had profound consequences, disproportionately impacting Black, Mexican American, Native American, and Asian American workers who were subsequently denied these basic workplace standards. This grave injustice set a disheartening precedent that reverberates through time, contributing to the persistent segregation into low-quality jobs that persists today.

Consider this: in 1890, a substantial 52 percent of Black women found themselves confined to domestic work. By 1940, this figure had soared to a staggering 70 percent. Fast forward to the present day, and while individual households are no longer the primary employers, the legacy of occupational segregation endures in roles centered around domestic and caregiving functions. Occupations such as home health aides, personal care aides, and childcare workers continue to disproportionately represent Black women's employment, with a staggering 1 in 5 individuals in these roles being Black women. Simultaneously, Black men often find themselves overrepresented in various driving and cleaning occupations.

DISCRIMINATION, HARASSMENT, AND STEREOTYPES

Systems and policy choices reflect stereotypes, bias, and perceptions of gender, racial, ethnic, and disability status, and they significantly influence and limit an individual's occupational choice. Florence Nightingale, credited with the professionalization of nursing in the late 19th century, created a new role for women in the workplace at a time when the concept was truly novel, proclaiming that nursing duties "could only satisfactorily be done by a woman." Today, characteristics seen as inherently "female" are associated with traditionally female-dominated occupations. For example, women are stereotyped as caring and domestic, and thus likely to be successful in teaching, nursing, or caregiving roles, or as physically weak and unauthoritative, and thus unsuccessful in construction and trades or management positions. Over time, these perceptions are strengthened and perpetuated by norms embedded in systems such as education and workplace recruitment.

Direct discrimination based on immutable characteristics is both a cause and an effect of occupational segregation. Landmark legislation enacted over the 20th century has moved the needle but cannot alone change behavior. The Equal Pay Act of 1963 prohibited employers from paying different wages based on sex, while the Civil Rights Act of 1964 prohibited workplace segregation and discrimination based on race, color, religion, sex, or national origin. Later, the Pregnancy Discrimination Act of 1978 prohibited discrimination based on pregnancy, childbirth, or related medical conditions. In 1990,

Title I of the Americans with Disabilities Act banned discrimination based on disability. Affirmative action and anti-discrimination enforcement initially led to an increase in workplace integration and narrowed wage gaps. However, due to a variety of intersecting factors, including declines in enforcement capacity and in political will and exclusions of certain industries from workplace protections, progress in this arena has plateaued.

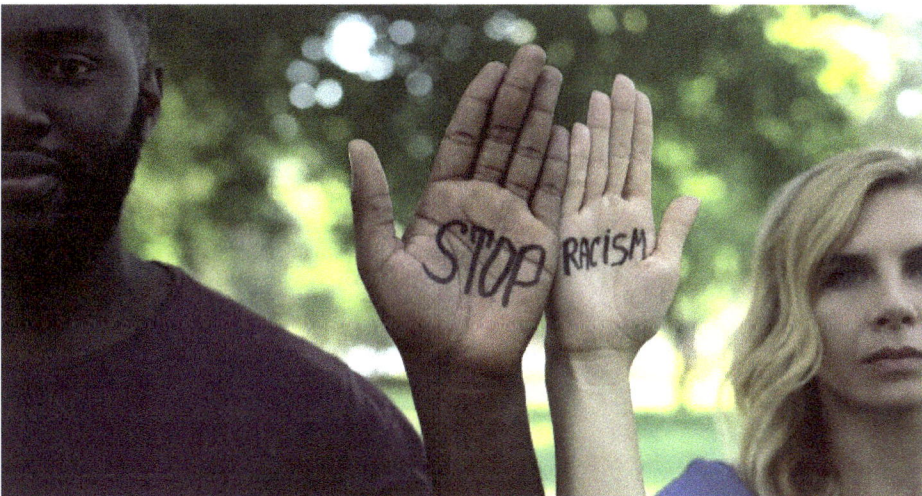

Today, women are most likely to report sexual harassment to the Equal Employment Opportunity Commission in industries that are the most male-dominated, such as construction, utilities, mining, and transportation and warehousing. This lessens the likelihood of integration, as women may opt out of joining or leave male-dominated jobs because of their experiences or concerns over harassment. Integration is most difficult for groups facing intersecting biases, such as women of color. For example, in corporate contexts, women of color—particularly Black women—are least likely to report having proactive or defensive support from managers, thus undermining promotability and leading to significant underrepresentation in corporate roles.

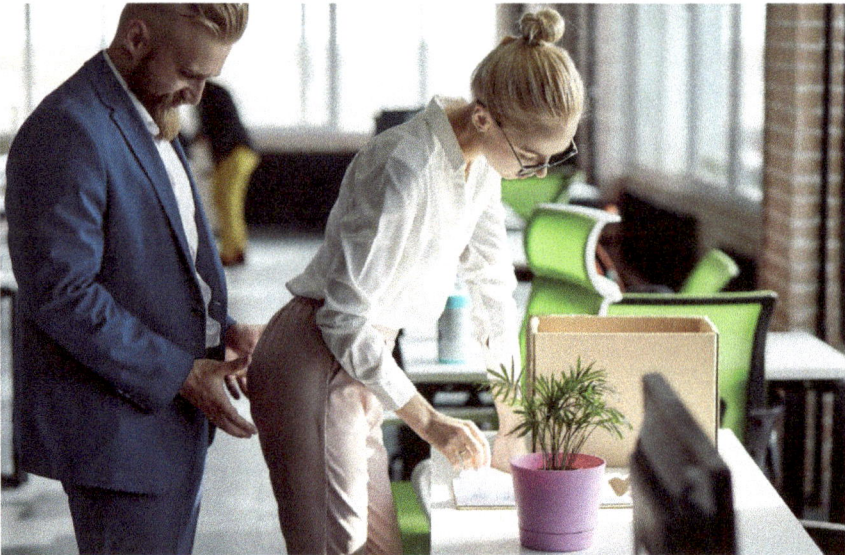

Occupational segregation within the labor market is intricately linked to the structure of K-12 and postsecondary educational systems. In the early years of education, girls perform on par with or even outperform boys in math and science exams from fourth to eighth grade. They also enroll in advanced math and science courses at equal rates as they progress into high school. However, a concerning gap begins to emerge during high school and continues through higher education. This gap is most pronounced among Black and Latino girls, who remain underrepresented in science and math professions.

The roots of this educational divide extend to the concept of vocational education, which can often channel or segregate students into specific career paths. Initially conceived as a solution to address labor shortages in burgeoning industrial settings and to educate a surge of new students, many of whom hailed from disadvantaged backgrounds, vocational training has historically directed lower-income students into occupational training programs. Meanwhile, traditional liberal arts education was predominantly reserved for wealthier, primarily white students.

Despite ongoing efforts to enhance the quality of vocational education and calls for universal access to career training in high schools, racial disparities persist. Black and Latino students are less likely to enroll in science, technology, engineering, and math (STEM) classes, which typically lead to higher-earning careers, and more likely to opt for hospitality and human services programs.

These discrepancies extend into postsecondary education as well. Hispanic and Black students remain significantly underrepresented in four-year STEM majors such as physical sciences, mathematics, and engineering. The gender gap further compounds the issue, with, for instance, only 17 Hispanic women and nine Black women earning bachelor's degrees in engineering for every 100 white men.

Furthermore, while higher education attainment is often linked to higher income, this correlation can mask a crucial underlying reality. Factors such as the cost of attendance, the prevalence of unpaid internships, and the time constraints of working for pay during school can make the eventual payoff of degrees unfeasible for some students. This disproportionately affects students of color, whose families typically have lower wealth compared to white families. Consequently, certain demographic groups find themselves overrepresented in jobs that do not require lengthy educational pathways. Shockingly, even among those with higher education, occupational segregation prevails, with workers of color and women often occupying different, frequently lower-paid roles compared to their white male counterparts.

Impacts of Occupational Segregation on Wages and the Economy

Social and institutional factors lead to pervasive occupational segregation in the labor market, with women and people of color frequently marginalized and segregated into those jobs that tend to offer the lowest compensation, provide less access to benefits, and limit workers' economic security. Two of these support these findings. The crowding hypothesis suggests that the concentration of one demographic, such as Black men or women, into a small number of occupations creates an oversupply of their labor within these occupations and reduces this group's wages. The devaluation theory suggests that work performed by certain groups, such as women, is devalued because they themselves are devalued in society, and market decisions about the economic value of a type of work are made after that job has been established to have a particular demographic composition. This is partly why equal pay advocates globally have moved away from frameworks of "equal pay for equal work" to "equal pay for work of equal value."

OCCUPATIONAL SEGREGATION CONTRIBUTES TO EXISTING GENDER AND RACIAL WAGE GAPS

73 cents Women's wage per every dollar a white, non-Hispanic man earns
58 cents Black women's wage per every dollar a white, non-Hispanic man earns
49 cents Latina women's wage per every dollar a white, non-Hispanic man earns
75 cents Asian American, Native Hawaiian, and Pacific Islander women's wage per every dollar a white, non-Hispanic man earns.

Occupational segregation plays a pivotal role in perpetuating enduring gender and racial wage disparities. When we examine income, we find that working women, on average, earn just 73 cents for every dollar earned by a white, non-Hispanic man. However, this pay gap becomes even more pronounced among women of color, with Black women earning a mere 58 cents and Latina women earning just 49 cents for every dollar earned by their white, non-Hispanic male counterparts.

Even though Asian American, Native Hawaiian, and Pacific Islander women appear to earn around 75 cents for every dollar earned by white, non-Hispanic men when we look at overall figures, the situation becomes more nuanced when we delve into specific communities within these groups. For instance, data reveal that certain subgroup, such as Burmese women, face some of the most substantial wage disparities along both racial and gender lines.

The wage inequality isn't confined solely to women. Black and Hispanic men consistently earn less than their white male counterparts. Furthermore, the adverse impact of wage suppression extends beyond the overrepresented group in a particular occupation. In sectors marked by high levels of occupational segregation, wages tend to be depressed for everyone working in those roles, irrespective of gender, race, or ethnicity.

This wage devaluation becomes particularly apparent as occupations move towards greater integration. Paradoxically, in some instances, as women become a larger proportion of the workforce in a particular occupation over time, the average pay in that occupation decreases, further underscoring the detrimental effects of occupational segregation.

Low wages limit the capacity of individuals to weather financial shocks, spend, save, and accumulate wealth and retire with dignity. This is particularly important in households where marginalized workers are the family's breadwinner—common for mothers of color. Occupational segregation negatively affects not only workers but also employers and the economy more broadly. Low wages are associated with high turnover within an occupation, a burden for employers who then must use resources for hiring and training, lowering productivity. Moreover, as occupational segregation limits an individual's choice to work where their skills are best matched, it can further lower productivity. Unsurprisingly, balanced, gender-integrated teams and management are more productive and profitable than segregated ones—and at a macro level, economies with labor markets with higher levels of gender segregation have experienced lower levels of economic growth since 1980.

Occupational Segregation Today: By the Numbers

The two datasets below—on occupational composition and demographic concentration— demonstrate how occupational segregation presents in the labor market today.

1. Occupational Composition

This interactive visualization explores what groups are over - or underrepresented in a specific job. Below are a few sample conclusions from this dataset:

• Asian American or Pacific Islander women across all levels of education constitute 3 percent of total employment and are most overrepresented as manicurists, at 51 percent of workers in this occupation, earning $21,228 per year.

• Black men with at least a bachelor's degree make up 1 percent of total employment and are most overrepresented as probation officers, at 8 percent of workers in this occupation, earning $56,013 per year.

• White men with at least a bachelor's degree constitute 14 percent of total employment and are most overrepresented as aircraft pilots and flight engineers, at 65 percent of workers in this occupation, earning $161,888 per year.

2. Demographic Concentration

The top five jobs in which selected demographic groups work demonstrate how occupation contributes to a group's overall economic security. For example, 18 percent of Hispanic or Latina women work in five occupations that pay an average wage of $23,196, while 14 percent of white men work in five occupations that pay an average wage of $59,670.

A Framework for Policy Solutions to End Occupational Segregation

Government at all levels must address occupational segregation by both raising the floor and making the ceiling more accessible. First, policy solutions must improve the quality of all jobs, particularly those where marginalized workers are overrepresented. This ensures that jobs are not devalued due to the composition of the sector's workers.

Policymakers can increase the quality of low-wage work in a variety of ways, including raising the minimum wage; ending the tipped minimum wage and subminimum wage; enhancing collective bargaining access and protections; and ensuring all workers have access to paid medical and family leave. Second, policymakers and government at all levels must diversify high-quality jobs to allow underrepresented workers to succeed in those roles. This can be done through ensuring equitable access to secondary and postsecondary education, workforce development, and apprenticeship programs; strengthening anti-harassment and anti-discrimination measures and enforcement; passing paycheck fairness laws; and setting incentives, goals, and requirements for employers to hire equitably.

Occupational segregation affects the personal and economic dignity of millions of Americans, particularly women and workers of color, and it depresses wages and limits economic growth. The product of intentional policy decisions, lawmakers, and government at all levels can mitigate its impacts through policies that acknowledge this labor market condition and actively work to address it.

FEMINISM AND HIGHER EDUCATION

The feminist movement, which advocates for gender equality and the rights of women, has had complex and varied effects on employment opportunities for males. It's important to note that the impact of the feminist movement on men's employment prospects is not a direct cause-and-effect relationship, but rather a result of changing social attitudes, policies, and economic dynamics. The feminist movement has influenced employment opportunities for men in the following manner:

1. **Evolution of Gender Roles**: The feminist movement has been instrumental in reshaping traditional gender roles and expectations, promoting greater equality between genders in various facets of life, including work. This shift in societal norms has fostered a more inclusive perspective on careers, encouraging men to explore a wider array of professional fields, transcending conventional male- dominated domains.

2. **Emphasis on Work-Life Balance:** Feminist advocacy has underscored the significance of achieving a harmonious work-life balance for both men and women. This emphasis has resulted in alterations to workplace policies, such as the implementation of parental leave and flexible work arrangements. These policies enable men to take on more active roles in caregiving responsibilities, granting them increased choices in balancing their

professional and family lives.

3. **Redefining Men's Roles in Caregiving**: The feminist movement's commitment to dismantling gender stereotypes has played a pivotal role in transforming societal attitudes toward men's caregiving roles. This transformation has fostered greater acceptance of men pursuing careers in fields traditionally associated with women, including nursing, teaching, and childcare.

4. **Impact on Male-Dominated Sectors**: With an intensified focus on gender equality, industries that have historically been male-dominated are now facing mounting pressure to diversify their workforce. While this shift presents enhanced opportunities for women in these sectors, it may also prompt men to consider professions they might not have contemplated previously.

5. **Combating Stereotypes and Biases**: The feminist movement's persistent efforts to challenge stereotypes and biases have yielded benefits for men as well. By dispelling negative assumptions about men's capabilities in various fields, these efforts have paved the way for men to pursue careers that were previously pigeonholed as traditionally female-dominated.

6. **Navigating Limited Opportunities**: Some critics argue that as more women enter the workforce and strive for leadership roles, men may perceive heightened competition for limited opportunities. However, it's crucial to recognize that this dynamic is often influenced by broader economic trends and specific industry factors rather than being solely a result of feminist movements.

7. **Policy Reforms**: Feminist advocacy has ushered in policy changes benefiting both men and women, including initiatives for equal pay and anti-discrimination laws. These policies are aimed at fostering fairer workplaces and dismantling barriers to career advancement, benefiting all employees alike.

Black women are seeking higher education at a much greater rate than black men. However, black women are less educated than white men and white women percentage-wise.

Black women are significantly less likely than white women to enroll in four-year colleges, graduate within six years, and go on to earn advanced degrees.

- The number of white women (39%) getting an associate or bachelor's degree by the age of 29 is nearly twice as high as for Black women (21%) and Latinas (20%). Among Black students in higher education, women are more likely than men to earn degrees: Black women get 64.1% of bachelor's degrees, 71.5% of master's degrees and 65.9%of doctoral, medical, and dental degrees.

- Fewer students of color attend four-year colleges than white students do: 30.6% of Latinx; 27.1% of Blacks and 39.3% white.

- Students of color are significantly more likely to attend for-profit colleges: 25.2% among Latinx to 28% among Blacks vs. 11.4% among whites.

- Black women are being awarded master's degrees at a significantly higher proportion than Black men at historically Black colleges and universities (HBCUs), a 1990-2015 National Center for Educational Statistics (NCES) shows.

- In the 2015 academic year, the most recent data available, 3,869 master's degrees were awarded to Black women compared to 1,545 master's degrees awarded to Black Men, a ratio of approximately 5 to 2.

- In the same academic year, 141,358 Black women were enrolled at HBCUs compared to 86,905 Black males, a ratio over 2 to 1.

- Black women also earn doctorates at a higher proportion at HBCUs. In 2015, women were awarded 1,084 such degrees whereas Black men earned were awarded 492. A ratio very close to 2 to 1.

- Paris Dennard, Senior Director of Strategic Communications, at the Thurgood Marshall College Fund proposed this is partly a reflection of the higher proportion of women enrolled at 4-year institutions nationwide.

- "I'm not certain of factors that contribute to why the disparity of enrollment exists, but I think looking at enrollment is a good place to start," Dennard wrote in an email to the AFRO.

- Kenneth K. Wong, Walter and Lenore Annenberg Professor for Education Policy and Director, Urban Education Policy Program at Brown University, provided three possible explanations for the disparity. Firstly, there are more opportunities outside of college for Black men and men in general when it comes to careers that do not require post-graduate or even post-high school degrees, the professor said. These careers include apprenticed and journeyman trades like construction and the military, both of which skew male participation.

- A second explanation that may be promoting women's enrollment as opposed to depressing men's enrollment is the types of work that require master's degrees.

- "Because I run a master's program of education policy at Brown, when I look at the statistics it's closely aligned with what I'm seeing in our program," Wong said. "That is, when you look at programs that are related to children or family services, in general, it's more likely that you'll have a higher representation of female students at the master's level."

- However, something may be happening, or not happening before enrollment, while students are still in high school.

- Dr. Brian K. Bridges, Vice President, Research and Member Engagement at United Negro College Fund, described a growing disparity over generations.

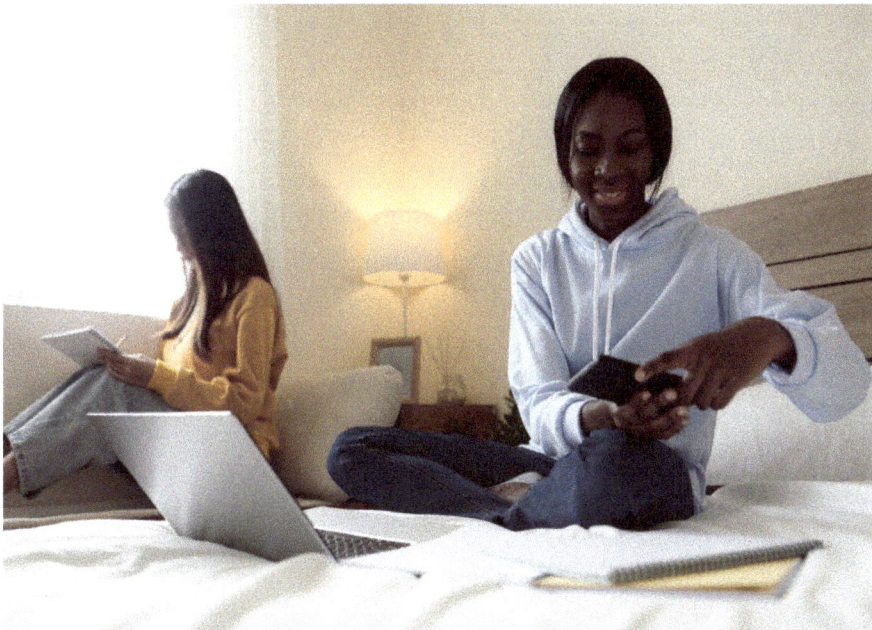

- More than 64.3% of white students finish a four-year degree within six years, compared to 55% of Latinx students and 39.8% of Black students.

- Enrollment at the open-access community colleges and four-year colleges and universities is 37% Black and Latinx, compared to enrollment at the top-funded and most selective four-year colleges and universities where enrollment is 75% white.

- Black and Latinx students are over-represented in the lower-earning majors.

- The top majors of Black students include: health and medical administration services (21%); human services and community organization (20%); social work (19%); public administration (17%); criminal justice and fire protection (15%); sociology (14%); computer and information systems (14%); human resources and personnel management (14%); interdisciplinary social sciences (13%); and pre-law and legal studies (13%).

- The top majors of Latinx students include: international business (22%); industrial and manufacturing engineering (17%); French, German, Latin and other common foreign language studies (16%); biomedical engineering (15%); international relations (15%); linguistics and comparative language and literature (14%); general education (12%); human services and community organization (12%); language and drama education (12%). Black women represent just under 7% of the population, but only 4.2% of biology sciences, 2.6% of computer sciences, 2.8% of physical sciences, 2.3% of math and statistics and 0.99% of engineering degrees.

- Black and Latinx students are more likely to leave STEM majors than white students. At the beginning of studies, around 20% of white, Latinx and Black students declared a STEM major, but the students of color switched out of STEM majors at higher rates: 37% for Latinx and 40% for Black students, compared to 29% of white students. About 20% of Latinx and 26% of Black STEM majors left the institutions without graduating compared, to 13% of white STEM majors.

- Some schools are creating scholars programs to attract and retain more students of color to earn STEM doctorates, such as the Meyerhoff Scholars Program at the University of Maryland, Baltimore.

There is an insufficient representation of people of color among college faculties and staff, resulting in a lack of diversity, equity, and inclusion in teaching methods, curriculum development, and the availability of mentors and student support services. To address this issue, some institutions like the University of California, Los Angeles, have implemented a requirement for faculty and staff candidates to provide information about their efforts to promote equity, diversity, and inclusion.

Economic disparities between black and white households in the United States persist significantly. Several factors contribute to this phenomenon, including limited upward mobility, labor market discrimination, significant disparities in incarceration rates, unequal access to quality education, historical obstacles to homeownership, and more. While higher education is often seen as a powerful tool for bridging racial divides, its effectiveness is constrained by four key factors:

- the gap in college achievement is as wide as ever.
- black Americans with an undergraduate degree are less wealthy than whites.
- marriage rates by race remain wide even for college graduates.

• the chances of both spouses having an undergraduate degree is lower for black couples.

1) Race Gaps in College Completion Remain Wide

To comprehend the income and wealth disparities based on race within households it is imperative to examine not just the individual-level factors of education and earnings, but also consider the dynamics of family structure and marital patterns.

There has been a significant increase in rates of four-year college completion among black Americans, especially women. But rates among whites have increased just as rapidly, again especially among women. Almost half (44.7 percent) of white women aged 25 to 35 in 2015 have completed four years of college. For black men the rate is just 17.2 percent:

The College Gap by Race and Gender

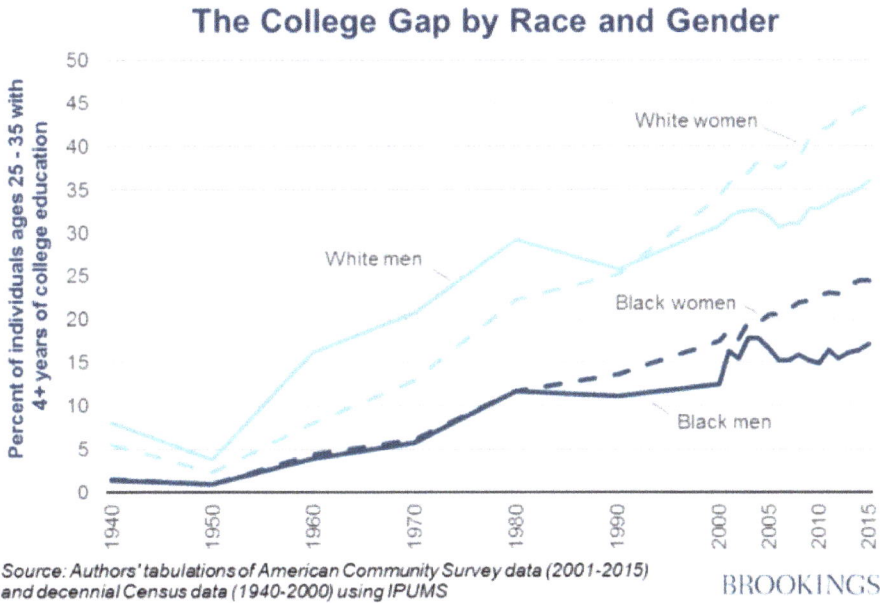

Source: Authors' tabulations of American Community Survey data (2001-2015) and decennial Census data (1940-2000) using IPUMS

BROOKINGS

Women are now outperforming men in terms of completing four years of college. Within racial categories, women are now more likely than men to complete college to the tune of 5 to 7 percentage points.

2) An Undergraduate Degree Is Not a Wealth Generator for Black Americans

So black Americans are still much less likely to get an undergraduate degree. But even when they do, they are less able to create greater economic security, at least as measured by household wealth, as new data from the Survey of Consumer Finances shows:

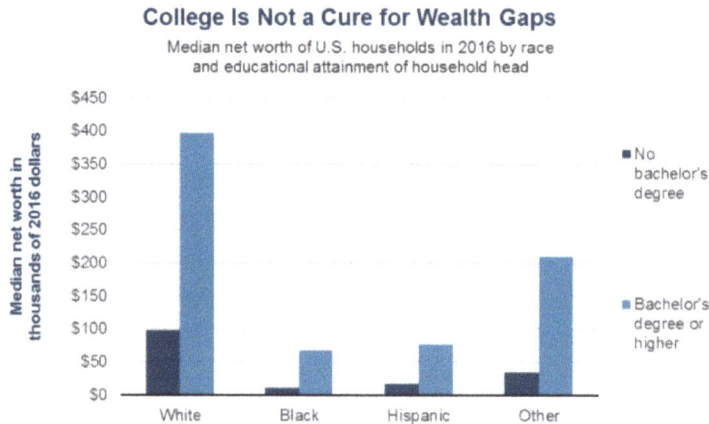

College Is Not a Cure for Wealth Gaps

Median net worth of U.S. households in 2016 by race and educational attainment of household head

Source: Lisa J. Dettling, Joanne W. Hsu, Lindsay Jacobs, et al. "Recent Trends in Wealth-Holding by Race and Ethnicity: Evidence from the Survey of Consumer Finances." Federal Reserve Board. September 27, 2017.

BROOKINGS

Indeed, households led by black college graduates possess lower wealth compared to white households with lesser educational attainment. Once more, a multitude of factors are undoubtedly influencing this phenomenon. Among these factors is the persistence of racial wage disparity, even among individuals who have completed college, particularly among men.

In 2015, college-educated white men over age 25 made a median of $32 per hour, compared to $25 for black men.

3) Black College Graduates Less Likely to be Married

U.S. Race Gaps in Marriage by Education

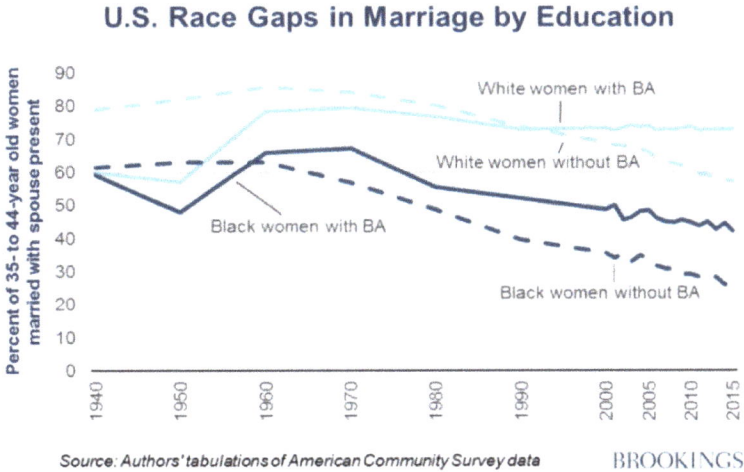

Source: Authors' tabulations of American Community Survey data   BROOKINGS

One contributing factor to the presence of well-educated individuals in more prosperous households is their higher likelihood of being married, resulting in a dual-income arrangement. Currently, women with a college education are more likely to be married compared to those without such credentials.

However, significant racial disparities are evident in this context. White women with an undergraduate degree maintain marriage rates nearly equivalent to those in 1960. In contrast, marriage rates have declined among black women regardless of their educational attainment. For instance, a black woman aged 35-45 with an undergraduate degree is 15 percentage points less likely to be married than a white woman without an undergraduate degree. The disparity in marriage rates between individuals without a college degree has remained consistent over time, showing similar declines for both white and black women. On the other hand, the gap in marriage rates among women with an undergraduate degree has expanded, increasing from 21 percentage points in 1970 to 31 percentage points in 2015.

4)   Black College Graduates Less Likely to Marry a College Graduate

The variations in marriage rates may partly be attributed to a shortage of eligible black men for marriage, stemming from elevated rates of incarceration and premature mortality. (It's important to note that while there has been an increase in interracial marriage, individuals of black ethnicity, particularly black women, still have the lowest likelihood of marrying someone from a different racial background.)

However, disparities reemerge when considering racial aspects. As highlighted in a 2015 publication titled "Single black female BA seeks educated husband: Race assortative mating and inequality," black women with an undergraduate degree have a lower likelihood of marrying a man with equivalent educational credentials compared to their white counterparts. Currently, white women are slightly more likely to have higher educational levels than their husbands. Nevertheless, the concept of marrying down is not a new phenomenon for black women.

Who Marries Down?

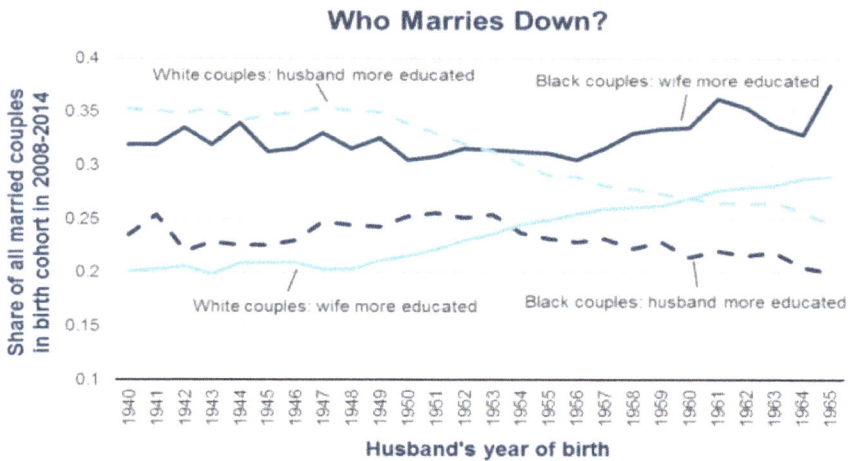

Source: Chiappori, Pierre-André, Bernard Salanié, and Yoram Weiss. 2017 "Partner Choice, Investment in Children, and the Marital College Premium." *American Economic Review*, 107(8), pp. 2109-2167

BROOKINGS

Hence, black women holding an undergraduate degree face decreased odds of entering marriage, and if they do so they are also less inclined to marry a man possessing similar educational qualifications. Consequently, advancements in the personal economic status of black Americans do not necessarily correspond to commensurate enhancements at the household level.

— October 21, 2016

EDUCATED BLACK HUSBANDS ARE KEY TO RACIAL EQUITY

The intricate interplay between race, gender, education, and marriage requires little emphasis, given its complexity and intimate nature. Yet, one fact remains evident: the educational and economic achievements of black men carry significant ramifications for the well-being of black families, the prospects of black youth, and the overarching pursuit of racial parity.

FEB. 24, 2022 — The U.S. Census Bureau released findings from the Educational Attainment in the United States: 2021 table package that use statistics from the Current Population Survey's Annual Social and Economic Supplement to examine the educational attainment of adults age 25 and older by demographic and social characteristics, such as age, sex, race, and nativity.

Data Highlights

● In 2021, the highest level of education of the population age 25 and older in the United States was distributed as follows:

- 8.9% had less than a high school diploma or equivalent.
- 27.9% had high school graduate as their highest level of school completed.
- 14.9% had completed some college but not a degree.
- 10.5% had an associate degree as their highest level of school completed.
- 23.5% had a bachelor's degree as their highest degree.
- 14.4% had completed an advanced degree such as a master's degree, professional degree, or doctoral degree.
- The high school completion rate in the United States for people age 25 and older increased from 87.6% in 2011 to 91.1% in 2021.
- The percentage of the population age 25 and older with associate degrees rose from 9.5% to 10.5% between 2011 and 2021.
- Between 2011 and 2021, the percentage of people age 25 and older who had completed a bachelor's degree or higher increased by 7.5 percentage points from 30.4% to 37.9%.

From 2011 to 2021, the number of people age 25 and over who's highest degree was a master's degree rose to 24.1 million, and the number of doctoral degree holders rose to 4.7 million, a 50.2% and 54.5% increase, respectively.

About 14.3% of adults had an advanced degree in 2021, up from 10.9% in 2011. In 2021, 29.4% of men aged 25 and older had completed a high school diploma or GED as their highest level of educational attainment, compared with 26.5% of women age 25 and older.

In 2021, of adults aged 25 and older who had completed a bachelor's degree or more, 53.1% were women and 46.9% were men.

From 2011 to 2021, the percentage of adults age 25 and older who had completed high school increased for all race and Hispanic origin groups. During this period, high school completion increased from 92.4% to 95.1% for the non-Hispanic White population; from 84.5% to 90.3% for the Black population; from 88.6% to 92.9% for the Asian population; and from 64.3% to 74.2% for the Hispanic population.

From 2011 to 2021, the percentage of adults age 25 and older with a bachelor's degree or higher increased from 34.0% to 41.9% for the non-Hispanic White population; from 19.9% to 28.1% for the Black population; from 50.3% to 61.0% for the Asian population; and from 14.1% to 20.6% for the Hispanic population.

Foreign-born people who recently came to the United States were more likely to have a college education than foreign-born people who arrived earlier or the native-born population. In 2021, among the foreign-born who arrived since 2010, 46.4% had a bachelor's degree or higher, compared with 38.2% of the native-born, and 32.9% of the foreign-born who arrived in the 1990s.

Naturalized citizens and the children of foreign-born parents both had high levels of educational attainment in 2021; 42.2% of naturalized citizens and 43.0% of children of foreign-born parents had a bachelor's degree or higher.

In 2021, a greater share of the foreign-born (15.4%) than native-born population (14.1%) held advanced degrees, such as master's degrees, professional degrees, or doctoral degrees.

The Current Population Survey, sponsored jointly by the Census Bureau and the U.S. Bureau of Labor Statistics, is the primary source of labor force statistics for the population of the United States.

Field of Degree: Women, Men, and Racial and Ethnic Groups: Bachelor's Degree:

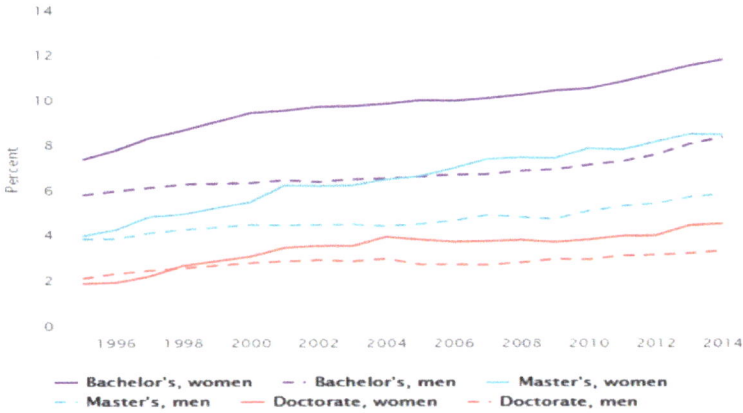

Minorities By Degree Share

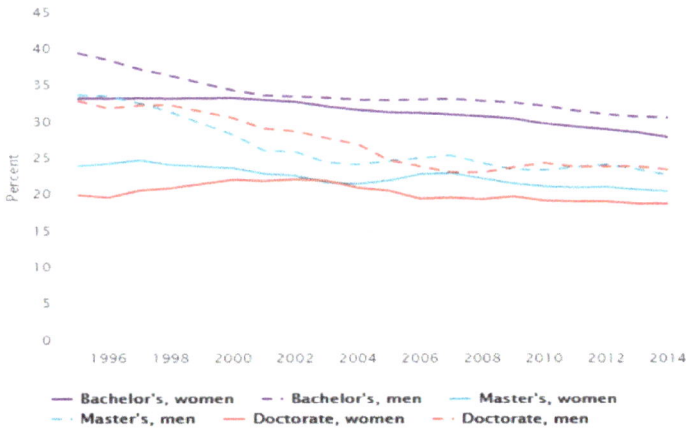

Whites By Degree Share

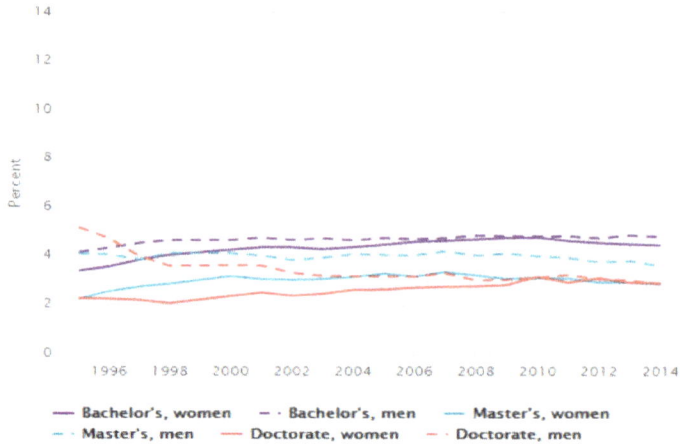

Asians By Degree Share

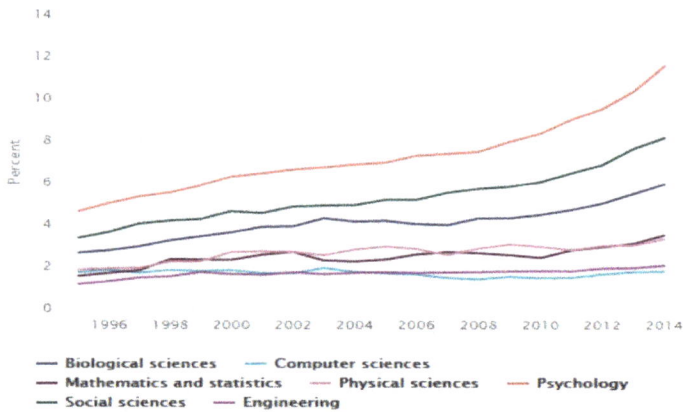

Hispanic Women, By Field

Among Black or African American women, much like Hispanic women, exhibit a greater proportion of bachelor's degrees conferred in psychology and social sciences compared to any other expansive field within science and engineering. Over the past two decades, the most substantial rise in the proportion of bachelor's degrees attained by black women has occurred in psychology, followed by social and biological sciences. Conversely, their portion of bachelor's degrees has diminished in the realms of computer sciences, mathematics and statistics and engineering.

Distribution of science and engineering bachelor's degrees achieved by Black or African American women, categorized by field: 1995-2014.

Percent Biological Sciences, Computer Sciences, Mathematics and

Statistics, Physical Sciences, Psychology, Social Sciences, Engineering 1996, 1998, 2000, 2002, 2004, 2006, 2008, 2010, 2012, 2014.

- Biological sciences: 4.73%

- Computer Sciences: 4.38%

- Mathematics and statistics: 2.79%

- Physical Sciences: 3.22%

- Psychology: 8.40%

- Social Sciences: 6.44%

- Engineering: 1.45%

Chart of Science and engineering bachelor's degrees earned by black or African American women, by field: 1995–2014.

—Note: Data not available for 1999.

Poverty refers to the condition of lacking sufficient material possessions or money. Absolute poverty, often referred to as destitution, is characterized by the inability to afford basic human needs. These necessities typically encompass access to clean fresh water, proper nutrition, healthcare, education, clothing, and shelter. Specifically, we can examine poverty among households headed by Black women, both with and without children under 18 years of age.

The pursuit of higher education has long been celebrated as a pathway to social mobility and economic prosperity. In recent years, the African American community has made impressive strides in accessing higher education, with more individuals enrolling in colleges and universities than ever before. However, a recent study from the Center on Education and the Workforce at Georgetown University shines a light on a troubling trend among African American college students. Despite their aspirations for higher education, they are more likely to choose majors that lead to lower-paying jobs, perpetuating a cycle of debt and underemployment. This phenomenon not only hinders individual financial success but also widens the persistent wealth and opportunity gap between African Americans and their white counterparts.

The mismatch between Education and Earnings Director Anthony Carnevale's analogy of African Americans attending the "right church but sitting in the wrong pew" aptly captures the issue at hand. African American students are leveraging education to climb the socioeconomic ladder, yet the choices they make regarding their majors significantly impact their future earning potential. While education is often celebrated as the great equalizer, the inherent disparities in major selection reveal a systemic flaw that requires attention.

Underrepresentation in Lucrative Fields: The underrepresentation of African Americans in high-paying fields, such as STEM (Science, Technology, Engineering, and Mathematics) and business, is a striking illustration of the problem. Within the realms of engineering, mathematics, and computer science, African Americans constitute only a fraction of the student population. For instance, they comprise merely 8 percent of engineering, 7 percent of mathematics, and 5 percent of computer science majors. This underrepresentation limits their access to industries with higher earning potential, perpetuating the cycle of economic inequality.

The Influence of Major Choice: Furthermore, even when African American students do pursue high-paying fields, they often gravitate towards the lowest-paying subfields within them. A prominent example is the field of STEM, where many African American women choose to study biology— a discipline with relatively lower earning potential compared to other branches of science. Similarly, among African American men in engineering, a significant portion opt for civil engineering, which typically yields lower incomes than other engineering disciplines.

Consequences for Economic Equity: The consequences of this trend extend beyond individual economic outcomes. Over time, the occupational choices made by African American college students contribute to the wealth and opportunity gap that spans generations between African Americans and white Americans. As African American graduates enter the workforce with limited earning potential due to their chosen majors, they are more likely to face financial hardships, struggles with repaying student loans, and an increased risk of underemployment.

Breaking the Cycle: Addressing this pressing issue requires a multi-faceted approach. First and foremost, there needs to be heightened awareness and education about the potential earning disparities associated with various majors. Students, parents, educators, and guidance counselors should collaborate to provide accurate information about career prospects and earning potential, enabling students to make informed decisions about their majors.

Additionally, creating pathways for African American students to access and excel in high-paying fields, such as STEM, demands concerted efforts. Initiatives that provide mentorship, scholarships, and targeted support can help break down the barriers that have historically limited their representation in these fields.

The trend of African American college students choosing majors with lower earning potential is a critical issue that demands our attention. While higher education remains a vehicle for social and economic advancement, the current trajectory risks perpetuating inequality rather than alleviating it. Addressing this challenge requires a comprehensive effort from educational institutions, policymakers, community leaders, and society at large. By fostering awareness, offering support, and creating equal opportunities, we can pave the way for African American students to not only attend the right church but also sit in the right pew—forging a path toward economic equity and a brighter future for generations to come.

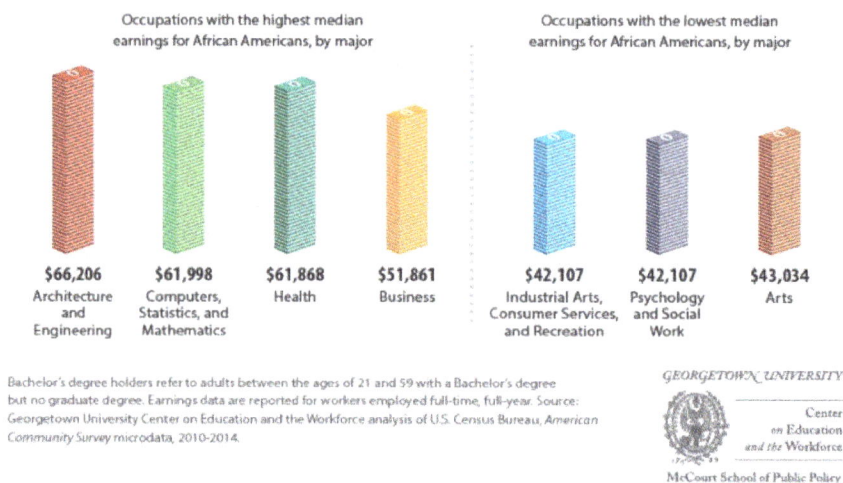

Occupations with the highest median earnings for African Americans, by major

Occupations with the lowest median earnings for African Americans, by major

| $66,206 Architecture and Engineering | $61,998 Computers, Statistics, and Mathematics | $61,868 Health | $51,861 Business | $42,107 Industrial Arts, Consumer Services, and Recreation | $42,107 Psychology and Social Work | $43,034 Arts |

Bachelor's degree holders refer to adults between the ages of 21 and 59 with a Bachelor's degree but no graduate degree. Earnings data are reported for workers employed full-time, full-year. Source: Georgetown University Center on Education and the Workforce analysis of U.S. Census Bureau, *American Community Survey* microdata, 2010-2014.

GEORGETOWN UNIVERSITY

Center
on Education
and the Workforce

McCourt School of Public Policy

African-American college students tend to have majors in public service, which are also some of the country's lowest-paying. As this chart shows, African-Americans are over-represented in majors that are some of the lowest paying. Image from Center on Education and the Workforce

THE IMPACT OF OCCUPATIONAL BIAS ON CAREER CHOICES OF BLACK COLLEGE STUDENTS

The pursuit of higher education has long been considered a pathway to personal growth, professional success, and upward mobility. However, a persistent trend among black college students has highlighted a significant contrast in their chosen majors compared to their white counterparts. They are often over-represented in service-oriented fields such as humanities, education, and social work, which tend to offer lower-paying career prospects. This discrepancy reflects broader societal biases against service-oriented occupations, raising questions about the valuation of these professions and the need to address systemic biases that influence career choices and contribute to economic disparities.

The Over-Representation in Service-Oriented Fields

A closer look at the distribution of black college students across different fields reveals a substantial over-representation in service-oriented disciplines, particularly humanities, education, and social work. While these fields play vital roles in shaping societies, nurturing minds, and providing essential services, their prevalence among black students is influenced by a complex interplay of historical, cultural, and economic factors.

Low-Paying Majors and Their Consequences

Among the majors chosen by black college students, some are associated with lower earning potential. For instance, early childhood education stands out as a poignant example, with a median annual earning of only $38,000. This underscores the financial challenges many individuals in these fields face. In stark contrast, majors such as computer science offer substantially higher median earnings of $65,000 annually, highlighting the glaring disparity in potential financial outcomes.

The Societal Devaluation of Service-Oriented Occupations

Anthony Carnevale's observation that American society often undervalues service-oriented occupations speak to a larger issue that extends beyond college campuses. Service-oriented fields, despite their essential contributions, are often characterized by lower pay scales and less prestige compared to other professions. This bias can discourage individuals from pursuing these careers, particularly when economic security is a concern. The undervaluation of these professions is deeply rooted in societal perceptions that often prioritize financial gain over the invaluable contributions made by those in service-oriented roles.

Addressing Systemic Bias and Creating Equitable Opportunities

To rectify the inequities arising from occupational biases, a multi-pronged approach is necessary. First and foremost, raising awareness about the significance of service-oriented fields and their impact on communities is essential. This can be achieved through educational campaigns, increased media representation, and highlighting success stories within these professions.

Efforts should also focus on elevating the compensation and recognition for service-oriented occupations. Governments, institutions, and organizations must reevaluate their funding and remuneration policies to reflect the importance of these fields. Scholarships, grants, and financial incentives for students pursuing careers in service-oriented sectors can help overcome the financial barriers that often deter individuals from entering these professions.

Furthermore, diversifying leadership within service-oriented sectors can play a pivotal role in challenging existing biases and fostering a more inclusive environment. When individuals from diverse backgrounds hold influential positions in these fields, it can reshape perceptions and promote inclusivity.

The over-representation of black college students in service-oriented fields, combined with the lower financial prospects associated with such careers, raises important questions about the value society places on these occupations. Addressing this issue necessitates a collective effort to challenge systemic biases, promote awareness, and provide equitable opportunities. By recognizing the vital role that service-oriented professions play in shaping societies and investing in their growth, we can pave the way for a more equitable and inclusive future for all individuals, regardless of their chosen career paths.

	Percentage African American	Median Earnings†
Health and Medical Administration Services	21%	$46,000
Human Services and Community Organization	20%	$39,000
Social Work	19%	$41,000
Public Administration	17%	$52,000
Criminal Justice and Fire Protection	15%	$48,000
Sociology	14%	$44,000
Computer and Information Systems	14%	$63,000
Human Resources and Personnel Management	14%	$51,000
Interdisciplinary Social Sciences	13%	$44,000
Pre-Law and Legal Studies	13%	$46,000

Bachelor's degree holders refer to adults between the ages of 21 and 59 with a Bachelor's degree but no graduate degree. Earnings data are reported for workers employed full-time, full-year. Source: Georgetown University Center on Education and the Workforce analysis of U.S. Census Bureau, *American Community Survey* microdata, 2010-2014.

† Earnings at the 50th percentile, ages 25–59

GEORGETOWN UNIVERSITY

Center
on Education
and the Workforce

McCourt School of Public Policy

As this chart shows, African Americans are over-represented in majors that are some of the lowest paying. Image from Center on Education and the Workforce

PART III: THE MOYNIHAN REPORT AND ITS HISTORICAL CONTEXT

In 1965, the issue of fatherlessness within the black community came to the forefront when Senator Daniel Patrick Moynihan released his report, shedding light on the "tangle of pathology" present in the community. This report sparked widespread controversy and public discussions by suggesting that cultural factors and family structure played significant roles in the challenges faced by the black community. It argued that family instability and the absence of fathers were root causes, igniting debates on whether this perspective blamed the victims or identified systemic issues.

Moynihan's insights challenged the prevailing social science theories of the time, which primarily focused on economic conditions as the main driver of social outcomes. He contended that the breakdown of the nuclear family and the absence of fathers were critical factors perpetuating the cycle of poverty and challenges within the black community. However, his viewpoint faced criticism for allegedly overlooking systemic racism and unequal opportunities.

THE SHIFT IN DISCOURSE AND POLICY

In the years that followed, the discourse around the issue of fatherlessness in the black community evolved. Influenced by black pride and feminism, some scholars redefined the role of the family and its impact on children's development. Rather than addressing the breakdown of the nuclear family structure, the focus shifted to discussions about teen pregnancy and the consequences of single motherhood.

In the 1980s and 1990s, conservative thinkers like Charles Murray, Lawrence Mead, and Thomas Sowell redirected attention to the original concerns raised by the Moynihan Report. They emphasized the detrimental effects of welfare policies on family structure, stressed personal responsibility, and called for behavioral change within the community. Policy changes also reflected this shift in perspective. President Bill Clinton's welfare reform initiatives and his emphasis on promoting two-parent families signaled a growing recognition of the importance of family structure. Despite the progress made, the persistently high rate of fatherlessness remains a significant challenge.

LESSONS AND HOPE FOR CHANGE

The crisis of fatherlessness in the black community is a deeply entrenched and multifaceted issue that demands a comprehensive and compassionate approach. The journey from the release of the Moynihan Report to the present day has witnessed shifts in public discourse, policy, and cultural perceptions. While progress has been achieved, the path forward remains intricate. The lessons drawn from the Moynihan Report underscore the significance of acknowledging the role of family structure in shaping social outcomes. Recognizing both the cultural factors contributing to fatherlessness and addressing systemic issues such as racism and economic inequality can pave the way for effective solutions. Initiatives that normalize healthy marriages, promote personal responsibility, and provide support to families represent steps in the right direction.

The endeavor to combat fatherlessness in the black community necessitates ongoing collaboration among policymakers, scholars, community leaders, and individuals. Ultimately, the goal is to create an environment where children can grow up with the support and guidance of both a mother and a father, breaking the cycle of challenges and contributing to a more equitable and thriving society.

THE CRISIS OF FATHERLESSNESS IN THE BLACK COMMUNITY: LESSONS FROM THE MOYNIHAN REPORT

Exploring Fatherlessness in the Black Community

The issue of fatherlessness within the black community has remained a contentious and multifaceted concern for decades, carrying profound social implications. Government statistics reveal a striking fact: a substantial 72 percent of black infants are born to unmarried mothers. To grasp the gravity of this statistic, it is crucial to delve into the underlying reasons, its repercussions on children, families, and society, and the historical context that has contributed to this enduring challenge. Additionally, we must consider the legacy of the Moynihan Report, its initial reception, and its lasting influence on the public discourse surrounding this issue.

Understanding the Statistics and Cultural Shift

While the stark figure of 72 percent of black infants born to unmarried mothers is undeniably concerning, it is imperative to move beyond mere numbers and explore the intricate cultural factors that have propelled this trend. One prevailing explanation is that, regardless of racial background, young women are increasingly viewing marriage as an optional institution. However, this shift in perception carries significant consequences, as children deserve the presence and support of both a mother and a father in their lives. The fatherlessness crisis in the black community warrants heightened concern due to its interconnectedness with various other challenges. Statistics indicate that black men constitute a disproportionate 60 percent of the prison population, despite comprising only 12 percent of the total population. Many of these men grew up in single-mother households. The absence of a paternal figure in the home can render children more susceptible to academic difficulties, legal entanglements, substance abuse, financial hardships in adulthood, and a perpetuation of single parenthood in the generations that follow.

FATHER'S CRITICAL ROLE

The Unappreciated Role of Dads: Shaping Children's Lives

In a rapidly evolving world where traditional gender roles are undergoing redefinition, it's remarkable to note that society still grapples with fully appreciating the vital role of fathers. Even as men increasingly take on caregiving responsibilities and women become primary breadwinners, there persists a tendency to view fathers as secondary caregivers, often overshadowed by mothers. Surprisingly, the phrase "babysitting" is still commonly used when fathers spend time with their own children, reflecting the enduring perception of paternal involvement as a sporadic favor.

Another telling sign of this prevailing notion is the presence of parenting forums predominantly populated by women, often bearing "mom" in their titles. Additionally, fathers often face an uphill battle when seeking equal custody rights post-divorce, further reinforcing the notion that children are primarily a mother's responsibility. This perspective is unfortunate, as fathers undeniably play a significant and unique role in their children's lives.

Active fatherly engagement in a child's upbringing brings about a remarkable difference, offering an array of benefits that are often underestimated. One distinct contribution that fathers make is in the realm of communication. Both mothers and fathers communicate differently with their children, and both styles are essential for a child's linguistic development.

Mothers tend to adapt their communication to the child's comprehension level, fostering a strong emotional bond. Conversely, fathers employ more intricate language and engage in discussions that encourage clarification, direction, and reference to past events. This variance is crucial since children exposed to diverse communication styles through involved fathers tend to excel in external communication, equipping them to thrive in social interactions beyond their familial environment.

Moreover, fathers significantly contribute to children's resilience. Multiple studies reveal that children with actively involved fathers exhibit greater self-confidence, resilience, curiosity, and adaptability. Fathers often comfort their children by promoting self-assurance and exploration, imparting valuable life skills. This divergent problem-solving approach, when combined with maternal care, contributes to emotionally well-adjusted children who are better prepared to confront life's challenges.

Notably, boys benefit from fatherly influence as they develop their concept of masculinity. Fathers establish the initial standard for masculinity, profoundly impacting their children's views on relationships, respect, and gender dynamics. Positive fatherly behavior influences a child's future approach to his own relationships, contributing to healthier marriages and respectful interactions.

Interestingly, a good father enhances a mother's well-being from the moment a child is born. A father's support significantly reduces a woman's vulnerability to postpartum depression. Throughout a child's life, an involved father alleviates maternal stress, enhancing the overall parenting experience, especially when fathers assume developmental roles such as reading to their children.

But is there concrete evidence to substantiate the claim that fathers wield a distinct and significant impact on their children's lives? Dr. David Popenoe, a prominent sociologist, firmly contends that involved fathers provide unique benefits that cannot be replicated by anyone else. This includes protection, economic support, male role modeling, and a distinctive parenting style that complements the mother's approach.

Fathers indeed parent differently from mothers, and this diversity is essential for children's holistic development. Fathers' tendency to engage in rougher play style encourages risk-taking and exploration, introducing children to a broader range of experiences and problem-solving techniques. Their emphasis on rules, justice, fairness, and duty imparts a sense of objectivity and consequences. These distinctive approaches together create a balanced foundation for a child's upbringing.

This isn't mere conjecture; a wealth of research supports these assertions. Numerous studies consistently demonstrate that positive father involvement correlates with improved child well-being, happiness, academic success, and social competence. Fatherly love has been found to be just as crucial as maternal love, and in some cases, even more influential, in promoting positive outcomes for children.

The implications of these findings are profound. As society increasingly recognizes the significant impact of fathers on children's lives, a collective effort must be made to disseminate this knowledge. Father involvement should not be perceived as a luxury but as a necessity. Ensuring that fathers are acknowledged and actively included in parenting discussions is not only equitable but also a critical step toward nurturing emotionally and socially resilient future generations.

THE LONG-TERM CONSEQUENCES OF GROWING UP WITHOUT A FATHER

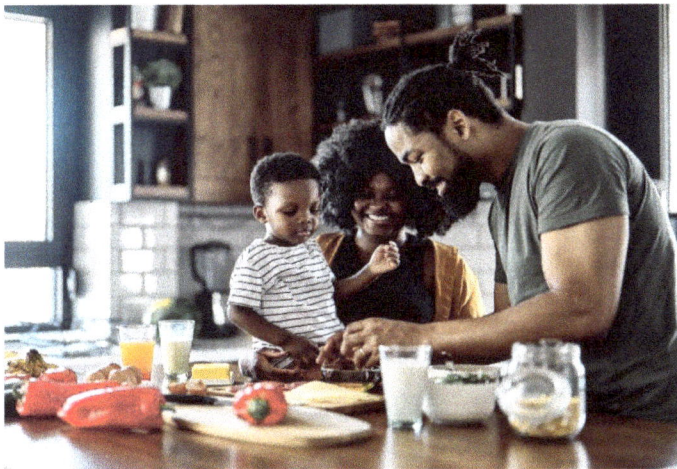

In today's rapidly evolving world, where societal dynamics continually shift, one undeniable truth remains: children need good fathers. Extensive research underscores this fact unequivocally, making it clear that father absence lies at the core of many of society's problems.

This issue has transcended individual concern; it has become a pressing public health challenge demanding immediate attention. A closer examination of the intricate web of consequences stemming from father absence reveals the compelling need for fathers' positive presence in the lives of their children.

The Impact of Fatherly Love

Bob Griffin's words highlight the urgency of the matter: "The need for a father is on an epidemic scale, and the 'father deficit' should be treated as a public health issue." This sentiment finds strong support in the 2020 U.S. Census, which reveals that a staggering 18.4 million children in the United States are growing up without their biological fathers. This alarming statistic translates to 23% of the total child population, a number that has doubled since 1968 and continues to rise. The pervasive absence of fathers paints a bleak picture of the future.

Research consistently underscores the vital role that fathers play in their children's lives. The "Father Facts Eight Edition," a comprehensive study published by the National Fatherhood Initiative in 2019, amalgamated findings from over 212 research projects and studies examining the effects of father absence on families and communities. The evidence is compelling: children thrive in the presence of engaged fathers.

The Facts of Father Absence

Father absence isn't just a statistic; it carries grave implications. The absence of fathers from children's lives has been linked to an array of negative outcomes. Children growing up in homes without a present father face heightened vulnerability to mental health issues such as depression, anxiety, and psychological distress. These children are also more susceptible to substance abuse, violence, and criminal activities, perpetuating a cycle of societal problems. Father absence casts a long shadow that touches not only children but also mothers, who bear the responsibilities of pregnancy, childbirth, and single-handedly raising a child.

The Positive Impact of a Present Father

Research unequivocally supports the powerful impact of a present father. Engaged fathers foster a sense of emotional security and well-being in their children, leading to better life outcomes. Fathers contribute a unique and complementary parenting style to mothers, encouraging risk-taking, exploration, and resilience. Their emphasis on justice, fairness, and duty teaches children valuable lessons in responsibility and ethical decision-making. Moreover, fatherly involvement has been shown to reduce the likelihood of intergenerational cycles of violence and abuse.

Effects of Father Absence on Children

The consequences of father absence ripple through generations. The void left by an absent father can lead to a cascade of detrimental outcomes, affecting children's emotional, social, and psychological development. Without a strong male role model, children may struggle to understand their own gender identity and navigate relationships with the opposite sex. These challenges can impair their ability to form healthy connections and may exacerbate feelings of loneliness and isolation.

Effects of Father Absence on the Mother's Well-being

Motherhood is already a complex journey, and when fathers are absent, the burden can be overwhelming. Single mothers face heightened stress and financial strain, often juggling multiple roles while striving to provide emotional stability for their children. The absence of a partner's support can lead to increased rates of maternal depression and anxiety, negatively affecting both the mother's well-being and her parenting capabilities.

Correlation Between Absent Fathers and Mass Shootings

A disturbing link between father absence and mass shootings has emerged. Numerous studies suggest that many perpetrators of mass shootings come from fatherless homes. While it's essential to acknowledge that not all individuals from fatherless homes become violent, the correlation underscores the importance of strong fatherly presence in shaping a child's emotional and psychological well-being.

The Cost to Society Due to Father Absence

The cost of father absence isn't just borne by individuals; it exacts a toll on society. Children growing up without a positive father figure are more likely to engage in risky behaviors, struggle academically, and require social services. The economic burden is significant, with increased healthcare expenses, higher rates of criminal justice involvement, and decreased workforce productivity.

Different Types of Fathers Bring Different Challenges

Recognizing that not all fathers are absent by choice is crucial. Economic factors, incarceration, and divorce contribute to father absence, presenting unique challenges for different segments of society. Addressing these challenges requires tailored strategies that provide fathers with the tools and support necessary to be active and positive contributors to their children's lives.

Predictors of Father Absence and Engagement

Understanding the predictors of father absence can help tailor interventions. Factors such as socioeconomic status, education, and cultural influences play a role in determining father involvement. Efforts to promote father engagement must take into account these variables and work toward creating supportive environments that enable fathers to be present in their children's lives.

WHAT THE BIBLE SAYS ABOUT FATHERS

For those seeking guidance from a spiritual perspective, the Bible emphasizes the importance of fathers in children's lives. The role of fathers as providers, protectors, and mentors is evident in numerous passages. The Bible's teachings underscore the significance of fatherly love and guidance in shaping children's character and values.

BUILDING FATHERS INTO REAL POPS

Building and nurturing positive fatherly involvement requires intentional efforts. Creating "POPS" - Positive Outcomes for Positive Support - involves providing fathers with education, resources, and mentorship to help them become actively engaged in their children's lives. Community organizations, schools, and government agencies all have roles to play in fostering father-child relationships.

Breaking the Cycle of Father Absence

Breaking the cycle of father absence requires a multi-faceted approach. Comprehensive sex education, accessible family planning resources, and support for fathers in challenging circumstances are essential components. Addressing systemic issues like incarceration rates and economic inequality can help create an environment where fathers can fulfill their roles effectively.

Next Steps

The research is compelling: children need good dads. Father absence has far-reaching consequences that touch upon every facet of society. It's a challenge that cannot be ignored, and addressing it requires a concerted effort from individuals, communities, and institutions. By recognizing the pivotal role fathers play and actively working to support and empower them, we can pave the way for a healthier, more resilient, and thriving future generation.

THE IMPACT OF FATHER LOVE

The Crucial Role of Fathers: Building Strong Families and Communities

In the book "Father Love – The Powerful Resource that Every Child Needs," author Eli Williams astutely defines the multifaceted role of a loving father. He portrays fathers not only as protectors, order keepers, and providers but also as stabilizers for both the family and the community. Williams seamlessly weaves together the essential elements of becoming a better father with a commitment to serve God faithfully. He highlights the transformative journey of becoming a stronger father by embracing the teachings of the Bible and surrendering one's life to Christ. Through this holistic approach, fatherhood is elevated to a divine calling, fostering a positive impact on children's lives and society as a whole.

The poignant verse from the book of Malachi, "And we will turn the hearts of the fathers to the children, and the hearts of the children to their fathers, Lest I come and strike the earth with a curse" (Malachi 4:6), encapsulates the profound influence fathers exert on their children's lives and the stability of society. This verse underscores the inseparable link between strong families and vibrant communities. Conversely, father absence perpetuates a cycle of challenges that reverberate through generations, casting shadows on children's futures and weakening the very fabric of society.

Understanding the Complex Causes of Father Absence

The causes of father absence are intricate and diverse, encompassing factors related to fertility, marriage, cohabitation, unexpected events, illness, and incarceration. Choices individuals make regarding relationships, education, and socioeconomic status play a significant role in determining the father's presence in a child's life. Different social classes experience fatherlessness differently, compounding the impact of absent fathers on marginalized communities.

The Call to Lead and Protect

A fundamental aspect of fatherhood is leadership and protection within the household. Fathers are entrusted with the responsibility to guide, nurture, and safeguard their families. Unfortunately, some fathers choose absence, neglecting their vital role as leaders and protectors. This abandonment has far-reaching consequences, affecting children's emotional, cognitive, and behavioral development.

Empowering Fatherhood Through Positive Role Models

The mission of organizations like Fathering Strong resonates with the impact statement laid out in Williams' book. Such networks play a pivotal role in uplifting fathers, enabling them to fulfill their responsibilities as committed leaders within their families. These organizations provide a platform for fathers to embrace the teachings of the Bible, anchor their lives in faith, and transform into positive role models for their children.

Consequences of Father Absence

At a national level, the statistics are alarming: 18.4 million children are living without their biological fathers. This absence disproportionately affects black children, with nearly a quarter of American children growing up in father-absent homes. The rise of unmarried parents cohabitating, and solo mothers underscores the shifting dynamics of fatherhood. The implications are far-reaching, as father involvement tends to decrease over time, hindering children's development and well-being.

The Power of a Present Father

Research unequivocally provides evidence of the positive impact of an involved father on a child's life. From academic success to emotional well-being, children with present fathers fare better in almost every aspect. Studies reveal that adolescents with resident biological or adoptive fathers demonstrate higher GPAs, underlining the role of fathers in educational attainment. Communication about school and active involvement yields positive influences on participants' grades, showcasing the pivotal role of fatherly engagement.

Unlocking Positive Outcomes Through Fatherhood

The National Fatherhood Initiative identifies eight key areas where a child's life improves with a present father. These include emotional regulation, physical health, healthier relationships, an increased sense of safety and confidence, a reduced likelihood of substance abuse, improved academic performance, decreased risk of poverty, and a reduced inclination towards harmful behaviors.

Impact on Society and Future Generations

The effects of father absence reverberate throughout society, impacting law enforcement and community challenges. Addressing this issue requires collective efforts from families, communities, and institutions. Recognizing fatherhood as a divine responsibility and aligning it with the teachings of the Bible can foster stronger fathers who serve as pillars of stability, fostering positive change in their families and communities.

In conclusion, the pivotal role of fathers cannot be overstated. From providing protection and guidance to nurturing emotional well-being and academic success, fathers shape the trajectory of their children's lives. The union of faith and fatherhood, as emphasized by Eli Williams, offers a transformative path, strengthening fathers' commitment to their families and faith communities. By understanding the complex causes of father absence and embracing the positive impact of a present father, we pave the way for healthier families, stronger communities, and a brighter future for generations to come.

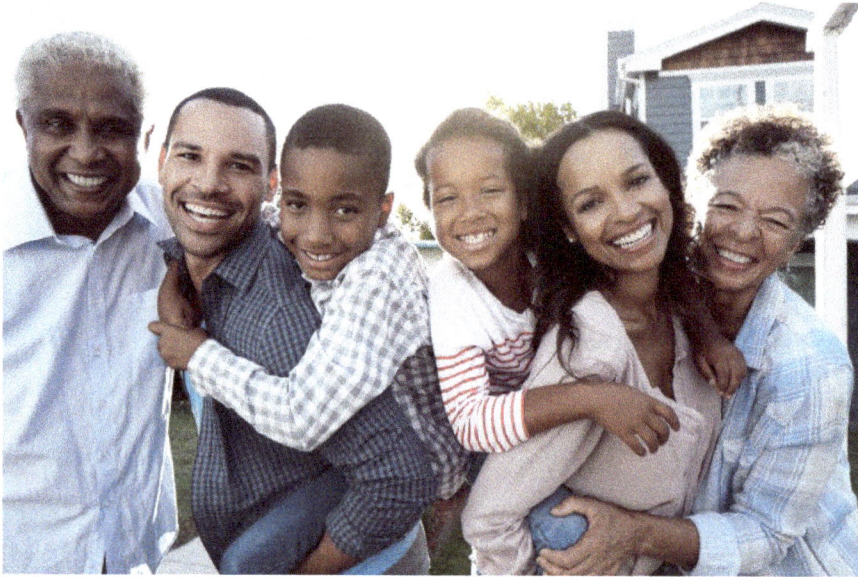

The data strongly indicates that a significant portion of societal problems today could be mitigated through the active presence and engagement of fathers in their children's lives. Research underscores the crucial role of father involvement as a protective factor against the following top five areas that impact a child's well-being:

• Elevated Rates of Depression and Suicide: The level of father involvement is closely linked to increased behavioral problems. Studies have demonstrated that children with stable father figures tend to exhibit improved cognitive and socio-emotional outcomes.

• Heightened Risk of Substance Abuse: The quality of a father's involvement is directly correlated with early substance abuse, irrespective of the child's gender. Children with absent fathers, those with abusive fathers, or those exposed to parental drug abuse face significantly elevated risks.

• Increased Likelihood of Criminal Activity: Father absence is strongly associated with criminal behavior among young men and serves as a predictor for higher rates of youth assault. Additionally, the quality of the father-child relationship plays a role in delinquency.

• Premature Sexual Activity: Research has linked early and risky sexual behavior to the absence of fathers. Adolescents from father-absent homes are 3.5 times more likely to experience pregnancy compared to their peers from father-present households.

• Subpar Educational Outcomes: The duration of a father's absence has been conclusively linked to a child's educational success. Adolescents without resident father figures are at the highest risk of academic underachievement and school failure.

EFFECTS OF FATHER ABSENCE ON THE MOTHER'S WELL-BEING

If the father is involved, it means good health outcomes for mother and baby.

Exploring the Extensive Consequences of Father Absence: Effects on Mothers and Society

Father absence extends beyond its impact on children's well-being and reaches into the lives of mothers and society. In our contemporary culture, which places a strong emphasis on autonomy and evolving definitions of freedom, promiscuity has become normalized, leaving many women to grapple with the complexities of single parenthood. In this discussion, we will delve into the broad-ranging ramifications of father absence, shedding light on how it affects both mothers and society.

Antenatal Depression and Maternal Stress

For mothers, the absence of a husband or partner can lead to antenatal depression, a silent struggle that often goes unnoticed. Research emphasizes that mothers who are married to or co-parenting with fathers experience less stress on their parenting journey. Even simple acts such as sharing household responsibilities or engaging with their children can significantly alleviate the stress burden for mothers. The presence of a supportive partner fosters a healthier maternal environment, resulting in improved emotional well-being and overall family harmony.

Partner Support and Birth Outcomes

Partner support during pregnancy demonstrates a direct correlation with positive birth outcomes. Studies reveal that pregnant mothers who receive support from their partners are more likely to achieve favorable birth outcomes, including a reduced likelihood of preterm birth and low birth weight. Father involvement in the pregnancy journey translates to improved health outcomes for both mother and baby.

The Cohesive Family Process

A 2018 study underscores the pivotal role fathers play in maintaining a cohesive family process. Father involvement, characterized by sensitivity, social engagement, and emotional support, contributes to a harmonious and collaborative family environment. Conversely, families with absent or uninvolved fathers exhibit less cohesion, highlighting the significance of fathers in promoting family unity and emotional well-being.

Father Absence and Mass Shootings

A striking correlation between absent fathers and mass shootings has emerged in contemporary society. Mass shooters, particularly young male perpetrators, often come from homes with father absence. These individuals exhibit signs of mental illness, delinquency, and violent tendencies. A study reveals that 85% of mass school shooters suffer from depression, emphasizing the profound impact of positive psychosocial influences in preventing such violence. A lack of stable family dynamics and a nurturing fatherly presence can exacerbate mental health challenges, contributing to a propensity for violence.

Societal Costs of Father Absence

Father absence imposes a staggering societal cost, amounting to nearly $99.8 billion annually. This financial burden arises from expenditures on programs supporting father-absent homes, including welfare, child support enforcement, food assistance, housing initiatives, and children's health insurance. The economic strain underscores the link between father absence and increased reliance on means-tested benefits. Addressing father absence becomes not only a moral imperative but also an economic necessity.

Diverse Types of Fathers and Their Challenges

Recognizing the diverse array of fathers and their unique challenges is integral to building stronger families and communities. Teen fathers contend with educational barriers and societal stigma, necessitating tailored support to ensure their involvement in parenting. Single fathers, often resulting from divorce, face varying levels of involvement that influence their children's outcomes. Divorced fathers navigating custody arrangements strive for productive involvement, leading to improved outcomes for their children.

Building Stronger Fathers: A Holistic Approach

Building stronger fathers requires a holistic approach that addresses the unique struggles faced by different types of fathers. Whether it's teen fathers, single fathers, divorced fathers, nonresident fathers, incarcerated fathers, military fathers, or stepfathers, tailored support systems are vital to empower fathers in their roles. Predictors of father involvement encompass living situations, marital status, and self-esteem, offering insights for comprehensive fatherhood programs.

The Transformative Impact of Marriage

Marriage emerges as a significant factor in enhancing father involvement. Fathers who are married to the mother or cohabitate demonstrate heightened levels of engagement. Marriage fosters a supportive environment, leading to increased father involvement and overall family stability. The influence of race and ethnicity on nonresidential fathers' involvement underscores the importance of cultural context in shaping family dynamics. In conclusion, the absence of fathers reverberates across mothers' emotional well-being and society's fabric, manifesting in economic burdens, societal challenges, and even acts of violence. The interplay between father absence and societal issues underscores the urgency of fostering strong father-child relationships. By acknowledging diverse fatherhood experiences, supporting positive psychosocial influences, and prioritizing marriage and family unity, we can collectively pave the way for healthier families, safer communities, and a brighter future for generations to come.

BIBLICAL AUTHORITY ON FATHERHOOD

Fatherhood was one of the first jobs given to man by God. Immediately after creating Adam and Eve, God commanded them to "be fruitful and multiply." (Genesis 1:28) One of His primary purposes for marriage was for man and woman to produce offspring who would fill the earth with God's praise and glory. However, providing sperm for conception is merely the beginning of God's expectations for fathers. The Bible provides many points of guidance on what God expects when it comes to being a good father.

I believe the following verses are illustrative of what I have described above:

• Colossians 3:21 – Fathers, do not provoke your children, lest they become discouraged.

• Proverbs 4:1-9 – Hear, O sons, a father's instruction, and be attentive, that you may gain insight, for I give you good precepts; do not forsake my teaching. When I was a son with my father, tender, the only one in the sight of my mother, he taught me and said to me, "Let your heart hold fast my words; keep my commandments and live. Get wisdom; get insight; do not forget, and do not turn away from the words of my mouth. …

• Proverbs 13:24 – Whoever spares the rod hates his son, but he who loves him is diligent to discipline him.

• Proverbs 22:6 – Train up a child in the way he should go; even when he is old, he will not depart from it.

• 3 John 1:4 – I have no greater joy than to hear that my children are walking in the truth.

• Psalm 127:3-5 – Behold, children are a heritage from the Lord, the fruit of the womb a reward. Like arrows in the hand of a warrior are the children of one's youth. Blessed is the man who fills his quiver with them! He shall not be put to shame when he speaks with his enemies in the gate.

• Psalm 103:13 – As a father shows compassion to his children, so the Lord shows compassion to those who fear him.

• Ephesians 6:4 – Fathers, do not provoke your children to anger, but bring them up in the discipline and instruction of the Lord.

The Characteristics of a Godly Father: Guiding Principles for Positive Fatherhood

Within the intricate tapestry of family dynamics, the role of a father holds unparalleled significance. An article published by Got Questions

Ministries sheds light on ten cardinal characteristics of a godly father, offering a timeless and universally relevant framework. These characteristics not only shape the course of fatherhood but also lay the cornerstone for the emotional, spiritual, and moral development of children.

A Relationship with God: The Inner Sanctum of Godly Fatherhood

At the heart of godly fatherhood lies an authentic relationship with God. Children often mirror their fathers' behavior, making a father's spiritual journey the starting point. By nurturing his own spiritual connection, a father sets an example that paves the way for his children's relationship with God.

Love and Honor for the Spouse: A Precious Gift to Children

The notion that a father's greatest gift to his children is his love for their mother holds profound wisdom. Regardless of marital status, a father's respectful and honorable treatment of the child's mother leaves a lasting impression. Children absorb these behaviors as a blueprint for their own relationships, fostering mutual respect and compassion.

Spiritual Training: A Guiding Hand in Faith

While material provision is vital, a godly father also embraces responsibility for the spiritual growth of his children. Encouraging Christian virtues through words, actions, and behavioral expectations shapes their moral compass. This active investment molds a generation that reveres God and embraces righteousness.

Aware of Influence: Every Action Matters

A godly father is acutely aware of his influence on his children's lives. Every word spoken, action taken, and decision made resonates deeply within the hearts of those he nurtures. His impact extends beyond verbal instruction, shaping his children through his behavior and choices.

Selfless Service: A Model of Christ-like Compassion

Following the example of Jesus, a godly father embodies selfless service. By involving his children in acts of kindness and service, he instills the importance of compassion and empathy. These actions become integral components of his children's character, transcending mere lessons.

Consistency: A Pillar of Security

Consistency stands as a pillar of stability in a child's life. A godly father understands that inconsistency breeds confusion and insecurity. By maintaining a steady demeanor, he cultivates an environment of trust and emotional security, laying the foundation for his children's well-being.

Appropriate Discipline: A Balancing Act

Discipline, when applied judiciously, molds character and fosters respect. A godly father recognizes its significance in child-rearing, acknowledging that it's not solely the mother's role. With the blend of love and correction, he mirrors the discipline of a Heavenly Father, nurturing growth through guidance.

Freedom from Outside Influences: A Path to Stability

A godly father liberates his family from the shackles of external addictions. Whether combating substance abuse or detrimental behaviors, he creates a haven free from fear, depression, and insecurity. By breaking the cycle of harmful behaviors, a godly father leaves a legacy of emotional well-being and wholeness.

Submission to Authority: A Humble Leadership

Humble submission to authority distinguishes a godly father. Embracing the example set by Jesus, he practices accountability and humility. By acknowledging his dependence on God and honoring authority, he becomes a beacon of strength and guidance for his family.

Leading with Wisdom: A Legacy of Leadership

A godly father leads not through domination but by example. He practices what he preaches, setting the pace for his family. Alert to potential dangers, he takes the initiative, thus shielding his family from harm. His leadership instills pride in his children, empowering them to embrace wisdom and responsibility. Within the fabric of family life, a godly father's role is woven with threads of faith, love, and selflessness. These ten characteristics serve as a compass, guiding fathers in nurturing a legacy marked by godliness, compassion, and strength. As fathers embody these virtues, they sow seeds that blossom into a future generation characterized by resilience, respect, and the pursuit of godly principles.

Empowering Fathers as Real POPS: Strengthening Society's Foundation

The vitality of a thriving society is intricately woven with the roles and contributions of its fathers. The "Building Fathers into Real POPS" program, encapsulating the roles of Protector, Order Keeper, Provider, and Stabilizer, represents a transformative approach. It empowers fathers to embrace their vital responsibilities and make a positive impact on their children, families, and communities. This initiative is not merely about individual growth but a collective effort to fortify the social fabric that binds societies together.

Protector – Safeguarding the Next Generation

Fathers bear the mantle of protectors, ensuring the physical and emotional well-being of their children. Their mature and responsible presence transforms homes, neighborhoods, and schools into sanctuaries where children can flourish without fear. By fully embracing their roles as protectors, fathers contribute to the construction of a society where safety is a foundational value.

Order Keeper – Nurturing Peace and Stability

A resilient society rests on the solid foundation of strong family units. Fathers play a pivotal role in upholding order and preventing family and

131

community turmoil. Their presence and leadership instill responsibility, discipline, and respect within their families. By fostering order and stability, fathers actively participate in creating a culture of peaceful coexistence and social harmony.

Provider – Fostering Holistic Development

Effective fatherhood extends well beyond material provision. Fathers serve as wellsprings of emotional, spiritual, and educational support for their children. Through active engagement in their children's lives, fathers provide guidance, encouragement, and empowerment. Their unwavering commitment sets them as role models, emphasizing the importance of comprehensive development. Fathers dedicated to catering to their children's diverse needs contribute to a society where growth and success are attainable for all.

Stabilizer – Anchoring Resilient Communities

Thriving communities are founded on stable and engaged families. Active and dedicated fathers act as stabilizers, fostering an atmosphere of encouragement and empowerment. Their involvement in their children's lives nurtures resilience, confidence, and a profound sense of belonging. As stabilizers, fathers play an integral role in creating cohesive communities that embrace diversity, strengthen relationships, and support collective progress.

Breaking the Cycle of Father Absence: A Unified Call to Action

The pressing need to address the pervasive issue of father absence cannot be overstated. Its consequences extend far and wide, impacting families, communities, and most crucially, children. This crisis exacts not only an emotional toll but also imposes a substantial financial burden on society. It is a challenge that demands a united and resolute response.

The "Building Fathers into Real POPS" initiative stands firm in its mission to reverse this prevailing trend. It offers a comprehensive platform that provides peer support, educational resources, and a nurturing community to empower fathers with confidence and determination. This journey is characterized by deliberate, incremental steps aimed at strengthening father-child relationships, guided by the principles of faith, responsibility, and compassion.

Within this program, fathers are not solitary figures but integral parts of a global network. The Fathering Strong community unites fathers from diverse backgrounds, enabling them to share their experiences, challenges, and victories. This collective endeavor underscores the importance of mutual support among fathers on their individual faith journeys.

The need for action is pressing, and the time for change is now. By involving stakeholders spanning from educators and law enforcement to parents and business leaders, the program highlights the critical significance of collaborative efforts. Just as the "Getting Down to Business" approach successfully transformed the campus learning environment, similar methodologies hold the potential to mitigate mass shootings in schools.

In conclusion, "Building Fathers into Real POPS" transcends being just a program; it is a movement deeply rooted in the core values of responsibility, nurturing, and unity. By empowering fathers to wholeheartedly embrace their roles as protectors, order keepers, providers, and stabilizers, the program fosters a society where families thrive, communities flourish, and the legacy of positive fatherhood is cherished for generations to come. It is a clarion call to acknowledge the pivotal role fathers play in shaping the destinies of societies and to collectively work towards a brighter future.

PART IV: GUN LAWS

The lack of investment in communities of color, coupled with weak gun laws, has resulted in devastatingly high rates of gun violence for Black and brown people.

Gun violence is a major problem in the United States as well as the key driver of the rise in violent crime across the nation. Notably, gun violence has a disproportionate impact on racial and ethnic minorities and is highly concentrated in a relatively small number of neighborhoods that have historically been under resourced and racially segregated. This is due to a combination of weak gun laws; systemic racial inequities, including unequal access to safe housing and adequate educational and employment opportunities; and a history of disinvestment in public infrastructure and services in the communities of color most affected by gun violence.

To reduce gun violence in these communities, U.S. policymakers must complement the enforcement of commonsense gun laws with investments in community-based violence intervention (CVI) initiatives and policies to address root causes of gun violence.

- Gun homicides are on the rise in the United States, with young Black and brown people experiencing the highest rates.

- Young Black Americans (ages 15 to 34) experience the highest rates of gun homicides across all demographics.

- Black Americans are 10 times more likely than white Americans to die by gun homicide.

• While Black Americans made up 12.5 percent of the U.S. population that year, they were the victims in 61 percent of all gun homicides.

• Black Americans are three times more likely than white Americans to be fatally shot by police.

• 60 percent of gun deaths among Hispanic and Latino people are gun homicides.

• Young Hispanic Americans (ages 15 to 29) represent 4 percent of the population yet are victims in 8 percent of all gun homicides.

• In 2015, half of all gun homicides took place in just 127 cities across the country:

> o Gun homicides are concentrated in a relatively small number of neighborhoods in these cities, which have historically been under resourced and racially segregated.

Women of color are more likely than their white counterparts to be shot and killed with firearms.

• Black women are twice as likely as white women to be fatally shot by an intimate partner.

• American Indian and Alaska Native women are killed by intimate partners at a rate of 4.3 per 100,000, compared with 1.5 per 100,000 for white women.

• Guns are used in more than half of all homicides of women and are disproportionately used against Black women.

• Even when firearms are not used to kill or injure, they are used to threaten women at alarming rates:

> o 4.5 million women alive today have reported being threatened with a firearm.

Ban Assault Weapons in Our Communities.

Nonfatal gun violence has a lasting impact on individuals and communities.

- For every gun homicide there are more than two nonfatal gun shootings.

- From 2009 to 2018, the rate of gun-related assaults against Black and Hispanic Americans was 208.9 and 128.7, respectively, per 100,000, compared with 90.5 per 100,000 for white Americans.

- Nine in 10 survivors of gun violence report experiencing trauma from their incident.

Solutions: In addition to stronger, commonsense gun laws, policymakers must address systemic racial inequities.

- Policymakers should dismantle racist policies in policing, access to housing, education, and employment to address root causes of gun violence.

- The country must invest in community violence intervention (CVI) programs:

> o CVIs focus on partnerships with those most affected by gun violence, government, and community stakeholders to bring community-specific solutions to gun violence.

- Domestic abusers must be prevented from accessing firearms:

> o Gaps in legislation, such as the "dating partner loophole," allow some abusers to access firearms even if they have been convicted of a domestic violence crime.

- In June 2022, President Joe Biden signed into law the Bipartisan Safer Communities Act, a gun violence prevention package that included some, but not all, priorities to curb gun violence across the country. This package partially closed the dating partner loophole by prohibiting some dating partners convicted of domestic violence misdemeanors from owning or purchasing a firearm. However, dating partners who are issued final protective orders can still possess firearms.

- Women in communities of color have unique needs and challenges that prevent them from both seeking help and accessing services. Solutions should, therefore, be driven by the needs of this group.

Frequently Asked Questions About Community-Based Violence Intervention Programs Jun 3, 2022

Communities of color disproportionately bear the brunt of gun violence in the United States. Commonsense gun laws as well as direct investments in the communities most affected by gun violence are crucial to ending gun violence and saving lives.

The issue of gun violence is pressing, intricate, and multi-dimensional, necessitating comprehensive and well-informed solutions. Psychology holds the potential to offer valuable insights into strategies for preventing gun violence. With this objective in mind, the American Psychological Association initiated this report in February 2013, enlisting a team of experts to present research-derived findings and suggestions (alongside pinpointing areas lacking substantial information) on effectively diminishing the occurrence of gun violence, encompassing instances of homicide, suicide, and mass shootings, across the entire nation.

Gun violence results from a complex interplay of factors that can either amplify or mitigate individuals' propensity to use firearms for harm. Consequently, there is no one-size-fits-all profile that can accurately predict who may turn to gun violence. Instead, the emergence of gun-related aggression is intricately linked to a web of diverse risk factors originating from individual traits, family dynamics, school environments, peer interactions, community influences, and the broader societal context. These factors evolve during childhood and adolescence.

While many young individuals outgrow aggressive and antisocial behaviors as they mature into their later teenage years, some remain at a heightened risk of becoming involved in or negatively affected by gun violence. The most consistent and influential predictor of future violence lies in an individual's history of past violent behavior. Efforts focused on prevention, driven by research on developmental risks, have the potential to reduce the likelihood of firearms being used in disputes within communities or families, as well as in criminal activities. These endeavors can also decrease instances where severe mental disorders contribute to homicides or where mental health issues contribute to suicides. The overarching goal of broader primary or secondary prevention and intervention strategies is to decrease incidents of gun violence stemming from criminal actions or self-inflicted harm.

To comprehensively address gun violence in the United States, it's crucial to explore why many males engage in such acts while most females do not. Initial indications suggest that changing male perceptions of societal norms tied to masculine traits and behaviors could potentially reduce instances of intimate partner and sexual violence. These interventions merit further evaluation to assess their potential effectiveness in mitigating gun violence.

The involvement of psychologists is indispensable in devising and evaluating initiatives and environments across various settings, including schools, workplaces, prisons, communities, and medical facilities. These endeavors aim to reshape gender-based expectations associated with masculinity, which often emphasize qualities like self-reliance, toughness, and aggression, including the use of firearms.

While it's imperative to recognize that most individuals grappling with mental illness do not pose a threat, those at risk of violence due to mental health issues, suicidal tendencies, or a sense of despair can often be prevented from committing acts of gun violence through proper mental health treatment. National attention should be directed towards policies and initiatives focused on identifying and providing treatment for all individuals affected by mental disorders. The inadequacy of current access to mental health services in the United States demands immediate and targeted attention.

Furthermore, it's essential to acknowledge that behavioral threat assessment is becoming a standard practice for preventing violence in educational institutions, colleges, workplaces, and against government and public figures. These assessment teams gather and evaluate information to determine whether an individual poses a threat of violence or self-harm, and if so, they take the necessary measures for intervention.

Violence prevention spans a spectrum of actions, starting in early childhood by supporting parents in nurturing emotionally well-adjusted children and extending to the identification and intervention with individuals who may pose a threat of violence. The mental health sector should take a leading role in advocating for collaborative problem solving models deeply rooted in the community to address gun violence prevention. These models should harmonize various prevention approaches to counteract the tendency of many community service systems to operate in isolation.

Significant progress has been achieved through community-centered programs, including initiatives such as police training in crisis intervention and educating community members in mental health first aid. These programs merit further testing and evaluation to facilitate their expansion into different communities as appropriate. Furthermore, public health campaigns emphasizing the secure storage of firearms are imperative. It is crucial that the practice of properly storing and locking firearms becomes the universally accepted social norm.

The utilization of firearms significantly increases the likelihood of violence resulting in a fatality, making it an issue demanding immediate attention. Implementing firearm restrictions for high-risk demographics – such as individuals with a history of domestic violence, those convicted of violent misdemeanors, and individuals with mental health conditions deemed a danger to themselves or others – has been proven to lower violent incidents. Approaches like licensing handgun buyers, enforcing background checks for all gun transactions, and closely monitoring retail gun vendors can curb the illicit distribution of firearms to criminals.

Efforts to decrease gun violence will necessitate interventions across various sectors, including the legal, public health, public safety, community, and healthcare realms. Enhancing the availability of data and funding will contribute to informing and assessing policies aimed at mitigating gun-related violence.

MASS SHOOTINGS BY WHITE MEN

Most recent mass shootings in the United States – including Newtown, Aurora, Fort Hood, Tucson, and Columbine – have been carried out by white men and boys. Yet, when the National Rifle Association (NRA), led predominantly by white men, held a press conference following the Newtown tragedy to offer advice on curbing gun violence, their viewpoints garnered significant attention.

When white men attempt to shift the discussion from gun control to mental health concerns, a portion of the populace buys into the notion that the United States faces a widespread mental health crisis, or that there are flawed systems for addressing such issues, which in turn contribute to mass shootings.

Women and girls with mental health challenges are not resorting to semiautomatic weapons to perpetrate school shootings. Even immigrants with mental health issues are not responsible for mall and movie theatre mass shootings. Latinos with mental health issues are not responsible for mall and movie theater mass shootings. Latinos with mental health issues are not continuously committing acts of violence against groups of strangers.

Educational institutions predominantly focus on American history that primarily revolves around the narratives of white men. Histories of other underrepresented groups, such as African American history, women's history, or Native American history, often require separate courses or limited recognition during designated months. Moreover, the notion of studying "Hispanic American History" does not inherently encompass the inclusion of "Asian American History."

This societal and cultural conditioning sets the stage for an environment in which conservative, white male-led organizations can effectively persuade the nation that groups like the NRA or the tea party movement, both predominantly led by white men, can advocate for the interests of the entire nation, despite primarily representing their own perspectives and experiences.

This leads us to ponder why there is a disproportionate involvement of white males in content play a role in the incidents involving white boys and white men committing mass shootings? Furthermore, why do white men tend to be overrepresented in activities related to buying, selling, and manufacturing guns for profit, attending gun shows, and advocating for unrestricted gun access, especially in comparison to other ethnicities? Lastly, why do white male legislators often take the lead in opposing gun control measures? These questions prompt us to examine the underlying dynamics contributing to these patterns.

These answers we need to find for the reasons for mass shootings by white men. We need these answers to help other white men and boys lead healthier and less violent lives. Newsweek ran an article with the headline, "White men have committed more mass shootings than any other group." The article stated that 54 percent of mass shootings since 1982 have been carried out by white males.

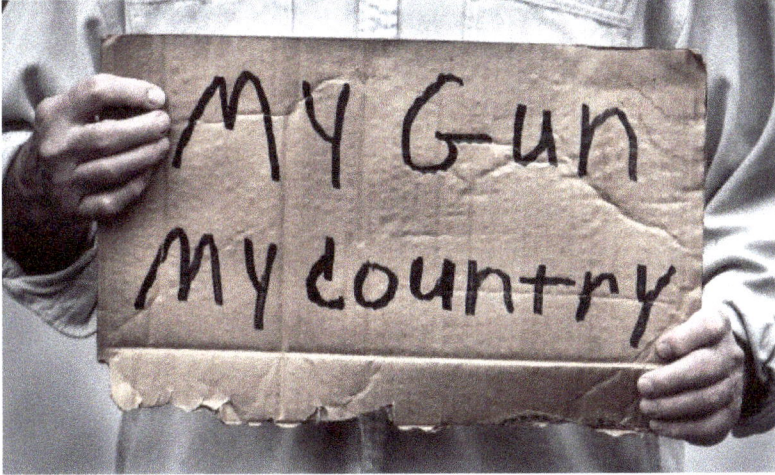

Discrepancies in the datasets stem partly from the absence of a universally agreed-upon definition of what constitutes a mass shooting. The number of recorded mass shootings can vary significantly depending on how the term is defined.

For example, the Gun Violence Archive, a nonprofit organization dedicated to tracking gun-related injuries and fatalities, defines a mass shooting as an incident in which "four or more individuals are shot and/or killed in a single event, occurring at the same general time and location, excluding the shooter." According to their data, there have been 274 mass shootings in the current year, nearly equivalent to one occurrence per day.

Mother Jones, which established a database in 2012 following the mass shooting at an Aurora, Colorado movie theater, characterizes a public mass shooting as an incident where the motive appears to be indiscriminate killing, and a lone gunman takes the lives of at least three people. This definition closely resembles a 2013 statute that defines "mass killings" as events where three or more individuals are killed in a single occurrence, regardless of the weapon used.

The Mother Jones database covers incidents from August 20, 1982, to the present day, documenting a total of 91 mass shootings, with 50 of them being committed by white men. In contrast, African Americans were responsible for 15 mass shootings, while both Latinos and Asians were linked to seven incidents each. Additionally, three attacks were carried out by women, including one of the two culprits behind the 2015 San Bernardino shooting.

It's important to note that some experts have expressed concerns that an excessive focus on mass shootings in discussions about gun violence may overshadow the reality that gun-related homicides disproportionately affect minorities.

According to Duwe, "There have been at least 184 mass public shootings in the U.S. since 1900, including the Las Vegas attack. Among these mass public shooters, non-Hispanic whites account for 63 percent, which closely mirrors the demographic makeup of the U.S. population. Consequently, the Mother Jones data actually underreports the extent to which white individuals are involved as mass public shooters."

Many mass shootings are perpetrated by males. When examining only the male population, some argue that statistical claims based on Mother Jones' data regarding the racial composition of mass shooters lack essential context. Critics contend that when considering that non-Hispanic white men make up about 63 percent of the male population, white men appear proportionally less likely to commit mass shootings. This contrasts with the Mother Jones statistics indicating that white men are responsible for 54 percent of mass shootings. (Duwe's finding that non-Hispanic white men account for 63 percent of mass shooters aligns closely with the white segment of the male population. White men make up approximately 31 percent of the total U.S. population.)

An alternate calculation, which encompasses a broader timeframe and a distinct definition of mass shooting, determined that non-Hispanic white men account for 63 percent of these incidents. Both definitions and datasets support the conclusion that white men have carried out more mass shootings than any other racial group. While Newsweek's statement is factually accurate, it's important to acknowledge the limitations of this data, and the proportion of mass shootings involving white men is lower than their representation within the male population, according to Mother Jones.

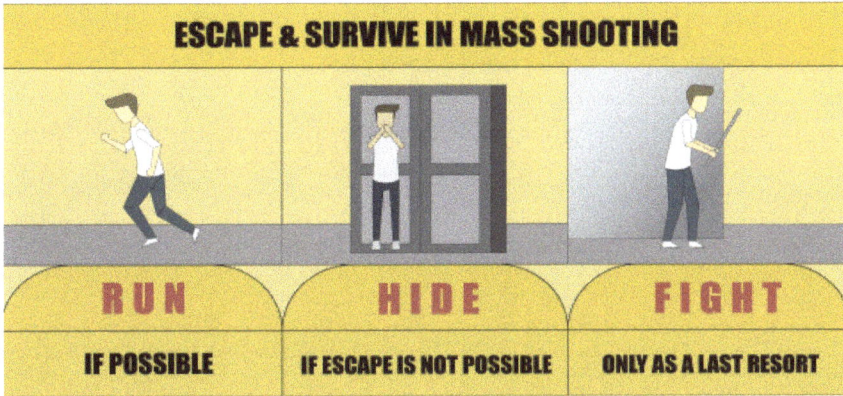

Factors that have been identified as potential contributors to such incidents include:

• Mental Health: Many individuals who engage in mass shootings may have underlying mental health issues that contribute to their actions. However, not all individuals with mental health challenges resort to violence.

• Ideology: Some mass shootings are driven by extremist ideologies, such as white supremacy or other forms of hatred and intolerance.

• Social Isolation: Feelings of loneliness and social isolation can be risk factors for various negative outcomes, including violence. However, not everyone who experiences loneliness becomes violent.

• Access to Firearms: Easy access to firearms can facilitate acts of violence, including mass shootings.

• Personal Grievances: Personal conflicts, grudges, or grievances against specific individuals, institutions, or society can also play a role.

• Copycat Behavior: Some individuals may be influenced by previous incidents of mass shootings, leading to copycat behavior.

• Media Influence: Media coverage of mass shootings can sometimes inadvertently glorify perpetrators and contribute to their motivations.

• Efforts to prevent mass shootings should involve a holistic approach that addresses mental health issues, promotes social inclusion, enacts responsible gun control measures, and addresses any underlying ideological or societal factors that may contribute to violence.

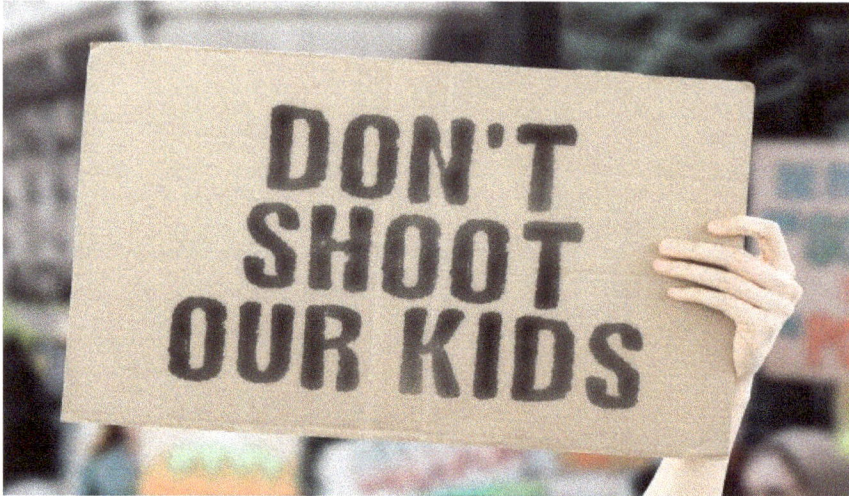

1. Columbine High School Shooting (1999): Location: Littleton, Colorado Date: April 20, 1999, Casualties: 15 killed (including the perpetrators), 24 injured.

2. Sandy Hook Elementary School Shooting (2012): Location: Newtown, Connecticut Date: December 14, 2012, Casualties: 28 killed (including the perpetrator), 2 injured.

3. Marjory Stoneman Douglas High School Shooting (2018): Location: Parkland, Florida Date: February 14, 2018, Casualties: 17 killed, 17 injured.

4. Santa Fe High School Shooting (2018): Location: Santa Fe, Texas Date: May 18, 2018, Casualties: 10 killed, 13 injured.

5. STEM School Highlands Ranch Shooting (2019): Location: Highlands Ranch, Colorado Date: May 7, 2019, Casualties: 1 killed, 8 injured.

6. Saugus High School Shooting (2019): Location: Santa Clarita, California Date: November 14, 2019, Casualties: 3 killed (including the perpetrator), 3 injured.

7. Freeman High School Shooting (2017): Location: Rockford, Washington Date: September 13, 2017, Casualties: 1 killed, 3 injured.

8. Oikos University Shooting (2012): Location: Oakland, California Date: April 2, 2012, Casualties: 7 killed, 3 injured.

9. Umpqua Community College Shooting (2015): Location: Roseburg, Oregon Date: October 1, 2015, Casualties: 10 killed (including the perpetrator), 8 injured.

The tragic events of school mass shootings have sparked debates about gun control, mental health, school safety, and related issues.

What nationality were the perpetrators of these mass shootings in schools?

> **1. Columbine High School Shooting (1999):** Nationality: United States
>
> **2. Sandy Hook Elementary School Shooting (2012):** Nationality: United States
>
> **3. Marjory Stoneman Douglas High School Shooting (2018):** Nationality: United States
>
> **4. Santa Fe High School Shooting (2018):** Nationality: United States
>
> **5. STEM School Highlands Ranch Shooting (2019):** Nationality: United States
>
> **6. Saugus High School Shooting (2019):** Nationality: United States
>
> **7. Freeman High School Shooting (2017):** Nationality: United States
>
> **8. Oikos University Shooting (2012):** Nationality: United States
>
> **9. Umpqua Community College Shooting (2015):** Nationality: United States

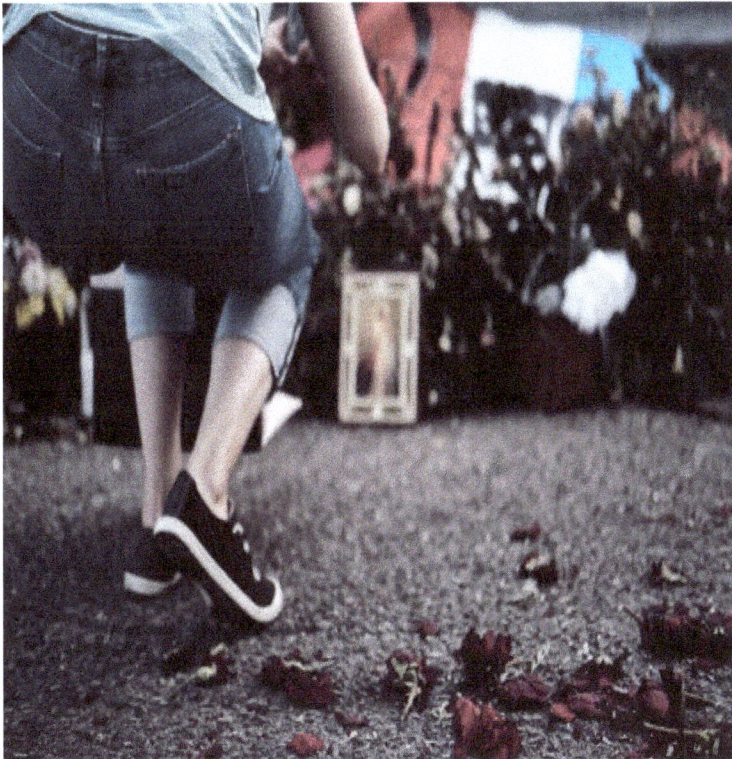

The perpetrators of mass shootings come from various nationalities, and the incidents can occur in different countries. Here's a breakdown of the nationalities of the perpetrators of some of the mentioned school mass shootings:

The incidents listed predominantly occurred in the United States, and the nationalities of the perpetrators reflect this context. Mass shootings can occur in various countries, and the motivations and backgrounds of the perpetrators can vary widely.

What racial background were the perpetrators of these mass shootings?

The racial backgrounds of the perpetrators of mass shootings can vary widely, reflecting the diversity of individuals involved in such incidents. Here's a breakdown of the racial backgrounds of the perpetrators of some of the mentioned school mass shootings:

---

1. **Columbine High School Shooting (1999):** Racial Background: White

2. **Sandy Hook Elementary School Shooting (2012):** Racial Background: White

3. **Marjory Stoneman Douglas High School Shooting (2018):** Racial Background: White

4. **Santa Fe High School Shooting (2018):** Racial Background: White

5. **STEM School Highlands Ranch Shooting (2019):** Racial Background: White

6. **Saugus High School Shooting (2019):** Racial Background: White

7. **Freeman High School Shooting (2017):** Racial Background: White

8. **Oikos University Shooting (2012):** Racial Background: Korean American

9. **Umpqua Community College Shooting (2015):** Racial Background: White

---

It's important to note that while the racial backgrounds listed above are based on available information, the motivations and factors contributing to each incident are complex and cannot be solely attributed to a person's racial background. Mass shootings are influenced by a combination of individual, social, psychological, and cultural factors.

1. Red Lake High School Shooting (2005): Location: Red Lake, Minnesota Date: March 21, 2005, Casualties: 10 killed (including the perpetrator), 5 injured.

2. Northern Illinois University Shooting (2008): Location: DeKalb, Illinois Date: February 14, 2008, Casualties: 6 killed (including the perpetrator), 21 injured.

3. Oikos University Shooting (2012): Location: Oakland, California Date: April 2, 2012, Casualties: 7 killed, 3 injured.

4. Marysville Pilchuck High School Shooting (2014): Location: Marysville, Washington Date: October 24, 2014, Casualties: 5 killed (including the perpetrator), 1 injured.

5. Umpqua Community College Shooting (2015): Location: Roseburg, Oregon Date: October 1, 2015, Casualties: 10 killed (including the perpetrator), 8 injured.

6. Townville Elementary School Shooting (2016): Location: Townville, South Carolina Date: September 28, 2016, Casualties: 2 killed, 2 injured.

7. Rancho Tehama Elementary School Shooting (2017): Location: Corning, California Date: November 14, 2017, Casualties: 6 killed (including the perpetrator), 18 injured.

8. Marshall County High School Shooting (2018): Location: Benton, Kentucky Date: January 23, 2018, Casualties: 2 killed, 14 injured.

9. Noblesville West Middle School Shooting (2018): Location: Noblesville, Indiana Date: May 25, 2018, Casualties: 2 injured.

10. University of North Carolina at Charlotte Shooting (2019): Location: Charlotte, North Carolina Date: April 30, 2019, Casualties: 2 killed, 4 injured.

The list includes incidents primarily from the United States and is not exhaustive. The tragic events of school mass shootings emphasize the importance of addressing factors such as mental health, gun control, and school safety to prevent further incidents.

What race were the perpetrators of these mass shootings? The racial backgrounds of the perpetrators of these mass shootings can vary, reflecting the diversity of individuals involved in such incidents. Here's a breakdown of the racial backgrounds of the perpetrators of the additional school mass shootings mentioned:

1. **Red Lake High School Shooting (2005):** Racial Background: Native American

2. **Northern Illinois University Shooting (2008):** Racial Background: White

3. **Oikos University Shooting (2012):** Racial Background: Korean American

4. **Marysville Pilchuck High School Shooting (2014):** Racial Background: Native American

5. **Umpqua Community College Shooting (2015):** Racial Background: White

6. **Townville Elementary School Shooting (2016):** Racial Background: White

7. **Rancho Tehama Elementary School Shooting (2017):** Racial Background: White

8. **Marshall County High School Shooting (2018):** Racial Background: White

9. **Noblesville West Middle School Shooting (2018):** Racial Background: White

10. **University of North Carolina at Charlotte Shooting (2019):** Racial Background: Asian American

PART V: GETTING DOWN TO BUSINESS

The stark reality remains unchanged since the 1990s when I served as principal at Centennial High and Compton High. The persistent issues surrounding gun violence, gang conflicts, and mass shootings bear an uncanny resemblance to what we faced then.

Nearly three decades have passed, and tangible results remain elusive. In fact, hate crimes have seen an alarming increase. What I'm about to say may not garner widespread popularity, but it's a truth that needs acknowledgment: African Americans must protest shootings and killings in their own communities with the same vigor as when a white police officer shoots a black individual.

Every day, crime plagues the urban neighborhoods where black and brown communities reside. Yet, these incidents rarely receive news coverage, and protests within the community over innocent lives lost to gun violence or gang-related activities are conspicuously absent. The issues I've highlighted are extensive and addressing them will require a Herculean effort. However, we have no choice if we wish to ensure our survival as a people, a nation, and a world.

Nonetheless, it's essential to recognize that schools alone cannot shoulder the burden. We need assistance from local government, state government, federal government, the community, the business community, parents, students, churches, and schools. The following recommendations largely reflect the methods I employed to combat school shootings and gang violence during my tenure. These are my suggestions, and I hope they can prove effective in your situation and community.

I recalled a meeting sometime in July 1991 with a fine young man I met in the Principal's Office at Centennial High School, a student by the name of John came (Knocking on the door) and he said, "May I come in?"

Me, smiling, said, "Of course, John! Come on in. Take a seat. What can I do for you today?"

John said, "Well, Mr. Gilliam, I wanted to talk to you about something that's been bothering me."

I responded saying, "Of course, John. I'm all ears. What's on your mind?"

John uttered, almost shamefully, "I've been hearing a lot of my friends talking about how they think they can make easy money by dealing drugs or getting involved in illegal activities. It's troubling, and I want to understand why they feel this way."

I responded by saying, "I understand your concern, John. It's unfortunate that some students may feel that way, especially in challenging environments. But let me assure you that there are much better and safer opportunities out there for you and your friends."

John: That's what I thought too. I want to believe there's a better path for all of us, but it's tough to convince them otherwise. They believe dealing drugs can provide quick money and escape from our financial struggles.

Mr. Gilliam: John, I understand their perspective, but it's essential to focus on the long-term consequences. Dealing drugs may seem tempting with the promise of quick cash, but it often leads to severe consequences – both legally and personally. Let's talk about the positive opportunities available to you.

John: I've been thinking about going to college or learning a skilled trade, but sometimes it feels like a distant dream. How can I make it a reality?

Mr. Gilliam: Your aspirations are commendable, John. Remember that education is your gateway to a brighter future. We have resources in school to help you explore career options, apply for scholarships, and find mentorship programs. We can also investigate vocational training and apprenticeships to prepare you for skilled jobs.

John: That sounds great, Mr. Gilliam, but how can we show my friends that there's more to life than what they're considering?

Mr. Gilliam: (Encouragingly) Leading by example can be powerful. By making positive choices and demonstrating the value of education and legitimate career paths, you can influence your friends positively. You can also share your aspirations and the opportunities you're exploring. Sometimes, inviting guest speakers or organizing workshops about successful people from different fields can inspire them as well.

John: I'd be willing to give it a try. I want my friends to realize that we can make a difference in our lives and our community without getting involved in illegal activities.

Mr. Gilliam: That's the spirit, John! Together, we can create a culture of positivity and empower our students to choose the path that leads to a successful and fulfilling life. Remember, I'm here to support you every step of the way.

John: Thank you, Mr. Gilliam. I appreciate your guidance and understanding. I'll do my best to make a positive impact.

Mr. Gilliam: I have no doubt you will, John. You have a bright future ahead of you, and I'm proud of your determination to make a difference. If you need any assistance or have more questions, don't hesitate to reach out. Let's work together to create a school community where every student can thrive.

I took great pride in a student who approached me to discuss these school-related issues. As a principal, I believed that conversations about steering clear of illegal activities and exploring legitimate career opportunities were essential topics that students should engage in more frequently with their teachers and principals. These discussions aimed to underscore the importance of providing guidance and support to students as they charted their future paths.

Over the next few weeks, I convened meetings with teachers in various locations, including the Cafeteria and Library at the High School. On one particular day, during a meeting with the teachers, I emphasized the need for strict adherence to the assertive discipline program we had established and urged them to actively pursue our school goals for the upcoming year.

Mr. Gilliam: Good morning, everyone. Thank you for being here today. I wanted to discuss a crucial topic that I believe requires our collective attention – guiding our students towards positive and fulfilling futures.

Ms. Johnson: (Nods) Yes, Mr. Gilliam. It's essential to help our students see beyond the challenges they face and understand the possibilities that await them.

Mr. Gilliam: Exactly, Ms. Johnson. Some of our students may be exposed to negative influences or believe that engaging in illegal activities is a viable way to improve their circumstances. We need to counter this perspective and offer them alternative paths.

Mrs. Thompson: I agree. It's about instilling a sense of hope and motivation, showing them the benefits of education and legitimate career options.

Mr. Gilliam: Precisely, Mrs. Thompson. We can start by incorporating financial literacy and practical money management skills into our curriculum. This will empower our students to make informed financial decisions and understand the importance of investing in their education.

Mr. Hernandez: I like the idea of emphasizing the real-world relevance of education. By connecting it to their lives, students may be more motivated to engage in learning.

Mr. Gilliam: Absolutely, Mr. Hernandez. We can also organize workshops or guest speakers from various industries to introduce our students to different career opportunities. This exposure will help them see the value of education in achieving their goals.

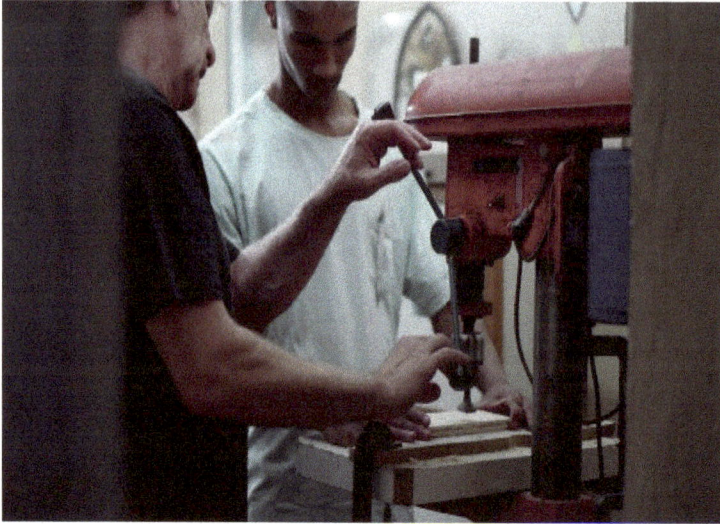

Ms. Johnson: I think it's essential to showcase successful individuals who come from similar backgrounds as our students. This way, they can relate to their experiences and see that success is achievable for them too.

Mr. Gilliam: Great suggestion, Ms. Johnson. Let's also encourage our students to explore vocational training and apprenticeships for those interested in skilled jobs. These paths offer lucrative and rewarding opportunities.

Mr. Lee: I agree. We should celebrate the achievements of our students who have pursued legal career paths and share their success stories as inspiration.

Mr. Gilliam: Excellent idea, Mr. Lee. We need to highlight positive role models within our school community and celebrate their accomplishments.

Mrs. Thompson: How about involving parents and the community in these efforts? It could help create a supportive environment for our students.

Mr. Gilliam: That's a fantastic suggestion, Mrs. Thompson. We can hold workshops for parents to discuss the importance of financial literacy and how they can support their children in pursuing their aspirations.

Mr. Hernandez: Additionally, involving community leaders and local businesses can open up internship opportunities for our students to gain practical experience in different fields.

Mr. Gilliam: Yes, Mr. Hernandez. Let's reach out to community organizations and local businesses to collaborate on providing valuable experiences for our students.

Ms. Johnson: I believe fostering a positive school culture where students feel supported and encouraged can also make a significant impact.

Mr. Gilliam: Absolutely, Ms. Johnson. Our school should be a place where every student feels valued, understood, and empowered to make positive choices.

Mr. Lee: It's exciting to see our school taking an active role in shaping the future of our students. I'm on board with these strategies.

Mrs. Thompson: I am too. Let's make a difference in the lives of our students and inspire them to pursue their dreams.

Mr. Gilliam: I'm thrilled to see your enthusiasm, and I know that together, we can create a lasting impact on our students' lives. Thank you all for your dedication and commitment to their success.

As principal, discussing with the school faculty strategies to guide students towards positive career paths and empower them to make informed decisions about their future was key to making positive changes. The dialogue highlights the importance of collaboration, community involvement, and fostering a positive school culture to support students in making positive choices for their lives.

About three weeks later, I met with heads of each department Ms. Johnson - English Teacher, Mr. Hernandez - Science Teacher, Mrs. Thompson - Mathematics Teacher, Mr. Lee - History Teacher, Mrs. Ramirez - School Counselor, Mr. Jenkins - School Security Officer. These meetings typically took place once every week on a Monday to get prepared for the week ahead.

Mr. Gilliam: (politely greeted his certificated staff) "Good morning, everyone."

Mr. Gilliam: I want to address a pressing matter today - the safety and security of our students. As we all know, school shootings are a serious concern, and we must do everything in our power to reduce the risk of such tragedies in our school.

Mr. Lee: Absolutely, Mr. Gilliam. The safety of our students should always be our top priority.

Ms. Johnson: I agree. We need to take proactive measures to ensure a secure learning environment for our students.

Mr. Gilliam: Precisely. I'd like to hear your thoughts on strategies we can implement to enhance school safety. Let's start with prevention. What can we do to identify potential issues before they escalate?

Mrs. Thompson: I think promoting a culture of open communication and trust is vital. Encouraging students and staff to report any concerning behaviors or signs of distress can help us intervene early.

Mr. Hernandez: We can also provide training for teachers and staff on recognizing warning signs of potential violence and how to respond appropriately.

Mrs. Ramirez: Yes, and let's not forget the importance of providing support services for students who may be struggling emotionally or socially.

Mr. Jenkins: Strengthening access control is crucial as well. We should ensure all entry points are monitored and limit access to the school building during the day.

Ms. Johnson: Agreed. Having a single point of entry with a staffed security checkpoint can help control who enters the premises.

Mr. Gilliam: Those are excellent suggestions. We should also consider implementing regular safety drills to ensure everyone knows how to respond in emergency situations.

Mr. Lee: And, Mr. Gilliam, we should review and update our emergency response plans regularly to address any changes in potential threats.

Mrs. Thompson: Absolutely. It's essential to be prepared for any scenario and have clear protocols in place.

Mr. Gilliam: We can also explore the option of increasing the number of security personnel on campus to provide a visible presence and swift response to any incidents.

Mr. Hernandez: And, Mr. Gilliam, we could consider installing security cameras in strategic locations for enhanced surveillance.

Mrs. Ramirez: Additionally, let's focus on fostering a positive and inclusive school climate. Strong connections between students and staff can help prevent violence.

Ms. Johnson: Yes, implementing anti-bullying programs and promoting respect and empathy among students can make a significant difference.

Mr. Gilliam: I appreciate all your input. These strategies will undoubtedly contribute to a safer environment for our students. Let's work together to implement them effectively and continue to prioritize the well-being of every student.

Mr. Jenkins: It's essential to remember that safety is an ongoing process. We need to stay vigilant and be prepared for any challenges that may arise.

Mr. Gilliam: You're right, Mr. Jenkins. We must stay proactive and adapt to changing circumstances. Let's form a safety committee to regularly review our security measures and ensure we're always improving.

Mrs. Thompson: That sounds like an excellent idea. Having a dedicated team focused on safety will help us address any issues promptly.

Mr. Gilliam: Thank you all for your dedication and commitment to our students' safety. With our collective efforts, we can create a secure and nurturing environment for everyone. It's crucial to emphasize the significance of obtaining buy-in from teachers and staff when implementing changes. Engaging in a dialogue with both the principal and the school staff to deliberate on strategies aimed at reducing the risk of violence and improving school safety was paramount. This underscores the essential principles of prevention, preparedness, and the cultivation of a positive school climate, all of which are essential for creating a secure learning environment that benefits all students.

Mr. Gilliam: Good morning, everyone. Today, I'd like to discuss an essential topic: leveraging technology to enhance school safety and reduce the risk of violence. As technology advances, we have new opportunities to create a safer learning environment for our students.

Mr. Hernandez: That's a crucial point, Mr. Gilliam. Embracing technology can help us address security challenges effectively.

Ms. Johnson: I agree. It's essential to explore innovative solutions that can support our existing safety measures.

Mr. Gilliam: Absolutely. Let's brainstorm ideas on how we can employ technology to enhance safety within our school community. Mr. Jenkins, as our security officer, I'd like to hear your thoughts first.

Mr. Jenkins: Thank you, Mr. Gilliam. One idea is to invest in advanced security camera systems that offer real-time monitoring and recording capabilities. These can help us track suspicious activities and respond promptly to any potential threats.

Mrs. Thompson: That sounds like a great step forward. We can cover blind spots and critical areas with these cameras.

Mr. Gilliam: Precisely, Mrs. Thompson. Having comprehensive coverage is vital. Additionally, we can explore the possibility of implementing facial recognition technology to identify unauthorized individuals on campus.

Mrs. Ramirez: That's a good idea. It would help us enhance access control and keep track of visitors, ensuring only authorized personnel could enter the premises.

Ms. Johnson: Along with that, we can also consider using mobile panic buttons for teachers and staff. In case of an emergency, they can send immediate alerts for assistance.

Mr. Gilliam: Excellent suggestion, Ms. Johnson. Panic buttons can expedite response times and provide a sense of security for our staff.

Mr. Hernandez: Another technology we can explore is gunshot detection systems. They can automatically identify the sound of gunshots and notify law enforcement.

Mr. Gilliam: That's an innovative solution, Mr. Hernandez. It can help speed up the emergency response process and potentially save lives.

Mr. Lee: Additionally, we should investigate anonymous reporting apps or platforms. These can empower students to report concerns or potential threats discreetly.

Mr. Gilliam: Agreed, Mr. Lee. Encouraging open communication while respecting students' privacy is crucial.

Mrs. Ramirez: In line with technology, we could also conduct regular safety drills using virtual reality (VR) or augmented reality (AR) simulations. It can offer a more immersive and effective training experience.

Mr. Jenkins: VR and AR simulations are excellent tools to help our staff and students familiarize themselves with emergency procedures in a realistic environment.

Mr. Gilliam: Absolutely. Let's also consider investing in digital safety training platforms that provide ongoing education for staff and students on various safety scenarios.

Ms. Johnson: Continuous training will ensure everyone is well-prepared to handle any situation that may arise.

Mr. Gilliam: I appreciate all your input. These technological solutions show great promise in enhancing school safety. Let's form a technology committee to research these options further and present a comprehensive plan for implementation.

Mr. Hernandez: That sounds like a solid plan, Mr. Gilliam. By collaborating as a team, we can make our school a safer place for everyone.

Mr. Gilliam: Precisely. Together, we can create a secure and nurturing environment that supports the academic and personal growth of all our students. Thank you for your dedication to their safety and well-being.

As Principal I was intent on inviting parents, students, staff and the school faculty to discuss technological solutions to enhance school safety and reduce violence. The discussions highlight the collaborative effort of the faculty in exploring innovative measures to create a safer learning environment for students.

During the first month of school, I established a Principal's Advisory Council. I asked the faculty and staff to identify the leaders on this campus besides the elected ASB officers. Once I had a list of students, I summoned each of those identified to attend a meeting in the auditorium.

Mr. Gilliam: (Welcoming the students) Good afternoon, everyone. Thank you for joining me today. As student leaders, your voices are essential in shaping the safety and well-being of our school community.

Lily: Thank you, Mr. Gilliam. We're honored to be here and contribute to making our school a safer place.

Mr. Gilliam: Safety is our top priority, and I believe working together is the key to success. Let's start by discussing your perspectives on the current safety measures and any ideas you may have to improve them.

Alex: We appreciate the safety measures in place, but we could benefit from more security personnel during after-school activities and events.

Carlos: (Nods) Yeah and having more staff around can also help prevent conflicts between students.

Mr. Gilliam: That's an important point, Carlos. Your presence and support during events can make a difference in maintaining a positive atmosphere.

Emily: I think it would be helpful to have regular safety workshops or assemblies for students, so we all know what to do in case of an emergency.

Jordan: I agree. It's crucial for all students to be informed about the safety protocols.

Mr. Gilliam: Those are excellent suggestions. Safety education is vital, and we can work with our staff to conduct regular safety drills and workshops.

Lily: Building a sense of community is also essential. If we all look out for each other, we can prevent conflicts and incidents before they escalate.

Mr. Gilliam: You're right, Lily. Encouraging a supportive and inclusive environment can foster a strong sense of community.

Carlos: (Eagerly) I want to help with that. I've been part of a gang in the past, but I've changed my ways. I want to be a positive influence and help others make better choices.

Mr. Gilliam: Carlos, that's commendable. Your personal journey can serve as an inspiration to others. We can work together to create mentoring and intervention programs that support students in making positive changes.

Alex: We also need to address the issue of bullying and conflicts between students. Sometimes, it gets out of control, and we don't know who to turn to.

Emily: Yeah, having a safe and confidential reporting system would be helpful.

Mr. Gilliam: Absolutely. We'll explore implementing anonymous reporting platforms, so students can share their concerns without fear.

Jordan: We should also focus on extracurricular activities and clubs that promote positive engagement and team building.

Mr. Gilliam: I couldn't agree more, Jordan. Extracurricular activities provide valuable opportunities for students to connect with their peers and develop leadership skills.

Lily: (Excitedly) As ASB, we can organize school-wide campaigns on safety and create events that bring students together.

Mr. Gilliam: Your involvement as ASB is crucial in promoting a safe and inclusive school culture. Let's collaborate on organizing events that promote unity and safety.

Carlos: I'll do my best to be a role model for others. I want to show them that we can make better choices.

Mr. Gilliam: Your dedication to positive change is commendable, Carlos. Your influence can help change lives.

Emily: We'll work together as student leaders to keep our campus safe and supportive for everyone.

Mr. Gilliam: I'm grateful for your commitment. Let's establish a Principal's Advisory Council that meets regularly to discuss safety initiatives and collaborate on making our school the best it can be.

Lily: Count us in, Mr. Gilliam. We're ready to make a difference.

Mr. Gilliam: Thank you all for your passion and dedication. Together, we can create a school community where every student feels safe, valued, and empowered to succeed.

I met with the Principal's Advisory Council weekly, typically on Monday of each week. The Principal's Advisory Council consisted of ASB officers, athletes, gang leaders, and other student leaders identified by staff and teachers. The purpose highlights their collaborative efforts to keep the campus safe and supportive through various initiatives and programs. The involvement of student leaders is emphasized to foster a sense of ownership and responsibility for the well-being of the school community.

Mr. Gilliam: Good morning, everyone. Thank you for gathering here today. As we all know, the safety and well-being of our students are paramount. Recent events have highlighted the need for us to address the risk of violence in our school. Let's have an open discussion about strategies to reduce the risk of children getting shot and killed in schools.

Ms. Johnson: It's a critical issue, Mr. Gilliam. We need to be proactive in ensuring our students' safety.

Mr. Hernandez: Agreed. It's essential to take a comprehensive approach to address this concern.

Mr. Gilliam: Precisely. So, let's start by discussing preventive measures. One of the most important things we can do is to foster a positive and supportive school culture. Building strong connections with our students can help identify early warning signs and intervene before any situation escalates.

Mrs. Thompson: I believe creating a safe and inclusive environment will encourage students to feel comfortable sharing their concerns with us.

Mr. Gilliam: You're right, Mrs. Thompson. Open communication is key. Let's encourage students to report any suspicious behavior or potential threats they may come across.

Mr. Lee: Regular safety drills can also prepare both students and staff to respond effectively in emergency situations.

Mr. Gilliam: That's an excellent point, Mr. Lee. Practicing safety procedures will help us all be better prepared.

Ms. Johnson: We should also consider training for teachers and staff on recognizing signs of distress or possible violence.

Mr. Gilliam: Absolutely, Ms. Johnson. Identifying early signs can enable us to provide the necessary support to students in need.

Mr. Hernandez: Strengthening access control is crucial too. Limiting access points and ensuring all visitors check in at the main office can enhance security.

Mr. Gilliam: I completely agree. Controlling access will help us maintain a secure environment.

Other Teacher: (Raises hand) What about utilizing technology? Can we implement surveillance systems or emergency alert apps to improve safety?

Mr. Gilliam: Technology can indeed play a significant role. Advanced security camera systems can provide real-time monitoring, and emergency alert apps can facilitate swift responses during crises.

Mrs. Thompson: And we could organize workshops or assemblies for students to educate them about safety and the importance of reporting concerns.

Mr. Gilliam: Wonderful idea, Mrs. Thompson. Education and awareness are vital components in enhancing safety.

Mr. Lee: (Nods) Additionally, we should involve parents in this process. Ensuring they understand our safety protocols will create a cohesive approach between school and home.

Mr. Gilliam: Excellent suggestion, Mr. Lee. A partnership with parents will reinforce our efforts.

Ms. Johnson: I think it's essential for us to be vigilant and observant in our daily interactions with students. Sometimes, they might need someone to listen to their concerns.

Mr. Gilliam: You're absolutely right, Ms. Johnson. Our attentiveness can make a significant impact on a student's well-being.

Mr. Hernandez: I believe involving students themselves in safety initiatives can also empower them to take an active role in creating a secure environment.

Mr. Gilliam: You're absolutely right, Mr. Hernandez. Our student leaders and student body, in general, can be valuable partners in promoting safety and positivity on campus.

Mr. Lee: It's essential for us as educators to lead by example and demonstrate empathy and kindness to our students.

Mr. Gilliam: Well said, Mr. Lee. Our collective efforts as educators will create a nurturing and safe learning environment.

Ms. Johnson: I'm glad we're addressing this issue together. We all play a vital role in keeping our students safe.

Mr. Gilliam: Indeed, Ms. Johnson. Let's continue to collaborate, share ideas, and support one another in our mission to ensure the safety and well-being of our students.

A discussion of strategies to reduce the risk of children getting shot and killed in schools with the school faculty was my highest priority. The dialogue highlights preventive measures, fostering a positive school culture, communication, technology, parental involvement, and the significance of student engagement in enhancing safety.

Setting: Principal's Office at Centennial High School

Characters:

Mr. Gilliam - Principal Assistant Principal,

Ms. Martinez - Assistant Principal,

Mr. Johnson.

Mr. Gilliam: Good morning, Ms. Martinez and Mr. Johnson. Thank you for joining me today. I wanted to discuss the matter of transferring some of our older students who are 18, 19, 20, and 21 years old to adult school and continuation school.

Ms. Martinez: Good morning, Mr. Gilliam. Yes, it's an important topic to address. Some of these older students might benefit from a different educational setting.

Mr. Johnson: I agree, Mr. Gilliam. The needs and challenges of these students might be better addressed in alternative schools.

Mr. Gilliam: Precisely. Our primary goal is to ensure the success and well-being of every student. Transferring these older students could provide them with more focused support and opportunities.

Ms. Martinez: For some of them, adult school might offer a more flexible schedule and tailored curriculum to help them catch up on credits.

Mr. Johnson: And for others, continuing their schooling might provide a more supportive and structured environment to help them thrive academically and personally.

Mr. Gilliam: Exactly. We need to assess each student's individual needs and consider the best fit for their educational journey.

Ms. Martinez: I suggest we meet with these students individually, along with their parents or guardians, to discuss the potential transfer and present the benefits of alternative schooling.

Mr. Johnson: Agreed. It's essential to involve the parents in the decision-making process to ensure their understanding and support.

Mr. Gilliam: I appreciate your proactive approach. It shows our commitment to considering the best options for our students.

Ms. Martinez: We should also collaborate with the teachers and counselors who know these students well. Their insights will be valuable in making informed decisions.

Mr. Johnson: I completely agree. Input from the teachers and counselors will help us create personalized plans for each student.

Mr. Gilliam: Our communication with the adult school and continuation school administrators is equally crucial. We must ensure a smooth transition for the students.

Ms. Martinez: Absolutely, Mr. Gilliam. We need to work closely with the receiving schools to provide them with the necessary information and support.

Mr. Johnson: And it would be beneficial to establish a follow-up system to monitor these students' progress and well-being in their new schools.

Mr. Gilliam: Excellent suggestion. Continuously monitoring their progress will allow us to make any necessary adjustments and provide additional support if needed.

Ms. Martinez: I think we also need to emphasize to the students that this decision is not a punishment but an opportunity for them to succeed in a more suitable environment.

Mr. Johnson: Agreed. We should highlight the positive aspects of the alternative schools and how they can benefit from this transition.

Mr. Gilliam: It's vital to approach this process with sensitivity and empathy. Our ultimate aim is to empower these students to achieve their full potential.

Ms. Martinez: I'm glad we're all on the same page, Mr. Gilliam. Working together, we can ensure a smooth and successful transfer for these students.

Mr. Johnson: Absolutely. I believe this will be a positive step in their educational journey.

Mr. Gilliam: Thank you both for your dedication and commitment to our students' well-being. Let's move forward with the necessary meetings and planning to make this happen.

Ms. Martinez: Sounds like a plan, Mr. Gilliam. We're ready to make a positive impact.

Mr. Johnson: Count us in, Mr. Gilliam. Our students' success is our priority.

Mr. Gilliam: Excellent. Let's work together to create the best opportunities for our students' academic and personal growth.

Note: The above dialogue is a conversation between Mr. Gilliam (the principal) and the assistant principals, Ms. Martinez and Mr. Johnson, discussing the transfer of older students to adult school and continuation school. The dialogue highlights the consideration of individual student needs, involving parents, teachers, and counselors in the decision-making process, and the importance of ensuring a supportive transition for the students. The approach is focused on providing the students with the best educational environment to thrive and succeed.

Mr. Gilliam: (Addressing the teachers) Good morning, everyone. Today, I'd like to discuss some exciting opportunities to enhance our curriculum and prepare our students for the future. Let's explore teaching AI, STEM education, health care, technology, and entrepreneurship.

Ms. Johnson: That sounds like a fantastic idea, Mr. Gilliam.

Incorporating these topics into our lessons will better equip our students for the evolving job market.

Mr. Hernandez: I agree. With the rapid advancement of technology, it's crucial for our students to have a strong foundation in AI and STEM subjects.

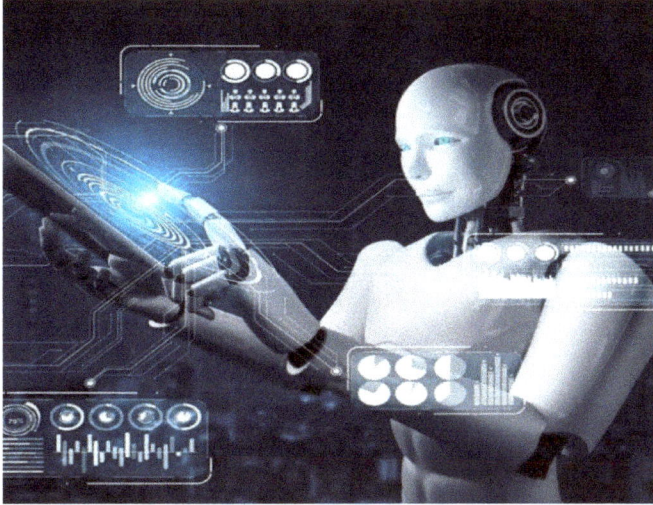

Mrs. Thompson: Absolutely. STEM education can foster critical thinking and problem-solving skills, which are essential in various fields.

Mr. Lee: I believe teaching our students about health care and technology will also make them more aware of potential career paths in the medical and tech industries.

Mr. Gilliam: You're absolutely right, Mr. Lee. We want our students to be well-informed about the diverse opportunities available to them.

Ms. Johnson: I suggest we collaborate with professionals in these industries to bring real-world perspectives into the classroom.

Mr. Hernandez: That's a great idea. Guest speakers and industry experts can offer valuable insights to our students.

Mr. Gilliam: Agreed. I'll reach out to our community and alumni network to find willing professionals to participate in our educational initiatives.

Mrs. Thompson: In addition to AI and STEM, teaching entrepreneurship is equally important. It can instill a sense of creativity and initiative in our students.

Ms. Johnson: I love the idea of encouraging our students to start a business and become future entrepreneurs.

Mr. Gilliam: That's an excellent point, Ms. Johnson. We can have business competitions or projects to nurture their entrepreneurial spirit.

Mr. Lee: And while we teach these subjects, let's make sure we promote inclusivity and encourage all students to explore their interests, regardless of gender or background.

Mr. Gilliam: Absolutely, Mr. Lee. Our goal is to provide an inclusive learning environment that supports every student's growth.

Ms. Johnson: To foster interest in these topics, we can also organize field trips to companies or research institutions related to AI, STEM, and health care.

Mr. Hernandez: Field trips are a fantastic way to show our students the real-world applications of what they learn in the classroom.

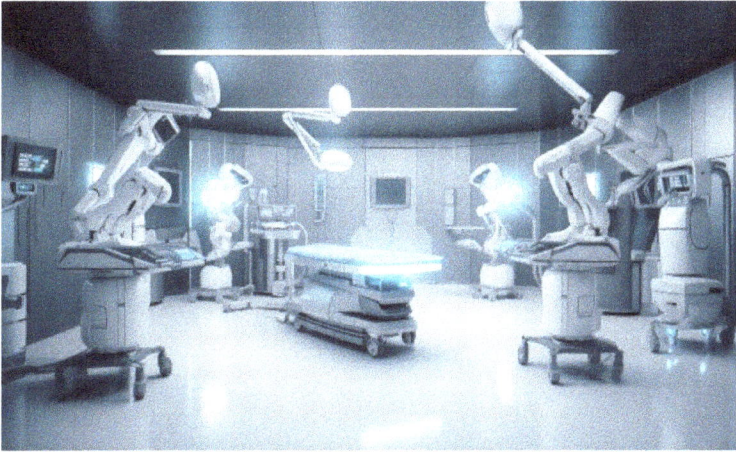

Mr. Gilliam: I'll work with our administration to ensure we have enough resources and support to make these field trips possible.

Mrs. Thompson: Additionally, we should encourage students to participate in science fairs, technology competitions, and entrepreneurship clubs.

Ms. Johnson: Yes, getting involved in extracurricular activities will further enrich their learning experiences.

Mr. Gilliam: I'm glad to see your enthusiasm, and I'm excited about the potential impact these changes can have on our students' future.

Mr. Hernandez: We should also seek feedback from the students themselves to understand their interests and adapt our approach accordingly.

Mr. Gilliam: Excellent point, Mr. Hernandez. Our students' input is valuable in shaping their education.

Ms. Johnson: In conclusion, these topics are not just about preparing students for jobs; they're also about empowering them to be informed and engaged citizens.

Mr. Gilliam: Well said, Ms. Johnson. Let's work together to integrate AI, STEM education, health care, technology, and entrepreneurship into our curriculum to create a dynamic and future-ready learning environment.

Please note that the school faculty engages in discussions regarding the incorporation of AI, STEM education, healthcare, technology, and entrepreneurship into the curriculum.

These conversations underscore the significance of offering students' opportunities to explore potential career paths while nurturing an inclusive and captivating learning environment. The suggestions and collaborative efforts of the teachers reflect a collective commitment to prepare students for the opportunities and challenges they will encounter in the future.

Mr. Gilliam: Good morning, everyone. Today, I'd like to address an urgent issue that affects some of our students: involvement in activities like selling drugs or engaging in prostitution. We must motivate our students to understand that they can make more money and have a brighter future by developing skills in technology, AI, health care, and business.

Ms. Johnson: This is a critical matter, Mr. Gilliam. We need to show our students the potential for success in legitimate and rewarding career paths.

Mr. Hernandez: Absolutely. By focusing on education and skills development, we can open doors to numerous opportunities for our students.

Mrs. Thompson: I believe it's essential to provide them with real-life examples of successful individuals in these fields who have risen above adversity.

Mr. Lee: Yes, showcasing role models who have achieved success through hard work and education can inspire our students to follow a similar path.

Mr. Gilliam: You're all correct. Our role as educators is to ignite their curiosity and passion for learning. We must help them realize their potential.

Ms. Johnson: Perhaps we can organize guest speakers or workshops where professionals from various fields share their experiences and career journeys.

Mr. Hernandez: That's a great idea. Hearing from real people who have found success in these areas can be incredibly impactful.

Mr. Lee: We should also emphasize the relevance of these skills in the modern job market, where technology and innovation play a significant role.

Mr. Gilliam: Excellent point, Mr. Lee. Let's emphasize that the demand for professionals in technology, AI, health care, and business will only grow.

Mrs. Thompson: I suggest we incorporate these fields into our classroom discussions, showing students how they relate to different subjects.

Ms. Johnson: Yes, we can create cross-disciplinary projects and activities to showcase the real-world applications of these skills.

Mr. Gilliam: We should also focus on mentoring and individualized support for students who may be struggling academically or facing personal challenges.

Mr. Hernandez: Building strong relationships with our students can provide the encouragement they need to overcome obstacles.

Mr. Lee: Let's celebrate the achievements of our students who excel in these fields and highlight their success stories.

Mr. Gilliam: Absolutely. Recognizing their accomplishments will motivate other students to strive for excellence.

Mrs. Thompson: Additionally, we should partner with local organizations and businesses to create internships or apprenticeship opportunities.

Ms. Johnson: That's a great way to provide practical experiences and expose them to potential career paths.

Mr. Gilliam: Lastly, let's collaborate with our school counselors to provide guidance and support in their academic and career planning.

Mr. Hernandez: Working together, we can ensure that our students have a clear vision of their future and the steps needed to achieve their goals.

Mr. Gilliam: I want to thank each of you for your commitment to our students' well-being. By motivating them to develop skills in technology, AI, health care, and business, we can help them build a better future. I discussed with the school faculty strategies to motivate students to pursue legitimate and rewarding career paths in technology, AI, health care, and business. The teachers' suggestions emphasize the importance of showcasing real-life examples, integrating these fields into the curriculum, providing support and guidance, and fostering positive relationships with students to help them make better choices for their future. My meetings highlight the teachers' dedication to creating a positive impact on their students' lives.

Mr. Gilliam: Good morning, everyone. Today, I'd like to discuss the possibility of replacing the wire fencing around our school with rod iron fencing. It's important to address safety concerns and ensure our campus remains secure.

Mr. Jenkins: I agree, Mr. Gilliam. Upgrading our fencing can play a significant role in enhancing campus security.

Ms. Johnson: Rod iron fencing would not only provide better security but also add a touch of elegance to our school's appearance.

Mr. Hernandez: That's true. It can make our campus look more inviting while still serving its primary purpose.

Mr. Gilliam: Precisely. We want our students to feel safe while also creating a positive learning environment.

Mrs. Thompson: I've heard that rod iron fencing is more durable and requires less maintenance than wire fencing.

Mr. Lee: If it's more durable, it can be a worthwhile long-term investment for our school.

Mr. Jenkins: And the added strength of the rod iron will act as a deterrent to potential intruders.

Mr. Gilliam: Agreed. Safety is our top priority, and we should take all necessary measures to protect our students and staff.

Ms. Johnson: How about involving the students in the decision-making process? It could make them feel more invested in the changes.

Mr. Hernandez: That's a good idea. We can discuss the reasons behind the upgrade with them and hear their thoughts.

Mr. Jenkins: Involving the students can also help raise awareness about the importance of campus security.

Mr. Gilliam: Excellent point, Mr. Jenkins. Engaging our students in such discussions empowers them to take ownership of their safety.

Mrs. Thompson: Before moving forward, we should also get estimates from contractors and review the costs.

Mr. Lee: That's a crucial aspect. We need to ensure that the budget allows for such an improvement.

Mr. Gilliam: I'll work with our administration to gather the necessary information, and we can discuss the financial feasibility.

Ms. Johnson: Once we have the estimates, we can present the proposal to the school board for their approval.

Mr. Hernandez: It would be beneficial to have their support in this endeavor.

Mr. Jenkins: In the meantime, we should assess the current fencing and identify any areas that might need immediate attention.

Mr. Gilliam: Agreed. Let's conduct a thorough inspection to address any security vulnerabilities promptly.

Mrs. Thompson: As we proceed, we should also keep the parents informed about the changes and the reasons behind them.

Mr. Lee: Transparent communication will help build trust and confidence among the parents.

Mr. Gilliam: You're all making excellent points. Let's form a committee consisting of faculty, security team members, and student representatives to work together on this project.

Ms. Johnson: I'd be happy to be part of that committee and involve some of my students too.

Mr. Hernandez: Count me in as well. It's essential to have diverse perspectives on the matter.

Mr. Jenkins: I'm on board too. Together, we can make our school a safer place for everyone.

Mr. Gilliam: Wonderful! I appreciate your dedication and enthusiasm. Let's move forward with this plan to improve campus security with rod iron fencing and ensure a safe environment for all.

The school faculty and security team members engaged in discussions regarding the potential replacement of the wire fencing around the school with either rod iron fencing or fencing that offers enhanced protection for our campus. This conversation underlines the advantages of opting for rod iron or impenetrable fencing, which not only improves security but also enhances the school's aesthetic appeal. Furthermore, it involves students and parents in the decision-making process. The commitment of the faculty to safety and their dedication to involving students in creating a safer school environment are key focal points of this collaborative effort.

Mr. Gilliam: Good morning, everyone. Today, I'd like us to focus on creating a comprehensive safety plan to ensure the well-being of our students and staff. Safety is our top priority, and we must work together to develop a robust plan.

Mr. Jenkins: Absolutely, Mr. Gilliam. A comprehensive safety plan will help us prepare for any potential emergencies and ensure a secure learning environment.

Ms. Johnson: I suggest we start by conducting a thorough assessment of our school's safety measures, including the current procedures and protocols.

Mr. Hernandez: That's a great starting point. Identifying our strengths and areas for improvement will guide us in crafting an effective plan.

Mr. Lee: We should also review our evacuation routes and emergency exits to ensure they are well-marked and easily accessible.

Mrs. Thompson: And let's involve the students in safety drills and practices regularly. Practice makes perfect, and it's crucial for them to know what to do in case of an emergency.

Mr. Jenkins: I agree. Conducting frequent drills will help students and staff be better prepared for any situation.

Mr. Gilliam: Additionally, we should focus on enhancing communication during emergencies. Implementing a reliable notification system can help us reach everyone quickly.

Ms. Johnson: We could also establish a crisis management team, consisting of faculty and staff members, to take charge during emergency situations.

Mr. Hernandez: Having a designated team with assigned roles will ensure a swift and organized response to any crisis.

Mr. Jenkins: I suggest we review and update our visitor management protocols. Restricting access to the school will enhance security.

Mr. Lee: And we should collaborate with local law enforcement to conduct safety assessments and receive their feedback on our safety plan.

Mrs. Thompson: Training our staff and teachers on recognizing signs of distress or potential threats can also be beneficial.

Ms. Johnson: We can create a safety handbook for students and parents that outlines our safety procedures and expectations.

Mr. Gilliam: Excellent suggestions, everyone. A comprehensive safety plan requires input from all of us. Let's form a safety committee with representatives from different departments to work on this plan.

Mr. Jenkins: I'd be happy to be part of that committee and share my expertise as the school security officer.

Ms. Johnson: Count me in too. Safety is a shared responsibility, and I want to do my part.

Mr. Hernandez: I'm on board as well. It's essential for us to be proactive in ensuring the safety of our school community.

Mrs. Thompson: I'll gladly join the committee too. Let's work together to create a safe and secure environment for everyone.

Mr. Gilliam: Thank you all for your commitment. I'm confident that with our collective effort, we will develop a comprehensive safety plan that ensures the well-being of our students and staff. Let's schedule our first committee meeting soon.

The emphasis here is the importance of conducting assessments, involving students in safety drills, enhancing communication, establishing a crisis management team, and collaborating with local law enforcement. The teachers' willingness to participate in the safety committee showcases their dedication to the safety and well-being of the school community.

Mr. Gilliam: Good morning, everyone. Today, I'd like to discuss an important aspect of our curriculum: teaching financial literacy and money management skills. How much should schools focus on teaching skills in investing, stock markets, bonds, insurance, bitcoin, balancing budgets, starting a business, and money management?

Ms. Johnson: Financial literacy is a crucial life skill, Mr. Gilliam. It's essential for our students to understand how to manage money effectively.

Mr. Hernandez: I agree. Understanding investing, stock markets, and other financial concepts will help them make informed decisions in the future.

Mrs. Thompson: Learning about bonds and insurance is equally important. It prepares them for different financial scenarios they may encounter.

Mr. Lee: And with the increasing popularity of bitcoin and other cryptocurrencies, our students should also be aware of these digital assets.

Mr. Gilliam: Precisely. We want our students to be financially literate and confident in navigating the complexities of the modern financial world.

Ms. Johnson: Financial education can empower our students to avoid debt and make smart financial choices.

Mr. Hernandez: Teaching them about balancing budgets can also help them set financial goals and plan for their future.

Mr. Gilliam: Agreed. It's crucial for them to learn early on about budgeting and responsible money management.

Mrs. Thompson: Additionally, knowledge of starting a business can open doors to entrepreneurship and self-employment.

Mr. Lee: Financial literacy isn't just about personal finance; it's also about understanding economic principles that shape our society.

Mr. Gilliam: You're absolutely right, Mr. Lee. Financial literacy contributes to a more informed and economically responsible society.

Ms. Johnson: We can incorporate financial concepts into various subjects to make learning more engaging and applicable.

Mr. Hernandez: I believe it's important for us as educators to receive training and resources on teaching financial literacy effectively.

Mrs. Thompson: I agree. We can collaborate with financial experts and institutions to provide our students with real-world insights.

Mr. Gilliam: Excellent suggestions. As a school, we need to take a comprehensive approach to financial literacy.

Ms. Johnson: In addition to classroom learning, we can organize workshops and seminars on money management for both students and parents.

Mr. Hernandez: Engaging parents in financial education will create a more supportive learning environment for our students.

Mr. Gilliam: I'm glad to see your enthusiasm for this initiative. Financial literacy is an investment in our students' future.

Mr. Lee: Let's also encourage students to participate in clubs or extracurricular activities related to finance and entrepreneurship.

Mr. Gilliam: Great idea, Mr. Lee. Clubs can provide hands-on experiences and foster their interest in financial matters.

Mrs. Thompson: And let's track their progress and measure the impact of financial literacy education on their overall academic and personal development.

Mr. Gilliam: I appreciate your dedication and commitment to our students' success. Let's work together to integrate financial literacy into our curriculum and equip our students with valuable life skills.

It was crucial for me to engage in a discussion with the school faculty about the importance of incorporating financial literacy and money management skills into the curriculum. This dialogue underscores the significance of comprehending various financial aspects such as investing, stock markets, bonds, insurance, bitcoin, budgeting, entrepreneurship, and financial concepts. The suggestions put forth by the teachers center on the integration of financial education across different subjects, offering training and resources, including parents, and arranging workshops and extracurricular activities. This conversation vividly highlights the teachers' enthusiasm and dedication to equipping students with the skills they need for financial responsibility and future success.

One morning I met with staff. I addressed the faculty one afternoon. I greeted them stating, "Good afternoon, everyone. Today, I'd like to discuss how judges, district attorneys, public defenders, and police officers can play essential roles in our school curriculum. Their involvement can enhance our students' understanding of the legal system, social justice, and community engagement."

Ms. Martinez: That's a fantastic idea, Mr. Gilliam. Having professionals from the legal field engage with our students will be a valuable learning experience.

Mr. Turner: I agree. Their expertise can bring real-world perspectives into the classroom discussions.

Officer Johnson: As the School Resource Officer, I believe that collaborating with these professionals can also foster positive relationships between law enforcement and our students.

Mr. Gilliam: Precisely, Officer Johnson. Let's explore some specific ways they can be involved.

Ms. Martinez: We can invite judges to speak about the legal system, the role of the judiciary, and the importance of due process. They can also share their personal experiences and insights.

Mr. Turner: And district attorneys and public defenders can offer workshops or mock trial events to introduce our students to the different aspects of the legal process.

Officer Johnson: I can help organize workshops on community policing, discussing the role of law enforcement in serving and protecting the community.

Mr. Gilliam: That's a great addition, Officer Johnson. It's essential for our students to understand the positive impact of law enforcement on the community.

Ms. Martinez: Additionally, we can collaborate with these professionals to develop curriculum materials that align with their areas of expertise.

Mr. Turner: Yes, having educational resources tailored to our students' needs and interests will make the learning experience more engaging. Make them feel more invested in the changes.

Officer Johnson: We can also arrange field trips to courts, police departments, or legal offices to give our students a firsthand look at the workings of the justice system.

Mr. Gilliam: Excellent suggestion, Officer Johnson. Field trips can provide invaluable learning experiences beyond the classroom.

Ms. Martinez: As part of our social justice curriculum, we can encourage these professionals to participate in discussions about equality, fairness, and advocacy.

Mr. Turner: And let's explore opportunities for community engagement projects where our students work alongside these professionals to address real-world legal and social issues.

Officer Johnson: That's a fantastic way to promote community involvement and empower our students to make a positive impact.

Mr. Gilliam: I'm thrilled with the enthusiasm and ideas you all have shared. This collaboration will enrich our students' education and inspire them to consider careers in law, criminal justice, or advocacy.

Ms. Martinez: It will also show our students that these professionals are approachable and invested in their success.

Mr. Turner: Definitely. Building these connections will benefit our students academically and socially.

Officer Johnson: I look forward to working with everyone to make these initiatives a success.

Mr. Gilliam: Thank you all for your support. Let's begin reaching out to these professionals and start planning their involvement in our curriculum.

Principal Gilliam, Assistant Principal Ms. Martinez, School Counselor Mr. Turner, and School Resource Officer Johnson. The dialogue discusses how judges, district attorneys, public defenders, and police officers can contribute to the school curriculum and enhance students' understanding of the legal system, social justice, and community engagement. The conversation highlights specific ways these professionals can be involved, such as guest speaking, workshops, field trips, curriculum development, and community engagement projects. The dialogue emphasizes the positive impact of such involvement on the students' education and their perception of law enforcement and the legal system.

Setting: Faculty Meeting at Centennial High School Conference Room

Characters:

Mr. Gilliam - Principal

Ms. Martinez - Assistant Principal

Mr. Turner - School Counselor

Officer Johnson - School Resource Officer

Other Teachers - School Faculty

Mr. Gilliam: Good afternoon, everyone. Today, I want to discuss an exciting opportunity to enhance our curriculum by involving judges, district attorneys, public defenders, and police officers. Their expertise can significantly impact our students' understanding of the legal system, social justice, and community engagement.

Ms. Martinez: I couldn't agree more, Mr. Gilliam. Having professionals from the legal field engage with our students will add depth and authenticity to our lessons.

Mr. Turner: Absolutely. It's crucial for our students to gain insights into the workings of the justice system and the impact it has on our society.

Officer Johnson: As the School Resource Officer, I think this collaboration can also foster a positive relationship between law enforcement and our students.

Ms. Johnson: I agree, Officer Johnson. We want our students to see law enforcement as a helpful resource and ally in the community.

Mr. Gilliam: Let's explore specific ways we can involve these professionals in our curriculum.

Mr. Hernandez: We can invite judges to speak to our social studies classes about the legal system, the rule of law, and the importance of due process.

Mrs. Thompson: And district attorneys and public defenders can offer workshops or mock trial events to introduce our students to the different aspects of the legal process.

Ms. Johnson: We can arrange field trips to courts, police departments, or legal offices to give our students a firsthand experience of the justice system.

Mr. Lee: As part of our English curriculum, we can discuss legal cases or court proceedings in literature to bring real-world relevance to our lessons.

Mr. Turner: In our counseling sessions, we can incorporate discussions about social justice, fairness, and advocacy, tying them to the experiences of these professionals.

Ms. Martinez: Let's also explore opportunities for community engagement projects where our students work alongside these professionals to address real-world legal and social issues.

Mr. Gilliam: Those are all excellent ideas. This kind of engagement will make our curriculum more dynamic and enriching for our students.

Officer Johnson: I'd be happy to assist in arranging workshops on community policing and discussing the role of law enforcement in serving and protecting the community.

Mr. Hernandez: We should also consider collaborating with these professionals to develop educational materials that align with their areas of expertise.

Mrs. Thompson: That's a great idea. Having resources tailored to our students' needs will make learning more engaging and effective.

Mr. Gilliam: I'm thrilled with the enthusiasm and support for this collaboration. Involving these professionals in our curriculum will inspire our students and broaden their perspectives.

Ms. Johnson: It will also show our students that these professionals are approachable and invested in their success.

Mr. Turner: Exactly. Building these connections will benefit our students academically and socially.

Ms. Martinez: I look forward to working together to implement these initiatives and create a more well-rounded educational experience for our students.

Mr. Gilliam: Thank you all for your dedication and support. Let's reach out to these professionals and start planning their involvement in our curriculum.

Note: Principal Gilliam, Assistant Principal Ms. Martinez, School Counselor Mr. Turner, School Resource Officer Johnson, and other school faculty members. The dialogue discusses the involvement of judges, district attorneys, public defenders, and police officers in the school curriculum, emphasizing specific ways they can contribute to the students' understanding of the legal system, social justice, and community engagement. The conversation highlights the positive impact of this collaboration on students' education, their perception of law enforcement, and their engagement with the legal system.

Setting: Centennial High School Auditorium

Characters:

Mr. Gilliam – Principal

Ms. Martinez - Assistant Principal

Mr. Turner - School Counselor

 Officer Johnson - School Resource Officer

Judge Anderson - Local Judge

Officer Davis - Police Officer

Students - High school students attending the event.

Mr. Gilliam: Good morning, students! Today, we have a special event planned to help us better understand the law and its importance in our lives. I'm excited to introduce our esteemed guests, Judge Anderson, and Officer Davis.

Judge Anderson: Thank you, Mr. Gilliam. It's an honor to be here with all of you today.

Officer Davis: Indeed. We are thrilled to have this opportunity to talk to you about the law and its role in our society.

Ms. Martinez: We believe it's essential for our students to gain insights into the legal system and how it affects their lives. Mr. Turner: That's right. Understanding the law can empower you to make informed decisions and be responsible citizens.

Officer Johnson: Throughout history, the law has played a significant role in shaping our society, ensuring justice, and protecting our rights.

Judge Anderson: Absolutely. The law provides a framework for resolving conflicts and maintaining order in our communities.

Officer Davis: And as law enforcement officers, we play a crucial role in upholding the law and ensuring public safety.

Mr. Gilliam: Students, today is an opportunity for you to ask questions and engage in a meaningful dialogue with Judge Anderson and Officer Davis.

Student 1: What inspired you to become a judge and a police officer?

Judge Anderson: For me, it was a passion for justice and a desire to ensure fairness in our legal system.

Officer Davis: I wanted to make a positive impact on my community and help keep it safe for everyone.

Student 2: What are some common misconceptions about the law that you'd like to clarify?

Judge Anderson: One common misconception is that judges are biased. In reality, we are bound by the law and committed to fairness and impartiality.

Officer Davis: Some people may also think that the police are out to get them. We're here to protect and serve, and building trust with the community is crucial to our work.

Student 3: How can we, as students, become more aware of our rights and responsibilities under the law?

Judge Anderson: Education is essential. Take advantage of your social studies classes and resources like our local library to learn about the law.

Officer Davis: Engage in conversations with your parents, teachers, and even law enforcement officers about your rights and responsibilities.

Ms. Martinez: We also have plans to incorporate more legal education into our curriculum to help you become better informed citizens.

Mr. Turner: Being aware of the law will empower you to make informed decisions and be responsible members of society.

Mr. Gilliam: I want to thank Judge Anderson and Officer Davis for taking the time to share their insights with us today.

Officer Johnson: And thank you, students, for your thoughtful questions and engagement.

Judge Anderson: Remember, knowledge of the law is not just for lawyers and law enforcement. It's essential for every citizen.

Officer Davis: That's right. Understanding the law empowers you to protect your rights and contribute positively to your community.

Mr. Gilliam: Let's give a round of applause to our guests for their valuable insights!

Students: *Applause*

Note: Judge Anderson, Officer Davis, and high school students attending an event at Centennial High School. The conversation focuses on the importance of understanding the law and its impact on society. Judge Anderson and Officer Davis share their motivations for pursuing their careers and clarify common misconceptions about the law and law enforcement. They also encourage students to become more aware of their rights and responsibilities under the law. The dialogue aims to inspire students to be responsible and informed citizens by engaging with legal education and community discussions.

Setting: Centennial High School Career Day Event

Mr. Gilliam: Good morning, students! Today, we have a fantastic lineup of guest speakers who will talk to you about exciting careers in the legal field and law enforcement.

Students: *Excited murmurs*

Ms. Martinez: We believe it's essential to expose you to various career paths so you can make informed decisions about your future.

Mr. Turner: Our esteemed guests are here to share their experiences and insights with you.

Officer Johnson: We're thrilled to be part of this event and hope to inspire some of you to consider careers in law enforcement.

Judge Anderson: And I'm excited to talk to you about the role of judges in our legal system.

District Attorney Ramirez: I'll be sharing what it takes to be a district attorney and the impact our work has on the community.

Attorney Martinez: As a defense attorney, I'll explain the importance of upholding the rights of the accused.

Officer Davis: And I'm here to talk about the different roles and opportunities in law enforcement.

Mr. Gilliam: Each of these professions plays a critical role in our justice system and community safety.

Student 1: What are the qualifications for becoming a judge?

Judge Anderson: To become a judge, you typically need a law degree and several years of legal experience. It's a position that requires a deep understanding of the law and a commitment to fairness and justice.

Student 2: What does a district attorney do?

District Attorney Ramirez: As a district attorney, I lead a team of prosecutors responsible for representing the state in criminal cases. We work to seek justice and protect the community from criminal activity.

Student 3: Is being a defense attorney challenging?

Attorney Martinez: It can be, but it's also incredibly rewarding. As a defense attorney, my role is to protect the rights of those accused of crimes and ensure they receive a fair trial.

Student 4: Officer Davis, what are the different roles within law enforcement?

Officer Davis: Law enforcement offers various career paths, from patrol officers to detectives, crime scene investigators, K-9 handlers, and more. Each role contributes to maintaining public safety.

Student 5: How can we prepare ourselves for careers in law and law enforcement?

Ms. Martinez: You can start by focusing on your studies, especially in subjects like history, government, and law. Engage in community service to understand the importance of giving back.

Mr. Turner: It's also helpful to seek internships or volunteer opportunities at legal offices or law enforcement agencies.

Judge Anderson: And never underestimate the power of good communication and critical thinking skills.

District Attorney Ramirez: Being passionate about justice and helping others will drive you in these careers.

Mr. Gilliam: We are incredibly fortunate to have these professionals with us today, sharing their expertise and guidance with you.

Officer Johnson: Remember, the legal field and law enforcement offer diverse and meaningful career options.

Students: *Thanks and applause*

Note: School staff, law enforcement professionals, and high school students attending a Career Day event at Centennial High School. The dialogue focuses on introducing students to careers as judges, district attorneys, defense attorneys, and police officers. Each professional provides insights into their roles and qualifications, and they encourage the students to pursue their passions and interests in the legal field and law enforcement. The conversation aims to inspire students to consider these meaningful and rewarding career paths and highlights the importance of education, community service, and critical skills development.

Title: Reevaluating "Scared Straight" Programs: A Comprehensive Approach to Juvenile Delinquency Prevention

Scene 1: Introduction to "Scared Straight" Programs [Location: Community Meeting]

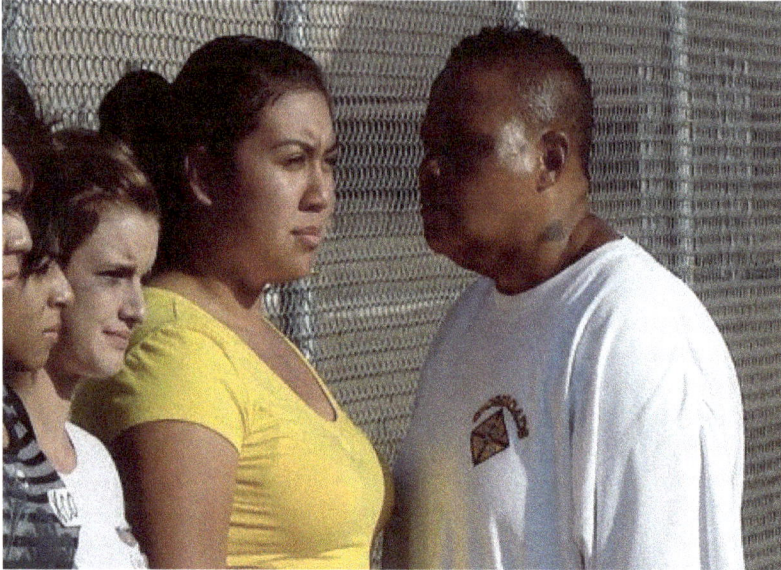

Narrator: "Scared Straight" programs have been used as an intervention strategy to deter at-risk or delinquent youth from engaging in criminal behavior. These programs involve taking young people to prisons to interact with inmates, hoping to shock them into making better choices.

[Visual: Youth visiting correctional institutions]

Narrator: The concept behind these programs is that witnessing the harsh realities of prison life and hearing inmates' stories will deter young people from pursuing a life of crime.

Scene 2: Mixed Research Findings [Location: Research Library]

Narrator: Research on the effectiveness of "Scared Straight" programs has yielded mixed results over the years.

[Visual: Researchers examining studies]

Narrator: Some studies suggest that while these programs might have short-term impacts, they often fail to produce lasting behavior change or reduce criminal activity among participants.

Scene 3: Unintended Consequences [Location: Classroom Discussion]

Narrator: Critics of "Scared Straight" programs voice concerns about potential unintended consequences.

[Visual: Students engaged in a discussion]

Narrator: There's a risk that exposure to the prison environment might romanticize criminal behavior or expose young people to manipulative individuals. The approach may not align with best practices in juvenile justice and education.

Scene 4: Evidence-Based Approaches [Location: Youth Center]

Narrator: Many experts advocate for evidence-based and comprehensive strategies to prevent juvenile delinquency.

[Visual: Youth participating in mentoring and counseling]

Narrator: These approaches prioritize education, mentoring, counseling, and providing positive alternatives to criminal activities, aiming for long-term positive impact.

Scene 5: Educators and Policymakers' Role [Location: School Board Meeting]

Narrator: Educators, policymakers, and communities play a crucial role in shaping effective interventions.

[Visual: Community leaders discussing strategies]

Narrator: It's vital to consider up-to-date research, expert recommendations, and best practices when deciding on the approach to take in preventing juvenile delinquency.

Scene 6: A Holistic Approach [Location: Community Workshop]

Narrator: To effectively address juvenile delinquency, we must adopt a holistic approach that recognizes the complexity of the issue.

[Visual: Workshop participants brainstorming]

Narrator: By combining evidence-based strategies, educational initiatives, and supportive resources, we can create a more positive environment for our youth.

Scene 7: Moving Forward Together [Location: Community Gathering]

Narrator: In conclusion, as we reevaluate "Scared Straight" programs, let's prioritize comprehensive strategies that promote positive behavior and offer alternatives to criminal activities.

[Visual: Diverse community members coming together]

Narrator: Together, we can create a safer and more nurturing environment for our young people, fostering their potential and helping them make positive choices.

[Screen fades to black with the message: "Investing in Youth for a Brighter Future"]

In the context of Centennial, I organized field trips for students to engage in direct conversations with various professionals, including Judges, District Attorneys, Parole Officers, Social Workers, and Police Officers, on a consistent basis. These professionals visited our classrooms to shed light on the opportunities within the criminal justice system, offering students a comprehensive understanding of it from different perspectives. Our program had a distinctive approach in this regard, and I believe it 189 played a pivotal role in the program's remarkable success. It's imperative not to overlook the value of providing students with such opportunities.

School principals and administrators play a crucial role in creating a safe and secure school environment to prevent incidents of school shootings. Here are some actions schools can take which I utilized at my schools:

1. Develop a Comprehensive Safety Plan

2. Create and regularly update a comprehensive safety plan that includes protocols for handling emergencies, crisis response, and

3. Communication procedures with staff, students, and parents.

4. Implement Security Measures: Enhance physical security measures, such as controlled access points, surveillance cameras, and security personnel. Conduct regular safety drills to ensure everyone knows what to do in case of an emergency.

5. Establish Threat Assessment Teams: Form a threat assessment team comprising school staff, mental health professionals, and law enforcement to identify and address potential threats or concerning behaviors early on.

6. Promote Mental Health Support: Offer mental health resources and counseling services to students. Encourage an open and supportive environment for students to express their concerns.

7. Conduct Safety Training: Provide training to staff and students on recognizing warning signs, reporting concerns, and responding to potential threats.

8. Encourage Anonymous Reporting: Establish a confidential reporting system that allows students and staff to report safety concerns anonymously.

9. Develop Partnerships with Law Enforcement: Collaborate with local law enforcement to establish a strong relationship, share information, and work together on safety initiatives.

10. Foster Inclusivity and Positive School Culture: Promote a positive and inclusive school culture that values every student and fosters a sense of belonging.

11. Monitor social media: Keep an eye on social media activities and monitor for potential threats or signs of distress.

12. Practice Effective Communication: Maintain open communication with parents, students, and staff about safety measures, protocols, and any changes in the safety plan.

13. Engage the Community: Involve parents, community members, and local organizations in school safety efforts.

14. Advocate for Gun Safety Legislation: Work with policymakers and advocate for sensible gun safety legislation and initiatives.

15. Continuous Assessment and Improvement: Regularly evaluate the effectiveness of safety measures and adjust based on lessons learned and emerging best practices.

By taking a proactive approach to school safety, principals and administrators can help minimize the risk of school shootings and create a secure learning environment for all students and staff.

A Comprehensive Safety Plan for schools involves a multifaceted approach that addresses various potential threats and outlines protocols for emergency response, prevention, and communication. Here are several examples of components that can be included in such a plan:

1. Emergency Response Protocols:

- Detailed procedures for different types of emergencies, including active shooters, natural disasters, medical emergencies, etc.
- Specific roles and responsibilities of staff members during emergencies.
- Evacuation routes and assembly points for students and staff.
- Guidelines for accounting for all students and staff after an emergency evacuation.

2. Crisis Communication:

- A system for rapid and effective communication with parents, guardians, and the community during emergencies.

- Clear channels of communication between school administrators, staff, and law enforcement agencies.
- Use of mass notification systems, email, text messages, and social media for disseminating critical information.

3. Security Measures:

- Controlled access points with secure entryways and visitor check-in procedures.
- Surveillance cameras at strategic locations throughout the campus.
- Identification badges for staff and students to distinguish authorized individuals.
- Regular review and updates of security infrastructure and measures.

4. Threat Assessment and Prevention:

- Establishment of a threat assessment team to evaluate and respond to potential threats.
- Early intervention and support for students displaying concerning behaviors or signs of distress.
- Promote a culture of reporting and anonymous tip lines for students and staff to report safety concerns.

5. Mental Health Support:

- Access to school counselors, psychologists, and mental health professionals for students.
- Training for staff to recognize signs of emotional distress and mental health issues in students.
- Partnerships with mental health organizations to enhance support services.

6. Training and Drills:

- Regular training sessions and drills for staff and students to practice emergency response protocols.
- Conduct active shooter drills and simulations in coordination with law enforcement.
- Review and debrief after each drill to identify areas for improvement.

7. Physical Safety Enhancements:

- Installation of safety glass and barricade devices on classroom doors to improve lockdown procedures.
- Structural assessments to identify and address potential safety hazards.

8. Bullying and Violence Prevention:

- Comprehensive anti-bullying programs that promote positive behavior and a respectful school culture.
- Conflict resolution training for students to manage interpersonal issues peacefully.

9. Parent and Community Involvement:

- Engage parents and the community in safety efforts through workshops and town hall meetings.
- Encourage community partnerships and collaborations with local law enforcement.

10. Continuity of Operations:

- Plans for maintaining essential school operations during emergencies or prolonged closures.
- Provision of educational resources and remote learning options during crises.

It's important to note that each school's safety plan should be tailored to its specific needs, geographic location, and community dynamics. A regularly reviewed and updated safety plan ensures that schools are prepared to respond effectively to any safety concerns or emergencies.

There are various types of technology that schools can utilize to enhance safety and prevent school shootings and violence. These technologies can complement existing security measures and aid in early detection and response. Some specific examples include:

1. Security Cameras:

High-quality surveillance cameras placed strategically around the campus can monitor entrances, hallways, common areas, and outdoor spaces. They act as a deterrent and can aid in identifying potential threats or suspicious activities.

2. Access Control Systems:

Implementing access control systems enables schools to regulate entry points. These systems can include key cards, biometric scanners, or electronic locks to restrict access to authorized personnel only.

3. Visitor Management Systems:

Schools can use visitor management systems to screen and track visitors entering the campus. These systems can help identify and prevent unauthorized individuals from gaining access.

4. Gunshot Detection Systems:

Advanced gunshot detection systems use acoustic sensors to detect the sound of gunfire and automatically alert school authorities and law enforcement, providing real-time information for a swift response.

5. Panic Buttons and Duress Alarms:

Panic buttons or duress alarms can be installed in classrooms or other areas to allow teachers and staff to quickly notify authorities in case of an emergency.

6. Two-Way Communication Devices:

Providing staff members with two-way communication devices, such as radios or mobile apps, facilitates immediate communication during emergencies.

7. Mass Notification Systems:

These systems allow schools to quickly disseminate emergency alerts and information to students, staff, parents, and law enforcement through multiple channels, including text messages, emails, and automated phone calls.

8. Biometric Identification Systems:

Biometric identification systems use fingerprint or facial recognition technology to verify the identity of individuals, enhancing security and access control.

9. AI-Powered Threat Assessment Tools:

AI-based systems can analyze data to identify potential threats, such as concerning social media posts or unusual behavior patterns, allowing schools to intervene early.

10. Metal Detectors:

Metal detectors at school entrances can help prevent weapons from entering the campus and serve as a deterrent against potential attackers.

11. Anonymous Reporting Apps:

Mobile apps or online platforms that allow students and staff to report safety concerns or potential threats anonymously can encourage a culture of reporting.

12. Social Media Monitoring Software:

Social media monitoring tools can track online activity for signs of potential violence or threats and provide early warning.

It's crucial to recognize that technology, although valuable in bolstering school safety, should be integrated as one component of a broader strategy that encompasses prevention, mental health assistance, training, and community engagement. Moreover, schools need to strike a balance between security measures and privacy considerations, ensuring that the implementation of any technology remains responsible and ethical.

When local law enforcement and police patrol the perimeters of schools, they can implement various techniques to prevent school shootings and violence. These strategies aim to deter potential threats, ensure a rapid response in case of emergencies, and build trust within the school community. Some of the techniques utilized include:

1. High Visibility Patrols:

Officers patrol the areas surrounding the school in marked police vehicles, increasing their visibility as a deterrent to potential attackers.

2. Random Patrol Patterns:

Police adopt unpredictable patrol routes and schedules to prevent predictability and make it challenging for anyone intending harm to plan an attack.

3. Building Relationships:

Officers build positive relationships with school staff, students, and parents, fostering a sense of trust and approachability within the school community.

4. School Resource Officers (SROs):

Having dedicated SROs assigned to schools allows for consistent law enforcement presence, fostering a proactive approach to addressing safety concerns and building strong connections with students.

5. Specialized Training:

Officers receive specialized training in school safety, crisis intervention, and de-escalation techniques to effectively handle situations in the school environment.

6. Threat Assessments:

Police collaborate with school administrators to conduct threat assessments and identify potential risks or concerning behaviors.

7. Coordination with School Administrators:

Regular communication between law enforcement and school administrators ensures that both parties are informed about security concerns and can respond appropriately.

8. Emergency Drills:

Police participate in school emergency drills, providing valuable guidance and feedback on the effectiveness of response procedures.

9. Active Shooter Training:

Officers and school staff undergo joint active shooter training to develop a coordinated response in the event of an emergency.

10. Community Engagement:

Police engage with the broader school community, including parents, neighborhood residents, and businesses, to build a network of support for school safety.

11. Intelligence Sharing:

Law enforcement agencies share information and intelligence related to potential threats or concerning activities in the community.

12. Mobile Command Centers:

In critical situations, mobile command centers can be deployed near the school to facilitate communication and coordination during emergencies.

13. Social Media Monitoring:

Police may monitor social media platforms to identify potential threats or concerning posts related to the school.

14. School Safety Assessments:

Police conduct regular safety assessments of school facilities to identify vulnerabilities and recommend improvements.

By employing these techniques, local law enforcement can work collaboratively with schools to enhance security, prevent violence, and ensure a safe learning environment for students and staff. The goal is to create a culture of safety, preparedness, and trust that promotes early intervention and reduces the risk of school shootings and violence.

Judges, district attorneys, public defenders, and police officers can play essential roles when involved in the school curriculum by contributing their expertise and perspectives to enhance students' understanding of the legal system, social justice, and community engagement. Here are some ways they can be involved:

1) Inviting Guest Speakers:

Judges, district attorneys, public defenders, and police officers can be invited as guest speakers in classrooms to share their expertise and real-world experiences within the legal system, criminal justice, and public service.

2) Engaging in Mock Trials:

These professionals can actively participate in organizing and conducting mock trials, allowing students to gain hands-on insight into courtroom procedures and the various roles played by legal stakeholders.

3) Hosting Legal Workshops:

The school can arrange workshops covering essential topics such as legal rights, the judicial process, and law enforcement procedures, promoting greater civic awareness and knowledge among students.

4) Providing Career Guidance:

By offering guidance on potential careers in the legal field or law enforcement, these professionals can inspire students to consider such paths and encourage them to excel academically.

5) Collaborating on Community Outreach:

Judges, district attorneys, public defenders, and police officers can collaborate on community service projects with students, imparting the value of civic engagement and the ability to make positive contributions to their communities.

6) Contributing to Criminal Justice and Social Justice Education:

These experts can play a pivotal role in developing educational materials and resources related to criminal justice and social justice issues, ensuring the curriculum remains accurate and up to date.

7) Utilizing Case Studies:

The use of real-life case studies can help students grasp complex legal matters and appreciate the consequences of decisions within the legal system.

8) Offering Law-Related Internships:

Students can be provided with internship or shadowing opportunities within the legal system or law enforcement agencies, offering practical exposure to the daily operations of these professions.

9) Fostering Debates and Discussions:

Encouraging debates and discussions on legal and ethical dilemmas can nurture critical thinking and empathy among students.

10) Implementing Restorative Justice Programs:

Collaboration with school administrators to introduce restorative justice programs can provide alternative disciplinary approaches and promote conflict resolution skills.

11) School Safety Education:

Police officers can actively participate in school safety education initiatives, providing valuable guidance on ensuring safety both within and outside the school environment.

12) Educating on Legal Rights:

Informing students about their legal rights and responsibilities can empower them to make informed decisions and engage responsibly in society.

Incorporating these professionals into the school curriculum offers students a comprehensive grasp of the legal system, enlightens them about their rights and duties, and cultivates a heightened awareness of the significance of law enforcement and the justice system within our society. Moreover, it facilitates a constructive connection between the legal community and the younger generation, fostering essential values like trust, respect, and active civic participation. My experience with implementing these strategies resulted in remarkable outcomes, enhancing trust and rapport not only with law enforcement but also within the broader community.

Involving all leaders of the student population, including gang members and other student leaders, in decision-making can have both challenges and potential benefits for fostering a safer and more inclusive school environment. Here are some key considerations:

1) Diversity and Representation:

Ensuring diverse student leadership, including individuals from various backgrounds and viewpoints, guarantees that decision-making processes reflect the entire student body's diversity and perspectives.

2) Empowerment and Responsibility:

Involving students in decision-making empowers them to take responsibility for their school environment, fostering a sense of accountability and ownership.

3) Addressing Student Concerns:

Engaging with student leaders, including those affiliated with gangs, can offer valuable insights into the concerns, needs, and challenges of different student groups.

4) Conflict Resolution:

Providing a platform for all student leaders, including gang-involved students, can promote dialogue and conflict resolution, potentially reducing tensions and creating a more peaceful school atmosphere.

5) Building Trust and Connection:

Active involvement of student leaders in decision-making communicates that their voices and viewpoints are valued, enhancing trust and building connections between students and school staff.

6) Targeted Support:

Engaging gang-involved students in decision-making can open doors to targeted interventions and assist in redirecting them toward positive engagement and away from harmful activities.

7) Social and Emotional Development:

Participation in decision-making processes can nurture essential social and emotional skills, such as effective communication, empathy, and teamwork.

However, it's vital to acknowledge potential challenges and risks:

1) Safety Concerns:

Involving gang members in decision-making may raise safety concerns for other students, staff, and the school community.

2) Power Dynamics:

Striking a balance in decision-making and ensuring equitable representation can be challenging, especially when power imbalances exist among student leaders.

3) Legal and Ethical Considerations:

Schools must navigate legal and ethical considerations when engaging students involved in illegal or harmful activities.

4) Confidentiality and Privacy:

Safeguarding the privacy and confidentiality of all students, particularly gang-involved students, is paramount.

5) Escalation of Tensions:

In some instances, involving gang members may exacerbate conflicts or tensions within the school community.

In summary, involving all student leaders, including gang members, in decision-making necessitates careful planning, effective communication, and a commitment to creating a safe and inclusive environment. Schools should establish clear guidelines and protocols while genuinely valuing and considering student input in decision-making. Collaboration with experienced professionals like school counselors, social workers, and community organizations is essential to provide necessary support and resources to all involved students.

When a principal takes on the role of being out of their office and shows extreme visibility and vigilance within the school, they play a crucial role in creating a positive and safe school environment. Here are some of the key roles a principal fulfills in this context:

1) Leading by Example:

The principal's active presence and engagement throughout the school premises set a powerful example, emphasizing the importance of accessibility and involvement.

2) Impact on School Climate:

The principal's visible engagement with students, staff, and parents significantly influences the overall school climate and culture, fostering a sense of community and belonging.

3) Enhancing Safety and Security:

The principal's vigilance and visibility contribute to the school's safety and security by enabling quick identification and resolution of potential concerns.

4) Building Strong Relationships:

Regular interaction with students, teachers, and staff allows the principal to build strong relationships, trust, and rapport, creating a supportive school community.

5) Proactive Issue Resolution:

Being visible and vigilant empowers the principal to proactively address issues, such as student conflicts or behavioral concerns before they escalate.

6) Boosting Student Engagement:

The principal's presence beyond the office positively influences student engagement and motivation, reinforcing their commitment to students' well-being and education.

7) Facilitating Conflict Resolution:

Accessibility and approachability make it easier for students and staff to seek resolution and support when conflicts arise.

8) Recognizing Achievements:

The principal's visibility enables them to personally celebrate student and staff achievements, acknowledging their hard work and accomplishments.

9) Encouraging Parent and Community Involvement:

Active participation in school events and activities by the principal encourages parent and community engagement, emphasizing the importance of collaborative partnerships.

10) Monitoring Academic Support:

The principal's vigilant presence allows them to assess the effectiveness of academic programs and support initiatives, making necessary adjustments to enhance student learning outcomes.

11) Enhancing Communication:

Improved communication between school stakeholders is facilitated by the principal's presence, ensuring everyone stays well-informed about school developments and initiatives.

12) Crisis Response:

In emergencies or critical incidents, the principal's immediate availability and responsiveness play a crucial role in coordinating an effective crisis response.

Overall, when a principal demonstrates extreme visibility and vigilance outside their office, they cultivate a dynamic and supportive school environment. This reinforces their dedication to the school community's well-being, promoting unity, safety, and accountability among students, staff, and parents. A principal can incentivize students to make good choices and help keep the school safe by implementing various positive reinforcement strategies and recognition programs. The aim is to create a culture where students feel motivated to contribute positively to their school community. Here are some effective ways a principal can achieve these goals:

1) Student Recognition Programs:

Establish programs that honor and celebrate students who consistently exhibit exemplary behavior, serve as positive role models, and actively contribute to school safety and well-being. Recognitions may include awards, certificates, or public acknowledgments during school events.

2) Leadership Opportunities:

Provide responsible and trustworthy students with leadership roles, such as safety ambassadors, peer mentors, or student council members. This empowers them to take ownership and responsibility for school safety initiatives.

3) Public Praise and Commendations:

Publicly acknowledge and commend students who report safety concerns, mediate conflicts, or assist in implementing safety protocols. Highlight their actions during morning announcements or school assemblies.

4) Safety Awareness Campaigns:

Engage students in safety awareness campaigns involving activities or events that promote a secure and respectful school environment.

5) Safety Contests and Challenges:

Organize contests or challenges related to safety, where students actively participate in solving hypothetical safety scenarios or suggest safety improvement ideas. Offer rewards or incentives to winners.

6) Positive Behavior Rewards:

Implement a positive behavior reward system wherein students earn points or tokens for making wise choices. These points can be redeemed for privileges, small rewards, or special activities.

7) Safety-themed Spirit Days:

Host spirit days or themed weeks centered around safety, addressing topics like anti-bullying, kindness, or conflict resolution. Encourage students to participate and reinforce positive behavior during these occasions.

8) Safety Training Incentives:

Offer incentives to students who actively participate in safety training sessions or drills, recognizing the importance of their engagement in preparedness efforts.

9) Peer-to-Peer Recognition:

Encourage students to acknowledge their peers' positive actions related to safety and responsible decision-making through shoutouts or nomination systems.

10) Positive Reinforcement from Teachers:

Promote teachers' positive reinforcement of good behavior and safety-conscious actions in the classroom. This reinforces the significance of responsible choices in all school settings.

11) Collaborative Safety Initiatives:

Involve students in the development and implementation of safety initiatives, such as creating safety posters or participating in safety committees. This nurtures a sense of ownership and engagement.

12) School-wide Goals:

Set collective school-wide goals related to safety and positive behavior, celebrating achievements when these goals are met.

By incentivizing students to make responsible choices and actively engage in school safety endeavors, principals can cultivate a culture of accountability and active participation in upholding a safe and nurturing learning environment. Positive reinforcement and recognition play pivotal roles in motivating students to contribute to the overall well-being of the school community.

Rewarding students for promoting a safe and violence-free school environment can be an effective way to encourage positive behavior and prevent violence. Here are some specific examples of how administrators and teachers can implement reward systems:

1) Good Behavior Incentive Programs:

Establish school-wide behavior incentive programs where students receive recognition, tokens, or points for demonstrating such positive behaviors as conflict resolution skills, kindness, and respectful communication.

2) Conflict Resolution Mediation:

Train selected students as conflict resolution mediators. Students who are trained and then who successfully mediate and resolve conflicts between peers then receive special recognition or rewards for their efforts in keeping the peace.

3) Anti-Bullying Initiatives:

Recognize students who actively participate in anti-bullying campaigns or take a stand against bullying behavior. These students could receive certificates or special privileges.

4) Peer Support Programs:

Reward students who actively participate in peer support programs, mentoring younger students or aiding their peers in need.

5) Positive Referral System:

Implement a positive referral system where teachers can refer students to the principal or administrators for demonstrating exemplary behavior, leadership, or acts of kindness. The referred students could receive commendations or small rewards.

I realize that the suggestions on possible reinforcers may seem too elementary; however, you would be surprised as to how many of the below items really work with kids in high school as well.

1) Safety Ambassador Program:

Establish a safety ambassador program where students are appointed as safety leaders. Reward these ambassadors for their vigilance and efforts to promote safety within the school community.

2) Reporting Safety Concerns:

Recognize and protect students who report safety concerns or suspicious activities. Implement an anonymous reporting system, and reward students who come forward with valuable information.

3) Safety Slogan Contest:

Organize a safety slogan contest where students can create catchy and meaningful slogans promoting school safety. The winning slogan can be displayed prominently, and the student receives recognition.

4) Safety Artwork Display:

Host an art contest where students create artwork representing school safety and violence prevention. The selected artwork can be displayed throughout the school, and the winning students can receive prizes.

5) Safety Patrol Program:

Reward students who actively participate in the school's safety patrol program, assisting with traffic control or monitoring safe pedestrian behavior during arrival and dismissal times.

6) Safety Drill Participation:

Recognize students who actively and responsibly participate in safety drills, such as fire drills or lockdown drills.

7) Positive Behavior Assemblies:

Organize periodic assemblies to celebrate positive behaviors and reinforce the importance of maintaining a safe and respectful school environment. During these assemblies, students who exemplify these behaviors can be publicly recognized.

By implementing such reward systems, administrators and teachers can positively reinforce students' efforts to keep violence away from their school. These recognition initiatives contribute to building a positive school culture and encourage students to actively engage in promoting a safe and supportive learning environment.

Field trips to various locations can be a powerful incentive for students to make good choices and contribute to a safe and positive school environment. These experiences offer several benefits that can positively influence student behavior and attitudes:

1) Reinforcement of Positive Behavior:

Field trips often serve as rewards for displaying positive behavior, achieving academic milestones, or actively participating in school initiatives. By associating these experiences with good choices and responsible actions, students are motivated to maintain their positive decision-making.

2) Team-Building and Social Skills:

Field trips offer valuable opportunities for students to interact beyond the classroom environment, promoting teamwork, cooperation, and the development of social skills. These positive social interactions can extend to how students interact with one another within the school community.

3) Sense of Belonging:

Engagement in field trips fosters a sense of belonging and inclusion among students. When students feel connected to their school community, they are more inclined to take ownership of the school's safety and overall well-being.

4) Exposure to New Experiences:

Field trips expose students to new places, cultures, and activities, broadening their horizons and enhancing their global awareness. These experiences can lead to more empathetic and respectful behavior.

5) Positive Memories and Motivation:

Exciting field trips create positive memories that students associate with their school experience. This motivation to earn additional enriching experiences can serve as an incentive for them to continue making positive choices.

6) Responsibility and Accountability:

To participate in field trips, students must meet specific expectations related to behavior and academic performance. This instills a sense of responsibility and accountability in students.

7) Appreciation for the School:

Field trips can instill a greater appreciation for the school and the opportunities it offers. Students are more likely to take pride in their school environment when they hold it in high regard.

8) Relationship Building with Teachers:

Spending time with teachers in a different context, such as on a field trip, can strengthen the teacher-student relationship. This connection can positively influence how students perceive and respect their educators.

9) Positive Peer Influence:

Field trips enable students to engage with their peers in a positive and enjoyable setting. This positive peer influence can reinforce good choices and behavior.

10) Celebration of Achievements:

Field trips can be utilized as celebrations of academic accomplishments, contributions to community service, or achievements related to school safety promotion. Recognizing these accomplishments encourages students to persist in their positive efforts.

Field trips can be carefully selected to align with the school's goals and values, reinforcing the importance of making good choices and contributing to a safe and positive school environment. When used strategically, field trips can be a valuable tool for incentivizing students to take ownership of their school community's well-being and contribute positively to its success, promote a sense of calmness, and foster a sense of pride in the school community. Here's how it can influence students:

1) Stress Reduction:

Playing soothing or enjoyable music during lunchtime can effectively reduce students' stress and anxiety levels. This calming musical backdrop creates a more relaxed atmosphere, allowing students to unwind and recharge.

2) Mood Enhancement:

Music possesses the ability to influence emotions. Incorporating uplifting or positive tunes into lunchtime can elevate students' moods, fostering a more optimistic and enjoyable environment.

3) Social Connection:

Music acts as a catalyst for conversations and shared interests among students. Discussing musical preferences and engaging in conversations about favorite songs strengthens social bonds and cultivates a sense of belonging.

4) Creating a Welcoming Environment:

Music contributes to the creation of a welcoming and inclusive lunchtime setting. Diverse genres can be played to cater to various tastes, ensuring that all students feel included and valued.

5) Encouraging Creativity:

Exposure to different music styles sparks students' creativity and imagination, motivating them to explore their artistic interests.

6) School Spirit and Pride:

Playing school anthems, fight songs, or music associated with school events fosters a sense of pride and school spirit among students. This enhances their connection to the school community.

7) Rhythm and Routine:

Music during lunchtime establishes a rhythm and routine in students' daily schedules, providing a predictable and comforting element in their school day.

8) Multicultural Awareness:

Incorporating music from diverse cultures and backgrounds promotes multicultural awareness and appreciation among students.

9) Reducing Noise Levels:

Playing background music at a moderate volume effectively reduces noise levels in the cafeteria, creating a more peaceful and focused lunchtime environment.

10) Enhancing Focus:

Soft, instrumental music can aid in improving concentration and focus, benefiting students during their lunch break and subsequent afternoon classes.

It's important to give due consideration to students' preferences and sensitivities when choosing lunchtime music. Some students may prefer a quiet environment, so providing options for different areas where they can eat, including a designated "quiet space," can cater to each contingent's specific needs.

Overall, playing music during lunchtime can contribute to a positive school culture, a sense of pride, and emotional well-being among students. By creating an enjoyable and inclusive lunchtime experience, schools can foster a more conducive learning environment for students throughout the day. Perforce, the music should not reflect Rap Music that glorifies or focuses on gang violence, such as drill or trap gangster rap music.

Parent participation in walking the campus in teams to assist in student supervision can play a significant role in enhancing school safety, fostering a sense of community, and promoting positive relationships between parents, students, and school staff. Here are some key benefits of this approach:

1) Increased Supervision:

Parent volunteers offer extra eyes and ears on campus, bolstering student supervision during critical times like arrival, dismissal, and lunch breaks.

2) Improved Safety:

A greater adult presence on campus acts as a deterrent to potential safety issues and ensures faster responses in emergencies or incidents.

3) Sense of Security:

The sight of parents on campus can boost students' feelings of security and overall well-being.

4) Community Involvement:

Engaging parents in school activities nurtures a stronger sense of community and underscores the school's appreciation for and encouragement of parental participation.

5) Positive Role Models:

Parent volunteers exemplify active involvement, becoming positive role models for students and reinforcing the importance of contributing to the school community.

6) Enhanced Communication:

Parent volunteers can facilitate improved communication between school staff and parents, leading to more effective collaboration in meeting students' needs.

7) Reducing Bullying:

The presence of parents on campus can deter instances of bullying, as students are less likely to engage in negative behaviors when parents are present.

8) Positive School Climate:

Parental participation contributes to a positive school climate, fostering a culture of trust and cooperation among all stakeholders.

9) Improved Parent-Teacher Relationships:

Walking the campus together strengthens relationships between parents and teachers, promoting open communication and mutual understanding.

10) Supporting School Staff:

Parent volunteers assist with student supervision, lightening the workload for school staff and enabling teachers to focus on instructional and academic responsibilities.

11) Celebrating Achievements:

Parent volunteers can join in school celebrations and events, making these occasions more meaningful and enjoyable for students.

12) Enhanced School Culture:

Parent involvement enriches the school's culture, infusing it with vibrancy and a shared commitment to student success and well-being.

It's essential to have clear guidelines and protocols in place for parent volunteers to ensure they understand their roles and responsibilities during campus walks. This includes maintaining appropriate boundaries and adhering to school policies.

By encouraging parent participation in walking the campus, schools can create a safer and more nurturing learning environment while fostering a strong partnership between parents and school staff. This collaborative approach supports the holistic development of students and reinforces the idea that education is a shared responsibility among all members of the school community.

Being able to offer an abundance of student activities plays an indispensable role in enhancing student achievement, participation, and attendance. These activities contribute to a well-rounded and engaging school experience, providing students with numerous benefits that positively impact their academic and personal growth. Here's how student activities contribute to these aspects:

1) Increased Engagement:

Student activities provide valuable opportunities for active participation and engagement outside the traditional classroom setting. When students engage in activities, they are passionate about, they become more motivated and dedicated to their education.

2) Sense of Belonging:

Joining clubs, sports teams, or other extracurricular groups nurtures a sense of belonging and connection within the school community. This feeling of belonging enhances overall satisfaction with the school experience and reduces feelings of isolation.

3) Skill Development:

Student activities enable students to develop a diverse set of skills, including leadership, teamwork, time management, communication, and problem-solving.

4) Confidence Building:

Participation in activities contributes to the development of self-confidence and self-esteem among students. This newfound confidence positively influences their academic performance and willingness to take on new challenges.

5) Improved Attendance:

Engaging and enjoyable student activities act as incentives for regular school attendance. Students are more likely to attend school when they anticipate participating in activities, they are passionate about.

6) Academic Improvement:

Involvement in extracurricular activities has been correlated with enhanced academic performance. Engaged students tend to refine their time management skills and demonstrate a higher level of commitment to their studies.

7) Social Skills:

Through participation in student activities, students can interact with peers from diverse backgrounds, fostering the development of essential social skills. This can lead to improved interpersonal relationships and a more positive school climate.

8) Stress Reduction:

Student activities serve as constructive outlets for stress and academic pressures, contributing to overall well-being and mental health.

9) College and Career Readiness:

Involvement in student activities enhances a student's readiness for college or career pursuits, as it showcases their commitment to personal growth and community involvement.

10) Sense of Pride:

Student activities instill a sense of pride in students for their achievements and contributions to the school community. This reinforces their identity as valued members of the school.

11) Positive School Culture:

A wealth of student activities fosters a vibrant and positive school culture, cultivating enthusiasm for learning and active engagement among students.

12) Long-lasting Memories:

Participating in student activities creates enduring memories of the school experience, nurturing positive associations with the learning environment.

Schools that offer a diverse range of student activities cater to different interests and talents, ensuring that all students have opportunities to get involved and thrive. By supporting and encouraging student engagement in activities, schools can create an enriching and rewarding educational experience that goes beyond academics and positively influences various aspects of students' lives.

Transferring older students in the ninth grade to Continuation School and Adult School can have several positive effects on school safety and a productive school climate. Here are some potential benefits:

1) Age-Appropriate Environment:

Continuation School and Adult School are purposefully designed to provide older students with an environment that suits their unique academic and social needs. This tailored setting promotes a more focused and conducive learning atmosphere.

2) Reduced Peer-Related Issues:

Segregating older students into separate school settings can effectively diminish potential conflicts and peer-related issues with younger students. This, in turn, contributes to a more harmonious and respectful school climate.

3) Tailored Instruction:

Continuation School and Adult School often excel in delivering individualized instruction tailored to meet the specific learning needs of older students. This customized approach enhances student engagement and academic progress.

4) Better Support Services:

These alternative schools frequently offer specialized support services, such as counseling and academic assistance, which play a vital role in helping older students overcome academic and personal challenges.

5) Increased Accountability:

By enrolling in schools specifically designed for their age group, older students may experience a heightened sense of accountability for their actions and academic performance. This instills a greater sense of personal responsibility.

6) Improved Attendance:

Placing older students in schools that align better with their needs and interests tends to result in improved attendance rates and reduced incidents of truancy.

7) Focused Learning Environment:

Continuation School and Adult School typically boast smaller and more focused academic and vocational programs, allowing older students to channel their energy into their studies.

8) Reduced Disruptions:

The separation of older students into distinct schools often leads to fewer disruptions in the classroom, creating a more conducive learning environment that benefits all students.

9) Personalized Transition Plans:

These alternative schools are well-equipped to develop personalized transition plans for older students, guiding them toward academic success, graduation, or post-secondary education and training opportunities.

10) Enhanced Safety Measures:

With a more concentrated student population, staff at these schools can implement targeted safety measures and provide tailored support to address individual student needs effectively.

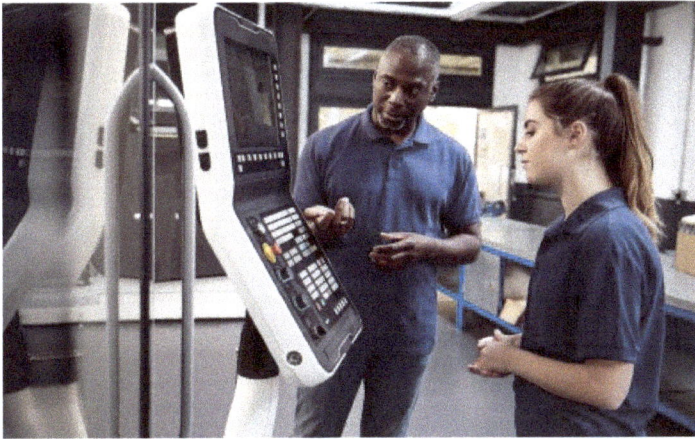

It's important to consider individual student circumstances and needs when making these decisions. Not all older students may benefit from transferring to alternative schools, and some may thrive in traditional settings with appropriate support and accommodations. Additionally, schools should ensure that Continuation School and Adult School have the necessary resources and programs to meet the diverse needs of their older student population.

A thoughtful, deliberate approach to transferring older students to alternative schools can lead to improved school safety, a more productive school climate, and increased opportunities for academic success and personal growth.

Schools must prioritize the integration of career and educational courses that align with emerging job trends in fields like artificial intelligence, STEM (Science, Technology, Engineering, and Mathematics) research, technology, healthcare, and other rapidly evolving industries. This emphasis on preparing students for future employment is crucial as it equips them with the necessary skills and knowledge to thrive in a swiftly changing world. Here's a breakdown of why this focus is of utmost importance:

1) Relevance and Real-World Application:

Schools enhance students' interest and engagement by including future-focused careers and educational courses, making learning more relevant and applicable to their lives.

2) Job Market Demands:

Preparing students for fields such as AI, technology, healthcare, and STEM research aligns their skills with the evolving job market, ensuring their readiness for employment.

3) Technological Advancements:

Incorporating relevant courses helps students grasp and adapt to the latest tools and technologies, keeping them up-to-date with ongoing advancements.

4) Global Competitiveness:

Education must meet the demands of the changing job landscape to keep students competitive on a global scale, ensuring they can thrive in diverse work environments.

5) Closing the Skills Gap:

Emphasizing future careers helps bridge skills gaps in industries facing shortages of qualified professionals, contributing to a more skilled workforce.

6) Job Diversity:

Focusing on diverse future careers exposes students to a wide array of opportunities, allowing them to explore their passions and interests across various fields.

7) Social and Economic Impact:

Preparing students for future roles enables them to positively influence society and contribute to economic growth in meaningful ways.

8) Innovation and Creativity:

Future careers often require creative and innovative thinking. Integrating related courses nurtures these essential skills among students.

9) Interdisciplinary Learning:

Fields like AI, healthcare, and technology often demand interdisciplinary approaches. Including these subjects promotes interdisciplinary learning and fosters problem-solving skills.

10) Long-Term Planning:

Education should encompass not only immediate job prospects but also students' long-term career trajectories, promoting a lifelong commitment to learning and adaptability.

11) Collaboration with Industry:

Emphasizing future careers can lead to valuable partnerships with relevant industries, offering students real-world experiences and access to industry expertise.

12) Career Guidance:

Schools can provide targeted career guidance and counseling by introducing students to potential future careers, assisting them in making informed decisions about their educational and career paths.

It's essential for schools to strike a balance between preparing students for future careers and providing a well-rounded education that includes the arts, humanities, social sciences, and critical thinking skills. By doing so, schools can ensure students are equipped not only for specific jobs but also for a lifetime of learning, adaptability, and success.

Schools should consider incorporating financial literacy and practical money management skills into their curriculum to empower students with essential knowledge for their future financial well-being. While the level of emphasis may vary depending on the school's resources and priorities, teaching these skills is crucial for several reasons:

1) Real-World Relevance:

Financial literacy skills hold direct relevance to students' daily lives.

Learning about investing, budgeting, and money management equips them with vital skills for making financial decisions as adults.

2) Financial Independence:

Equipping students with money management skills encourages financial independence and cultivates responsible financial behavior.

3) Long-Term Financial Security:

Teaching investment strategies and financial planning contributes to students' long-term financial security and prepares them for retirement planning.

4) Consumer Awareness:

Understanding financial concepts empowers students to become informed consumers, enabling them to make wise financial choices.

5) Entrepreneurship:

Introducing entrepreneurship and business skills stimulates innovation and empowers students to explore potential career paths in the business world.

6) Economic Understanding:

Financial literacy provides a foundation for a broader understanding of economic principles and how financial markets operate.

7) Risk Management:

Learning about insurance, investments, and financial risk equips students to make informed decisions to protect themselves and their assets.

8) Reduced Debt and Financial Stress:

Financial literacy can lead to reduced student debt and improved personal finance management, resulting in lower financial stress.

9) Empowerment:

By teaching money management skills, schools empower students to take control of their financial futures, fostering self-reliance and responsibility.

10) Lifelong Skills:

Financial literacy is a lifelong skill that students will carry with them into adulthood and throughout their careers, ensuring they can navigate various financial situations effectively.

11) Addressing Financial Inequalities:

Providing financial education helps bridge gaps in financial knowledge and contributes to economic empowerment for all students, addressing financial inequalities.

12) Parental Engagement:

Financial literacy education can extend to parents and caregivers, fostering a community-wide focus on financial well-being and strengthening family financial practices.

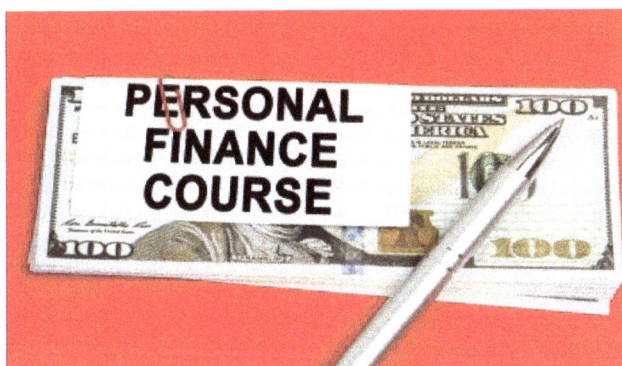

While the level of focus on financial literacy may vary across schools, it's essential for educators to consider age-appropriate curriculum content and teaching methods. Financial literacy education can be integrated into existing subjects, such as mathematics, social studies, or home economics, to ensure a comprehensive approach. Schools can also partner with financial institutions or local organizations to provide additional resources and support for financial education initiatives.

Overall, incorporating financial literacy skills in the curriculum helps prepare students for economic challenges and opportunities they will encounter in their personal and professional lives.

Young men should develop self-confidence and a sense of responsibility, believing they can provide for their families. Young women, too, should acquire financial literacy, enabling them to contribute to family well-being when coupled with a partner. Therefore, it is imperative for schools to integrate financial literacy and practical money management skills into their curriculum. While the extent of emphasis may differ based on a school's resources and priorities, teaching these skills holds critical importance for the following reasons:

1) Real-World Relevance:

Financial literacy skills hold direct relevance to students' daily lives. They encompass essential knowledge about investing, budgeting, and money management, preparing students for informed financial decision-making as they transition into adulthood.

2) Financial Independence:

Equipping students with money management skills nurtures financial independence and encourages responsible financial behavior.

3) Long-Term Financial Security:

The instruction of investment strategies and financial planning contributes to students' long-term financial security and prepares them for retirement planning.

4) Consumer Awareness:

A grasp of financial concepts empowers students to become well-informed consumers, enabling them to make judicious financial choices.

5) Entrepreneurship:

Introducing entrepreneurship and business skills not only fosters innovation but also empowers students to explore diverse career paths.

6) Economic Understanding:

Financial literacy widens students' comprehension of economic principles and the intricacies of financial markets.

7) Risk Management:

Learning about insurance, investments, and financial risk equips students with the knowledge to make informed decisions safeguarding their assets and financial well-being.

8) Reduced Debt and Financial Stress:

Financial literacy can alleviate student debt burdens and enhance personal financial management, leading to reduced financial stress.

9) Empowerment:

By imparting money management skills, schools empower students to take charge of their financial futures, cultivating self-reliance and responsibility.

10) Lifelong Skills:

Financial literacy is a skill that accompanies students throughout their lives, benefiting them in both personal and professional contexts.

11) Addressing Financial Inequalities:

Providing financial education helps bridge gaps in financial knowledge, contributing to economic empowerment for all students, regardless of their background.

12) Parental Engagement:

Extending financial literacy education to parents and caregivers fosters a community-wide focus on financial well-being and responsible financial practices.

While the level of focus on financial literacy may vary across schools, it's essential for educators to consider age-appropriate curriculum content and teaching methods. Financial literacy education can be integrated into existing subjects, such as mathematics, social studies, or home economics, to ensure a comprehensive approach. Schools can also partner with financial institutions or local organizations to provide additional resources and support for financial education initiatives. Overall, incorporating financial literacy skills in the curriculum helps prepare students for economic challenges and opportunities they will encounter in their personal and professional lives.

Setting: Centennial High School hallways during passing period

As the school bell rings, students rush through the hallways to get to

their next classes. The atmosphere is bustling and energetic. Principal Gilliam stands at a central point in the hallway, holding a bullhorn. Assistant Principal Mr. Martinez is nearby, observing the situation.

Principal Gilliam: (using bullhorn) Good morning, Centennial High! Just a reminder, you have 12 minutes between classes. Make sure you're in your seats by the time the bell rings. Let's start this period strong!

The students hurriedly continue on their way, some exchanging smiles as they pass Principal Gilliam.

Mr. Martinez: (to Principal Gilliam) It's impressive how quickly this program has caught on. The students seem to be responding positively.

Principal Gilliam: Absolutely. We've seen a significant improvement in students' punctuality and the overall discipline on campus since we started this initiative.

As the passing period comes to an end, the bell rings for the start of the next class.

Students are in class not wandering around on campus and in the hallways.

By the time the bell rings. Let's avoid any unnecessary consequences.

Students hustle to their classrooms, making sure to get to their seats before the bell rings.

Scene Transition: Inside a Classroom

The scene shifts to a classroom where students are taking their seats just as the bell rings.

Teacher: Good morning, everyone. Great job getting here on time. Let's make the most of this class.

Scene Transition: Courtyard Area

In the school's courtyard, there are no students lingering around. The area is clean and quiet, with students either heading to class or engaging in conversations in an orderly manner.

Student 1: Have you heard about the new hall sweep program? They're really strict about getting to class on time now.

Student 2: Yeah, I heard. I don't want to risk getting detention, so I'm making sure I'm in my seat before the bell rings.

Scene Transition: Principal Gilliam's Office

Later in the day, Principal Gilliam and Mr. Martinez discuss the program's impact.

Mr. Martinez: The hall sweep program has made a remarkable difference, Mr. Gilliam. The students are more punctual, and the campus feels more organized.

Principal Gilliam: It's been incredible to witness. Our students are now equipped to better understand the importance of time management and accountability.

Mr. Martinez: And the disciplinary measures have proven effective too. The threat of detention or suspension has encouraged them to be on time.

Principal Gilliam: Our main goal is to create a focused and respectful environment for learning. I'm glad the students are taking this initiative seriously.

The two administrators share a satisfied nod, knowing that their efforts to instill discipline and responsibility in the students have yielded successful results.

Note: The scene described above depicts the implementation of a hall sweep program at Centennial High School. The program aims to ensure that students are in class on time before the bell rings, promoting punctuality and discipline. Principal Gilliam and Mr. Martinez observe the positive impact of the program, leading to a more organized and focused school environment. Students respond by doing their best to be on time, and the disciplinary measures associated with the program are proven effective in maintaining the desired behavior.

Setting: The bustling school campus during passing period.

Mr. Gilliam is standing near the entrance, keeping an eye on students. As students rush to their next classes, Mr. Gilliam notices a male black student who doesn't appear to be part of the school's student body. The student is riding a bicycle through the campus.

Mr. Gilliam: (firmly) Excuse me, young man. Are you a student at Centennial High School?

Male Black Student: (stops his bicycle) Nah, I ain't no student. Just passin' through.

Mr. Gilliam: I'm sorry, but this campus is for our students. I'm going to have to ask you to leave immediately.

The male black student looks at Mr. Gilliam with defiance.

Male Black Student: Man, I ain't leavin'. Who you think you are?

Mr. Gilliam: I'm the principal of this school, and I have the responsibility to ensure the safety and security of our students. You're not allowed to be here.

School Resource Officer Johnson approaches the scene, aware of the situation.

SRO Johnson: Everything okay here, Mr. Gilliam?

Mr. Gilliam: We have a non-student on campus. I've asked him to leave.

Male Black Student: (getting confrontational) I said I ain't goin' nowhere. This my hood too. **Mr. Gilliam:** This campus is for our students. If you're not a student here, you have no reason to be on our property.

SRO Johnson: Sir, I need to ask you to leave the campus immediately. If you refuse, we'll have to escort you off the premises.

Male Black Student: (angry) You think you can tell me what to do? I'll show you!

The male black student picks up his bicycle and holds it above his head in a threatening manner.

Male Black Student: I'll bash your head in with this if you don't get outta my way, Principal!

Mr. Gilliam: (calmly but assertively) Put the bicycle down. I'm not here to escalate anything. But I won't stand for threats or violence on this campus.

SRO Johnson: (positioning himself) Sir, if you don't put the bicycle down and leave, we'll have to take appropriate action.

Mr. Gilliam: (directly to the student) Listen, I understand there might be frustrations, but we won't tolerate violence here. I'm asking you one last time: put the bicycle down and leave the campus peacefully.

The student hesitates for a moment, then lowers the bicycle.

Male Black Student: Fine, whatever. Y'all ain't worth my time.

The male black student turns and walks away, pushing his bicycle.

SRO Johnson: Thank you for handling that, Mr. Gilliam. You did the right thing.

Mr. Gilliam: Our students' safety comes first. We can't allow anyone to disrupt that.

Students who had been watching the exchange from a distance look on with a mixture of awe and respect.

Student 1: Did you see that? Mr. Gilliam's fearless!

Student 2: He stood up to that guy without backing down. That was impressive.

Note: The above scene portrays an encounter where Mr. Gilliam, the principal, confronts a male black student who is not part of the student body and is riding a bicycle on the school campus. Despite this outsider's threats, Mr. Gilliam remains firm and unyielding in ensuring the campus remains safe for students. With the support of the School Resource Officer, they manage to deescalate the situation and encourage the intruder to leave peacefully. The scene reflects Mr. Gilliam's commitment to maintaining a secure and respectful environment for the students, even in the face of potential danger.

> **Setting:** Mr. Gilliam's office, where he meets with Frank, a gang member recommended to him for a potential positive role.

Frank enters Mr. Gilliam's office, his demeanor a mix of curiosity and apprehension. Mr. Gilliam welcomes him with a friendly but serious expression.

Mr. Gilliam: Thank you for coming in, Frank. Have a seat. I wanted to talk to you about something important.

Frank: (nervously) Yeah, sure. What's this about, Mr. Gilliam?

Mr. Gilliam: I've heard a lot about you, Frank. You have influence with the Piru Bloods, right?

Frank: Yeah, I'm part of that, but I ain't no leader or anything.

Mr. Gilliam: Well, I'm interested in your potential as a leader. You see, I have an idea that could benefit both the school and your community.

Frank: (confused) Benefit? How?

Mr. Gilliam: I want to see positive changes in our school environment, Frank. I've noticed graffiti on the school grounds, especially in the bathrooms. It's not a good look, and it doesn't reflect the pride we should have in our school.

Frank: Yeah, I get that. But what's it got to do with me?

Mr. Gilliam: I'd like to enlist your help, Frank. I believe you have the influence and respect among your gang members. I want you to lead them in a positive direction.

Frank: (surprised) You want me to do what?

Mr. Gilliam: I'd like you to work with your gang members to paint murals over the areas that are usually covered in graffiti. Turn that negative energy into something creative and uplifting. Show that your gang can make a positive impact.

Frank: (thoughtful) Murals? I mean, that's different. But why?

Mr. Gilliam: I want to develop pride in our school and our community. I want students to walk into our bathrooms and see beautiful artwork that represents their school, not mindless tags. I believe in the potential of our students, and you can help lead the way.

Frank: And what's in it for us? What's the catch?

Mr. Gilliam: The catch is that we're all part of this community. If we work together, we can create an environment that we're all proud of. In return, I'll work with you and your gang to address concerns and help keep outsiders off our campus. Your gang can play a positive role in ensuring the safety and well-being of our students.

Frank: This is some unexpected stuff, Mr. Gilliam.

Mr. Gilliam: I know it might seem unusual, but sometimes unexpected alliances can lead to remarkable changes. Will you consider my proposal, Frank?

Frank: (pauses) Yeah, I will. Let me talk to my guys, see what they think. I'll let you know.

Mr. Gilliam: That's all I ask, Frank. Let's work together to make a difference, not just for us, but for the future of this school and community.

Note: The above scene portrays a conversation between Mr. Gilliam and

Frank, a gang member with influence. Mr. Gilliam discusses his idea of enlisting Frank's help in leading his gang members to create positive changes in the school environment, including painting murals over graffiti and maintaining campus security. The scene reflects Mr. Gilliam's determination to improve the school and foster community pride while also showing how unexpected alliances can lead to positive transformation.

Scene: Mr. Gilliam's Office at Centennial High School

Characters:

Mr. Gilliam - Principal

Frank - Gang Member

Setting: Mr. Gilliam's office, where he meets with Frank, a gang member recommended to him for a potential positive role.

Frank enters Mr. Gilliam's office, a mix of curiosity, skepticism, and wariness in his eyes. Mr. Gilliam greets him with a welcoming smile, sensing the tension in the air.

Mr. Gilliam: Frank, thank you for coming in. Have a seat. I wanted to discuss something with you, something that could potentially make a significant impact on our school and community.

Frank: (guarded) Alright, Mr. Gilliam. What's this all about?

Mr. Gilliam: I've heard quite a bit about you, Frank. About your involvement with the Piru Bloods and your influence among your peers.

Frank: Yeah, well, I'm just one of many, you know?

Mr. Gilliam: That's true, but it's precisely that influence that I'm interested in. I believe that a leader, even in unconventional circumstances, can drive positive change.

Frank: (raising an eyebrow) Positive change? In what way?

Mr. Gilliam: Let's talk about the graffiti that's been appearing on our school grounds, especially in the bathrooms. It's a constant battle to remove it, and it creates a negative atmosphere. But imagine if those walls were covered in murals, vibrant artwork that speaks to the pride we should all have in our school.

Frank: Murals? That's different, I'll give you that.

Mr. Gilliam: I want to harness the power of your influence, Frank. I want you to lead your peers, your gang members, in transforming those graffiti-ridden spaces into works of art that represent the unity and strength of your community.

Frank: (thoughtful) Unity? Strength? You really think we can do that?

Mr. Gilliam: I absolutely believe in your potential, Frank. You have a chance to show your gang's positive impact, not just in art but in our school's culture.

Frank: And what's the school offering in return? Why should we care?

Mr. Gilliam: Good question. The school, me included, wants to work with you to address your concerns, your needs. We'll be allies in creating a safe environment for all students. And those murals you create? They'll be a reminder of what your gang can achieve when you focus on uplifting your community.

Frank: The bathrooms... they're terrible, to be honest. It's like no one cares.

Mr. Gilliam: That's exactly what I want to change. By turning these spaces into something beautiful and meaningful, we're making a statement that we care, that we're invested in our school.

Frank: This ain't what I expected coming in here.

Mr. Gilliam: Sometimes unexpected partnerships can lead to remarkable outcomes. Will you consider being a part of this positive change, Frank?

Frank: Yeah, I'll talk to my guys about it. If we're gonna do this, we'll do it right.

Mr. Gilliam: That's all I ask, Frank. Let's work together to prove that we can create something extraordinary.

Note: The elaborated scene continues the conversation between Mr. Gilliam and Frank, a gang member. Mr. Gilliam discusses his vision of transforming graffiti-laden spaces into vibrant murals and harnessing Frank's leadership and influence for positive change. The dialogue delves into the reasons behind the proposal, the potential benefits for both parties, and the idea of unity and pride in the community. The scene showcases the careful negotiation and possibility for unexpected alliances to bring about meaningful transformation.

Scene: Centennial High School, Mr. Gilliam's Office

Setting: Mr. Gilliam's office, where he meets with Mrs. Ahmed, a concerned parent who is part of the Muslim community. Mrs. Ahmed enters Mr. Gilliam's office, a warm smile on her face. Mr. Gilliam rises from his desk, extending his hand in a welcoming gesture.

Mr. Gilliam: Welcome, Mrs. Ahmed. Thank you for taking the time to meet with me. Please, have a seat.

Mrs. Ahmed: Thank you, Mr. Gilliam. I appreciate the opportunity to discuss something important with you.

Mr. Gilliam: Of course, I'm here to listen and work together to ensure the safety and well-being of our students. What's on your mind?

Mrs. Ahmed: Well, Mr. Gilliam, I've been thinking about the safety of our school. There have been instances of outsiders, particularly rival gang members, coming onto campus and causing disruptions. I'm concerned about the safety of our children.

Mr. Gilliam: I share your concern, Mrs. Ahmed. The safety of our students is a top priority for us.

Mrs. Ahmed: In my community, we believe in being proactive when it comes to security. I was wondering if we could organize a group of Muslim parents and students to walk the perimeter of the school during certain times to deter outsiders from entering.

Mr. Gilliam: (thoughtful) That's an interesting proposal, Mrs. Ahmed. I appreciate your willingness to be involved in the safety of our school. It's not about your religious background; it's about concerned parents taking action to protect their children.

Mrs. Ahmed: I'm glad you understand, Mr. Gilliam. We're all part of this community, and we want to contribute positively.

Mr. Gilliam: I fully support parents' involvement in ensuring a safe environment for our students. Having a visible presence can be a powerful deterrent. And if it fosters a sense of unity and cooperation among different backgrounds, that's a wonderful bonus.

Mrs. Ahmed: Thank you for being open-minded about this, Mr. Gilliam.

Mr. Gilliam: Of course, Mrs. Ahmed. We're all working toward the same goal - a safe and nurturing environment for our students. Your proposal aligns perfectly with that mission.

Mrs. Ahmed: So, would it be possible to organize these walks? We can work with our community to schedule regular patrols.

Mr. Gilliam: Absolutely. Let's collaborate on a plan. I'll work with you to coordinate the times that would be most effective. We can even involve other concerned parents from different backgrounds if they're interested.

Mrs. Ahmed: That sounds wonderful, Mr. Gilliam. I believe that together, we can make a positive impact.

Mr. Gilliam: I have no doubt about that, Mrs. Ahmed. Your involvement and concern are invaluable to our school community.

Mrs. Ahmed: Thank you for your understanding and support, Mr. Gilliam.

Mr. Gilliam: Thank you for your dedication to our students' safety. Let's move forward together to create a safer environment for everyone.

Note: The scene portrays a conversation between Mr. Gilliam and Mrs. Ahmed, a Muslim parent, discussing her proposal to organize a group of parents and students to walk the school perimeter as a safety measure. Mr. Gilliam expresses appreciation for her concern and willingness to participate, emphasizing that safety is a shared goal that transcends religious background. The scene highlights collaboration and unity among parents from diverse backgrounds for the greater good of the school community.

> **Setting:** Staff meeting in the school's conference room at Centennial High School, where Mr. Gilliam addresses the incident and its impact. The staff meeting is in session, the atmosphere tense as teachers and staff sits around the conference table. Mr. Gilliam stands at the front, addressing the room.

Mr. Gilliam: Thank you all for being here today. I understand that last year was incredibly challenging for us as a school community. The incident along Central Avenue was a stark reminder of the challenges we face regarding safety.

Ms. Johnson: (softly) It was truly terrifying. Bullets flying, chaos everywhere. We had to take cover in our classrooms.

Mr. Gilliam: I know, Ms. Johnson. It was a traumatic experience for all of us - teachers, staff, and most importantly, our students. I want to acknowledge the fear and concern that this incident has left us with.

Mrs. Remy: And it's not just about us. The students were genuinely scared. Many transferred out to find a safer environment.

Mr. Gilliam: That's right. Our primary responsibility is to provide a safe learning environment for our students. The fact that they felt unsafe here is deeply troubling.

Mr. Hamm: What are we doing to prevent something like that from happening again?

Mr. Gilliam: We're taking this incident as a wake-up call. I've been working with law enforcement, district officials, and our security team to enhance our safety protocols. We're investing in better surveillance, improving communication systems, and coordinating with local law enforcement for quick responses.

Ms. Johnson: What about counseling and support for those who were directly affected by the incident?

Mr. Gilliam: We've implemented counseling services for both students and staff who were affected. Trauma support is crucial, and we want everyone to have the resources they need to cope and heal.

Dr. Weinstein: (concerned) What about our own safety during such incidents? We need a plan.

Mr. Gilliam: Absolutely. We're conducting drills and training sessions to ensure that everyone knows their roles in emergencies. Our teachers, staff, and students need to be prepared to respond effectively.

Ms. Johnson: It's going to take more than just protocols and drills. We need to rebuild a sense of security and trust in our school.

Mr. Gilliam: You're absolutely right, Ms. Johnson. It's not just about procedures; it's about fostering an environment where everyone feels safe and supported.

Ms. Kelley: What can we do to help with that? How can we reassure students and each other?

Mr. Gilliam: We're working on initiatives to promote a sense of community and safety. We'll have open forums, meetings with students and parents to address their concerns, and we'll continue to involve law enforcement and community leaders in our efforts.

Ms. Johnson: It's going to take time, but I'm glad we're addressing this head-on.

Mr. Gilliam: It won't be easy, but we're in this together. Our commitment to our students' well-being is unwavering.

Staff Members: (in agreement) We're with you, Mr. Gilliam.

Note: The scene takes place during a staff meeting where Mr. Gilliam addresses the shooting incident that occurred near the school and its impact on staff and students. The dialogue revolves around the staff's concerns, their reactions to the incident, and the steps being taken to enhance school safety and rebuild trust within the school community. It emphasizes the importance of collaboration, communication, and support in creating a secure and nurturing environment for everyone.

Setting: Mr. Gilliam's office, where a staff meeting is held to discuss ongoing issues affecting the school environment.

The staff meeting continues, with Mr. Gilliam at the head of the table and staff members seated around.

Mr. Gilliam: I appreciate all of you being here today to discuss the various challenges we're facing at Centennial. It's clear that the violence and vandalism we are witnessing are urgent matters that demand our attention, but we must also address the other issues that contribute to the negative atmosphere in our school.

Mr. Rodriguez: (with frustration) That's right, Mr. Gilliam. We can't ignore the daily verbal abuse, the chaos in the hallways, and the disrespect some students show towards teachers and staff.

Ms. Thompson: It's disheartening. We're here to educate and support these students, and yet some of them treat us like we're the enemy.

Mr. Gilliam: I completely understand your frustrations. Every educator deserves respect and a safe working environment. We can't let these challenges overshadow our commitment to providing quality education.

Ms. Kelley: But what can we do about it? It feels like we're constantly putting out fires without addressing the root causes.

Mr. Gilliam: You're right. We need a multi-pronged approach. First, we need to strengthen our disciplinary measures. Consistency is key. We should work together to establish clear consequences for disruptive behavior and enforce them uniformly.

Ms. Rodriguez: And we should involve parents in this process too. If we had their support, it could make a significant difference.

Mr. Gilliam: Precisely. I'm planning on organizing meetings with parents to address these concerns and collaborate on solutions. Their involvement is crucial for creating a positive school culture.

Ms. Remy: But what about the vandalism? Last week, your car was targeted, Mr. Gilliam. How can we ensure our safety and protect our property?

Mr. Gilliam: It's deeply concerning, I know. We're working on enhancing security measures, including installing cameras in the parking lots. We're also involving local law enforcement to patrol the area during school hours.

Ms. Thompson: I appreciate those efforts, Mr. Gilliam. It's important for us to feel safe at school, not just physically but emotionally too.

Mr. Gilliam: Absolutely. We can't effectively teach and support our students if we're constantly worried about our well-being. I want you all to know that your concerns are valid, and I'm committed to making necessary changes.

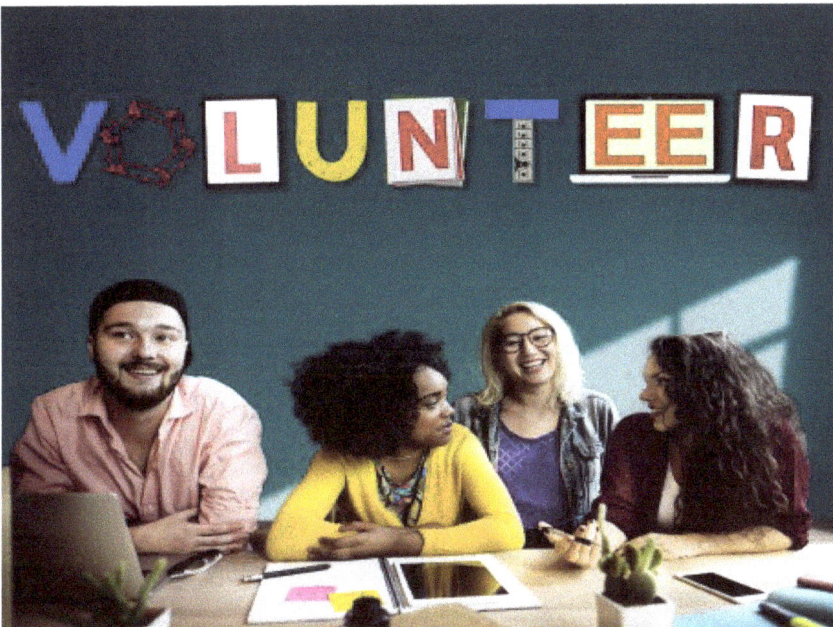

Mr. Rodriguez: It's good to hear that, Mr. Gilliam. We need to work together to create a positive environment for both students and staff.

Mr. Gilliam: You're all vital to our school's success. Let's collaborate on solutions, communicate openly, and ensure that Centennial becomes a place where both teaching and learning thrive.

Note: The scene portrays a staff meeting where Mr. Gilliam addresses the challenges of verbal abuse, hallway chaos, and vandalism faced by the staff. The dialogue emphasizes the importance of consistent discipline, involving parents, enhancing security measures, and fostering a positive school culture. The conversation reflects a collective commitment to creating a safe and supportive environment for both students and staff.

Scene: Mr. Gilliam's Home - Evening

Characters:

Mr. Gilliam – Principal,

Lark - Mr. Gilliam's Wife,

Robin - Mr. Gilliam's Daughter

Setting: Mr. Gilliam arrives home after a challenging day at the school, seeking comfort and support from his family.

Mr. Gilliam enters his home, the weight of the day evident on his face. He's met by his wife, Lark, and daughter, Robin, in the living room.

Lark: (concerned) Edward, you look exhausted. How was your day?

Mr. Gilliam: (with a sigh) It was one of those days, Lark. The challenges at school seem to be escalating. Mr. Gilliam embraces Lark and Robin tightly, seeking solace in their presence.

Robin: Daddy, are you okay? You look upset.

Mr. Gilliam: I'm fine, sweetheart. Just a lot on my mind. Lark holds Mr. Gilliam's face gently, looking into his eyes.

Lark: Edward, you know we're here for you. Whatever you're facing, we're in this together.

Mr. Gilliam: (softly) I know, Lark. It's just... The threats, the violence, the constant pressure. I worry about the safety of the students and staff.

Robin: What can we do to help, Dad?

Mr. Gilliam: (smiling) The fact that you are here, asking that question, is already a tremendous support. But we're facing some tough decisions to make the school safer.

Lark: You've always been the one to find solutions, Edward. What do you think needs to be done?

Mr. Gilliam: (reflecting) First, we need to replace that wire fence with a sturdy rod iron fence. We must secure the entrances and exits, have visible security patrols, and install cameras throughout the campus. Discipline also needs to be firm and consistent.

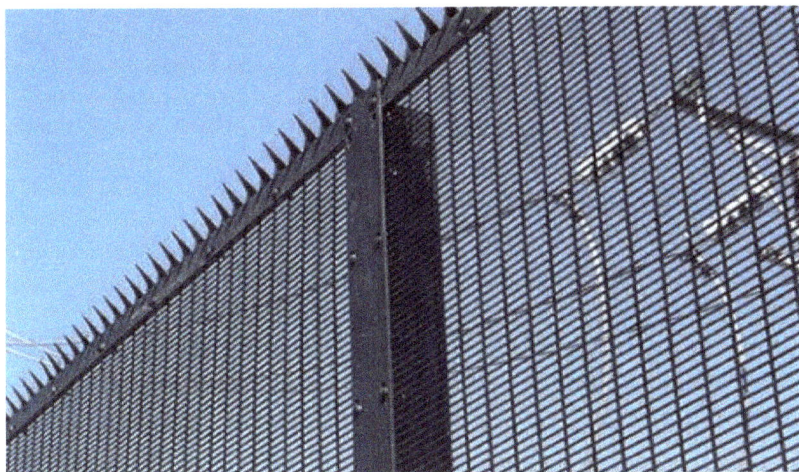

Robin: Are you worried about the threats you've been receiving?

Mr. Gilliam: It's a concern, Robin. But I can't let fear dictate my actions. I need to focus on what's right for the school and its community.

Lark: We stand by you, Edward. Whatever decisions you make, we're with you every step of the way.

Mr. Gilliam: I'm grateful for that, Lark. These challenges won't be easy to overcome, but with the support of my family, my staff, and the community, we can make a positive change.

Robin: And don't forget, you're a strong leader, Dad. You'll find a way.

Mr. Gilliam: Thank you both. Your faith in me means the world.

Lark, Mr. Gilliam, and Robin share a moment of unity, reminding each other of the strength they have as a family.

Note: The scene portrays a touching moment where Mr. Gilliam seeks comfort and support from his wife, Lark, and daughter, Robin, after a challenging day at school. The dialogue highlights the family's unity, their willingness to stand by him, and Mr. Gilliam's determination to address the safety challenges at the school.

Scene: Centennial High School - Administrative Office

Characters:

Mr. Gilliam - Principal

Security Team - Officers Johnson, Martinez, and Williams

Administrators - Ms. Rodriguez and Mr. Thompson

Setting: Administrative office at Centennial High School, where Mr. Gilliam addresses the security team and administrators.

Mr. Gilliam gathers the security team and administrators in the office, a stern expression on his face.

Mr. Gilliam: Thank you all for being here. I want to address a critical issue we're facing regarding campus security and administrative presence.

Security Officers and Administrators exchange glances, sensing the seriousness of the situation.

Mr. Gilliam: It's come to my attention that our security team isn't as visible and proactive as we need them to be. And I believe the administrative team can also play a more active role on campus.

Officer Johnson: Mr. Gilliam, we do our best to ensure safety, but...

Mr. Gilliam: (interrupting, firmly) Officer Johnson, I'm not here to assign blame. I'm here to discuss a new approach to improve the safety and atmosphere of our school.

Ms. Rodriguez: And what approach would that be?

Mr. Gilliam: Effective immediately, I'm redefining the roles of our security team and administrators during school hours. Security officers will no longer have an office to sit in. Instead, you'll be patrolling the halls and the entire campus, ensuring visibility and vigilance.

Officer Martinez: That's a significant change, Mr. Gilliam.

Mr. Gilliam: Yes, it is. But our students and staff deserve a safe and secure environment. You'll each receive walkie-talkie radios so that communication between us is seamless. I want to know where you are at all times during the school day.

Officer Williams: Understood, Mr. Gilliam.

Mr. Gilliam: As for the administrators, our focus needs to shift. Administrative work can be done after school hours. During the school day, I expect you to be out on the campus, interacting with students and staff.

Ms. Rodriguez: Does that mean...

Mr. Gilliam: Yes, Ms. Rodriguez. No more retreating to your office. Our students need to see our presence, our commitment.

Mr. Thompson: But paperwork...

Mr. Gilliam: Will be done after 3 O'clock. Our priority is the well-being and safety of our school community. We need to be visible, engaged, and responsive.

Officer Johnson: This is a bold change, Mr. Gilliam.

Mr. Gilliam: Bold, but necessary. We're in this together, and I believe this shift in approach will make a significant difference.

Officer Martinez: We're on board, Mr. Gilliam.

Ms. Rodriguez: Count me in too.

Mr. Thompson: Agreed.

Mr. Gilliam: Thank you all. Let's work together to create an environment where everyone feels safe and supported.

Note: The scene depicts a meeting where Mr. Gilliam addresses the security team and administrators, outlining a new approach to enhance campus security and administrative presence. The dialogue emphasizes the importance of visibility, vigilance, and active engagement to ensure the safety and well-being of the school community.

Scene: Centennial High School - Assistant Principals' Office

Characters:

Mr. Gilliam - Principal

Assistant Principal 1 - Ms. Ramirez

Assistant Principal 2 - Mr. Anderson

Setting: Assistant Principals' office, where Mr. Gilliam is addressing the assistant principals regarding a decision to remove certain students from the 9th grade.

Mr. Gilliam enters the assistant principal's office, a determined expression on his face. Ms. Ramirez and Mr. Anderson are seated at their desks.

Mr. Gilliam: Good morning. I've come to a decision that I believe is necessary for the betterment of our school community.

Ms. Ramirez: Good morning, Mr. Gilliam. What decision are you referring to?

Mr. Gilliam: I've decided that we need to remove over 500 students from the 9th grade who are 18, 19, and 20 years old. They're causing significant disruption and challenges on our campus.

Mr. Anderson: Remove them? Where will they go?

Mr. Gilliam: I want them transferred by the end of the week. I want the cumulative files of these students on my desk, ready to be transferred to either continuation school, adult school, or out of the district. These students are creating more problems than they're here to learn.

Ms. Ramirez: (concerned) Mr. Gilliam, this is a substantial decision. We need to ensure that we follow proper protocols and consider the students' individual situations.

Mr. Gilliam: I understand the gravity of this decision, but we cannot let a small percentage of students disrupt the education and safety of the majority. This action will send a clear message that we're committed to a positive learning environment.

Mr. Anderson: What if some of them genuinely want to learn and improve?

Mr. Gilliam: We need to consider the greater good of our school. For those who want to learn, they'll have opportunities in continuation school or adult school. Our responsibility is to safeguard the well-being of all students and staff.

Ms. Ramirez: (hesitant) Understood, Mr. Gilliam. We'll start the necessary procedures immediately.

Mr. Gilliam: Thank you. I know this isn't an easy decision, but it's essential for the progress of Centennial High.

Mr. Anderson: We'll do our best to ensure a smooth transition for everyone involved.

Mr. Gilliam: That's what I expect. Let's work together to create an environment where all students can thrive.

Note: The scene portrays a meeting between Mr. Gilliam and the assistant principals, where he informs them of his decision to remove over 500 9th-grade students who are 18, 19, and 20 years old. The dialogue highlights the challenges and concerns surrounding the decision, as well as Mr. Gilliam's determination to prioritize the overall well-being of the school community.

Scene: Inner City Community

Characters:

Luis - Latino Student

Jamal - Black Student

Ms. Rodriguez - School Counselor

Maria - Luis's Mother

Tyrone - Jamal's Older Brother

Setting: An inner-city neighborhood, where Luis and Jamal live. The scene depicts their challenges and interactions with school personnel and family members.

Luis and Jamal are sitting on a stoop, deep in conversation.

Luis: Man, it's tough out here. My mom's been struggling to find work, and our apartment is falling apart.

Jamal: I feel you, Luis. My brother got caught up in that gang violence last year, and things ain't been the same since.

Luis: (sighs) And school... It's hard to focus when you're hungry or stressed about what's happening at home.

Ms. Rodriguez, the school counselor, approaches them.

Ms. Rodriguez: Hey, Luis, Jamal. How are you guys doing?

Jamal: Just trying to get by Ms. Rodriguez.

Ms. Rodriguez: I know it's tough, but remember, your education can be your way out of these challenges.

Luis's mother, Maria, walks over.

Maria: Luis, I've been trying to find work, but it's been tough. And the hot water isn't working again. I'm sorry.

Luis: (softly) It's okay, Mom. We'll figure it out.

Jamal's older brother, Tyrone, joins the conversation.

Tyrone: Jamal, I've been looking out for you, little bro. But it's hard when jobs are scarce and the streets ain't safe.

Jamal: I know, Tyrone. I just want things to get better.

Ms. Rodriguez: We're here to support you both. Remember, you're not alone. There are resources and people who care about your future.

Luis: It's just frustrating, you know? We want to succeed, but it feels like the odds are stacked against us.

Jamal: Yeah, we want a better life, but it's hard when there's so much going on around us.

Ms. Rodriguez: I understand your frustration. But don't underestimate your resilience and strength. Your stories matter, and we're working to create an environment where you can thrive.

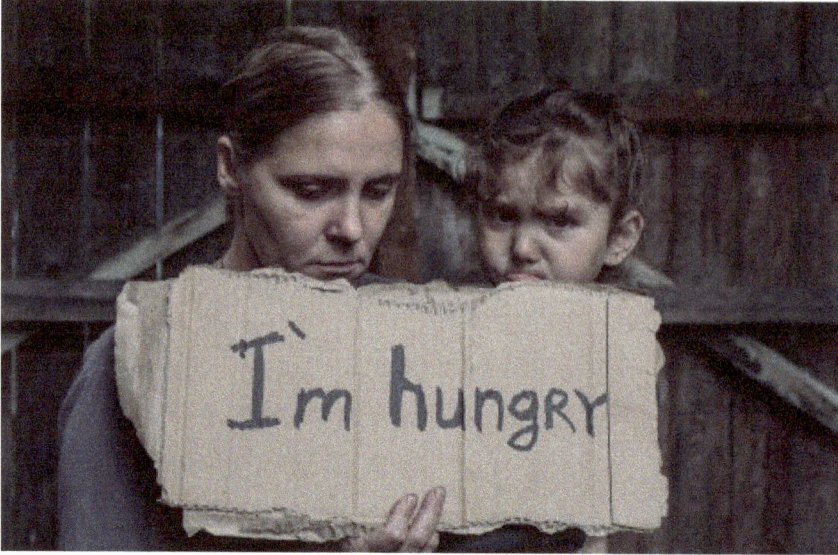

Maria: (teary-eyed) Thank you for caring about our kids, Ms. Rodriguez.

Tyrone: Yeah, we need all the support we can get.

Ms. Rodriguez: We're in this together. Let's work together to overcome these challenges and create a brighter future for everyone.

Note: The scene portrays a conversation between Luis, Jamal, Ms. Rodriguez, Maria, and Tyrone, highlighting the challenges faced by Black, White and Latino students in the inner city. The dialogue emphasizes the difficulties related to poor housing, family violence, financial struggles, and lack of parental education. The school counselor's presence represents the supportive role that educators play in understanding and addressing these complex issues.

Scene: Centennial High School - Principal's Office

Characters:

Mr. Gilliam - Principal

Assistant Superintendent Cynthia Greer

Setting: Principal's office at Centennial High School, where Mr. Gilliam and Assistant Superintendent Cynthia Greer have a conversation about Mr. Gilliam's busy schedule and decisions at the school.

Mr. Gilliam is at his desk, reviewing documents and making notes. Assistant Superintendent Cynthia Greer enters the office.

Cynthia Greer: (with a concerned tone) Good afternoon, Mr. Gilliam. I hope you're well.

Mr. Gilliam: Afternoon, Ms. Greer. I'm keeping busy, as you can imagine.

Cynthia Greer: I can see that. Mr. Gilliam, I wanted to talk to you about a few matters.

Mr. Gilliam: Of course, what's on your mind?

Cynthia Greer: First, I'd like to commend you for the remarkable turnaround you've achieved at Centennial High. Your dedication is evident, and the school is on the right track.

Mr. Gilliam: Thank you, Ms. Greer. It's been a team effort.

Cynthia Greer: Absolutely. Now, I wanted to discuss the conference in Sacramento. I believe it could be beneficial for you to attend and network with other educators.

Mr. Gilliam: I appreciate the suggestion, but with the amount of work here, I'm afraid I won't be able to make it.

Cynthia Greer: (slightly frustrated) Mr. Gilliam, I understand the workload, but professional development is crucial too.

Mr. Gilliam: I understand the importance, but my priority is the school and its community. I can't afford to be away right now.

Cynthia Greer: Very well. Moving on, there's the matter of the security team's office. I've received feedback that they need their space back.

Mr. Gilliam: I understand, but having them visible and patrolling is more important. We can't afford to have them sitting in an office all day.

Cynthia Greer: (raising an eyebrow) I've also heard some concerns about your working hours, Mr. Gilliam. You're here from 5 am till midnight, even on weekends?

Mr. Gilliam: It's what's necessary to ensure the school's success. These hours are a testament to the dedication of my staff and myself to creating a safe and productive environment.

Cynthia Greer: I appreciate your dedication, but burnout is a concern. You need to take care of yourself as well.

Mr. Gilliam: I understand your concern, Ms. Greer. But until we're in a better place, I can't afford to slow down.

Cynthia Greer: Just remember, Mr. Gilliam, maintaining balance is essential for long-term success.

Mr. Gilliam: I'll keep that in mind, Ms. Greer.

Note: The scene depicts a conversation between Mr. Gilliam and Assistant Superintendent Cynthia Greer regarding Mr. Gilliam's busy schedule, his decision not to attend a conference, and the security team's office. The dialogue emphasizes Mr. Gilliam's commitment to the school's success and the challenges he faces in managing his time effectively.

Scene: Community Meeting

Characters:

Mr. Gilliam - Principal

Community Members - Maria, Tyrone, Luis, Jamal

Ms. Rodriguez - School Counselor

Setting: A community meeting hall, where concerned citizens, including Mr. Gilliam, Ms. Rodriguez, and community members, gather to discuss the challenges faced by students and the cycle of violence and dysfunction.

The meeting hall is filled with concerned community members. Mr. Gilliam stands at the front, addressing the crowd.

Mr. Gilliam: Thank you all for being here today. We're facing a monumental challenge that affects the lives of our children and our community.

Maria, Tyrone, Luis, and Jamal sit among the audience, nodding in agreement.

Mr. Gilliam: The cycle of violence, disengagement from education, and the sinking into drugs and crime is a harsh reality for many of our youth.

Ms. Rodriguez: (standing up) We're here to break that cycle. Our students are not statistics; they are the future of this community.

Maria: It's true. Our children deserve better than this cycle of despair.

Tyrone: Our schools should be places of hope, not breeding grounds for chaos.

Jamal: We need a way out of this mess.

Mr. Gilliam: I couldn't agree more. Our children are products of their environment. We need to provide them with the tools, guidance, and support they need to rise above their circumstances.

Ms. Rodriguez: Education is a key to breaking this cycle. We need to show them that there's a way forward through learning and self-improvement.

Luis: And we need positive role models. Too many of us have grown up without them.

Mr. Gilliam: That's why I'm here, and that's why each of us must be actively involved. We can't turn a blind eye to the challenges our students face.

Maria: It starts with strong leadership in our schools. We need administrators who are committed to safety and education.

Tyrone: And we, as a community, need to step up. We can't just blame the schools. We need to support our children and hold them accountable.

Jamal: We also need opportunities. Jobs, mentorship programs, after-school activities – things that keep us engaged positively.

Mr. Gilliam: Exactly. Our schools should be safe havens, places where children can learn and grow without fear.

Ms. Rodriguez: Together, we can change this narrative. It won't be easy, but it's possible.

Maria: Let's break this cycle for our children's sake.

Community Members: (in unison) Yes!

Mr. Gilliam: Thank you all for your passion and dedication. Let's work together to build a brighter future for our community.

Note: The scene depicts a community meeting where Mr. Gilliam, Ms. Rodriguez, and community members discuss the challenges faced by students and the cycle of violence and dysfunction. The dialogue emphasizes the need for collective effort, positive role models, education, opportunities, and strong school leadership to break the cycle and create a better future for the youth and the community.

Scene: Community Forum

Characters:

Mr. Gilliam - Principal

Community Members - Maria, Tyrone, Luis, Jamal

Ms. Rodriguez - School Counselor

Dr. Johnson - Community Activist

Setting: A community forum, where concerned citizens, including Mr. Gilliam, Ms. Rodriguez, community members, and Dr. Johnson, discuss societal challenges and the need for educational initiatives to address them.

The community forum is in session, with a diverse group of attendees. Mr. Gilliam stands at the front, addressing the crowd.

Mr. Gilliam: Thank you all for joining us today. We're here to have an open dialogue about the societal challenges we face and how education can be a catalyst for change.

Community members nod in agreement, and Dr. Johnson stands up to speak.

Dr. Johnson: Indeed, we can't ignore the harsh realities that exist within our communities. Mass shootings, family instability, and educational disparities are pressing issues.

Ms. Rodriguez: Education plays a critical role in breaking these cycles. We need to empower our youth with knowledge that can steer them away from destructive paths.

Maria: Teen pregnancy and single-parent households are prevalent concerns. Our schools must provide comprehensive education on relationships, contraception, and family planning.

Tyrone: And we need to address the lack of positive role models for young men. Many are vulnerable to gangs and violence due to a lack of guidance.

Jamal: Education is the way out. We need programs that expose us to different industries and careers, giving us hope for a better future.

Dr. Johnson: We must engage successful individuals from various industries as mentors. Young men need to see that there are alternatives to gangs and violence.

Mr. Gilliam: Exactly. Our schools should offer life skills, financial literacy, and character development. It's about preparing our students for a successful and responsible adulthood.

Ms. Rodriguez: It's also important to provide a safe space for open discussions. Let's break the stigma around mental health and teach students how to cope with stress and challenges.

Dr. Johnson: Schools can be the catalyst for change, but we need the support of the entire community. Government, businesses, families – we must all work together.

Maria: And we need to address the economic disparities. Education alone isn't enough if families are struggling to make ends meet.

Tyrone: Our schools can partner with community organizations to provide resources like job training, access to affordable housing, and financial assistance.

Jamal: We need a holistic approach. Education isn't just about academic subjects; it's about preparing us for life.

Mr. Gilliam: Thank you all for sharing your insights. Let's continue this dialogue and work collaboratively to create a brighter future for our communities.

Note: The scene depicts a community forum where Mr. Gilliam, Ms. Rodriguez, community members, and Dr. Johnson discuss societal challenges and the role of education in addressing them. The dialogue emphasizes the need for comprehensive education, mentorship, economic support, and community collaboration to break cycles of violence, family instability, and educational disparities.

CONCLUSION

Based on the discussions and insights provided above, I believe that the following are some key steps that schools, and various levels of government should consider taking to address the challenges related to gang violence, mass shootings, education, family dynamics, and community support:

For Schools:

1. Comprehensive Curriculum:

Develop a comprehensive curriculum that addresses not only academic subjects but also life skills, mental health, relationships, financial literacy, and conflict resolution.

2. Mentorship Programs:

Establish mentorship programs where successful individuals from various industries engage with students, providing guidance, role models, and insights into alternative paths to success.

3. Community Engagement:

Collaborate with community organizations to provide resources such as job training, housing assistance, and support for families in need.

4. Counseling and Mental Health Services:

Offer accessible and stigma-free counseling and mental health services to help students cope with stress, challenges, and emotional well-being.

5. Parental Engagement:

Facilitate workshops and resources for parents, focusing on effective parenting techniques, communication, and family support.

6. Alternative to Gangs:

Provide extracurricular activities, clubs, and programs that offer positive outlets for creativity, teamwork, and skill-building, as alternatives to gang involvement.

7. Career and Life Skills:

Integrate practical skills such as resume writing, job interview preparation, and budgeting into the curriculum to prepare students for real-world challenges.

For Local and State Governments:

1. Funding and Resources:

Allocate sufficient funding and resources to schools in disadvantaged communities, ensuring they have the necessary tools for effective teaching and student support.

2. Community Partnerships:

Foster partnerships between schools, community organizations, law enforcement, and businesses to create a network of support for students and families.

3. Youth Employment Programs:

Create opportunities for part-time jobs, internships, and apprenticeships to empower young people and provide them with valuable work experience.

4. Affordable Housing:

Collaborate with housing agencies to ensure that families have access to affordable housing, reducing the impact of unstable living conditions on education.

5. Community Centers:

Establish community centers that offer after-school programs, vocational training, and recreational activities for youth, creating safe spaces for growth.

For Federal Government:

1. Education Reform:

Advocate for educational reform that prioritizes equity, teacher training, and the development of modern curricula, tailored to meet the specific needs of diverse communities.

2. Mental Health Support:

Allocate funding for school-based mental health services and provide training for educators to recognize and address mental health challenges among students.

3. Parental Support Programs:

Invest in initiatives that offer parenting education, family counseling, and support programs to strengthen family dynamics and increase parental involvement in education.

4. Job Training Initiatives:

Establish federal programs dedicated to providing job training and skill development opportunities for young individuals, equipping them for a competitive job market.

5. Youth Mentorship:

Create national mentorship initiatives connecting successful professionals with young people to serve as sources of inspiration and guidance.

6. Research and Data Collection:

Invest in research efforts aimed at identifying the underlying causes of issues such as violence, dropout rates, and family challenges, using the findings to inform the development of effective policies.

As of August 27, 2023, when this manuscript was written, there has been no change in the frequency of mass shootings and gang violence. Unfortunately, another tragic incident occurred in Jacksonville, Florida, serving as a somber reminder of the potential for violence in unexpected places. On that fateful day, the peace of a dollar store was shattered by an individual who had carefully armed himself, resulting in a devastating loss of lives. The events that unfolded and the subsequent response from law enforcement shed light on the complex challenges faced by authorities and the community.

According to reports, the shooter obtained body armor from a nearby college before carrying out the act at the dollar store. The premeditated nature of the crime, with the shooter taking the time to plan and protect himself, raises disturbing questions. Did he intend to maximize harm and prolong the standoff with law enforcement? Or did he anticipate resistance and prepare accordingly? These unsettling questions demand answers to understand the depth of this tragedy.

Jacksonville, a city with a substantial police and Sheriff's Department, responded swiftly to the incident, despite the toll on human lives. The integration of city and county law enforcement agencies into a single metropolitan department underscores the need for a coordinated and efficient response to such incidents.

The shooter's motives, actions, and fate also highlight the complexities of police work in such circumstances. The uncertainty surrounding whether the shooter took his own life or was subdued by law enforcement adds further ambiguity to the already disturbing situation. If confirmed, the involvement of a sniper raises ethical and tactical questions about the use of force. Balancing the public's demand for transparency with the sensitivity of victims' families and the integrity of an ongoing investigation is a challenging task.

The response to the incident extended beyond local law enforcement, as the FBI quickly joined the investigation. Federal agencies' involvement underscores the gravity of the incident and the commitment to uncovering the truth. Categorizing the incident as a hate crime reflects the recognition that such acts of violence target not only individuals but also entire communities.

In the aftermath of such an event, communities unite in mourning and reflection. The tragedy in Jacksonville serves as a stark reminder that violence can strike anywhere, affecting us all. It underscores the urgency of preventing such incidents, whether through mental health support, addressing societal factors contributing to violence, or strengthening gun control measures.

While we await further details from the press conference and the ongoing investigation, our focus must remain on the lives lost and the families forever impacted by this violence. It reminds us that despite preparation and law enforcement expertise, we must strive to better understand the factors that lead to such acts and work collectively to prevent them.

The urgency of addressing gun violence cannot be understated, and the methodologies I used to deal with gang violence serve as a reminder that progress requires unity and collaboration. The discussions surrounding gun violence prevention go beyond political divides; they speak to the shared values of protecting lives and communities. Americans can come together to address complex challenges, even amidst differing viewpoints. On a sobering note, the segment highlighting the commercial promotion of a child-sized assault rifle, even if satirical, underscores the gravity of the gun violence issue. Such absurd marketing strategies shock the collective conscience and highlight the incongruence between the need for gun safety and the irresponsible distribution of firearms. The message here is clear: society must prioritize measures to protect lives over profits and ensure the safety of vulnerable communities.

In conclusion, it is hoped that the ideas and recommendations in this book serve as a beacon of hope and an urgent call for change in the realm of gun violence prevention. With total community involvement, participation, and advocacy, the imperative of enacting effective gun safety laws both at the state and federal levels must be given top priority. As communities continue to grapple with the devastating effects of gun violence, it is incumbent upon lawmakers, activists, and citizens alike to unite, collaborate, and push for the comprehensive solutions that will save lives and build safer schools and communities for all.

The topic of fatherhood and its impact on social issues, especially within the African American community, demands thoughtful consideration due to its complexity and significance. The points presented here underscore the importance of family structure, economic incentives, and systemic factors in comprehending the challenges faced by various American communities.

Central to this argument is the assertion that the breakdown of intact nuclear families, particularly the absence of fathers, significantly contributes to social problems. The data presented highlight a concerning statistic: a significant number of black children grow up in households without fathers. Research has consistently shown correlations between absent fathers and adverse outcomes for children, including higher rates of crime, school dropout, and incarceration.

Providing historical context by discussing Lyndon Johnson's policies and the War on Poverty sheds light on the government's role in shaping social dynamics. The shift towards incentivizing women to rely on government support and men to shirk their financial responsibilities has contributed to the destabilization of family structures. It's essential to recognize that these policies might not have aimed at promoting fatherlessness but rather to aid struggling families.

Furthermore, discussing the disparity in crime rates among racial groups, with a focus on black communities, highlights the pivotal role of absent fathers in these higher crime rates. While family dynamics and socioeconomic conditions certainly influence crime rates, we must also consider other systemic factors, such as limited access to quality education, economic opportunities, and adequate healthcare. These factors contribute to a cycle of poverty and crime.

This perspective also addresses systemic racism and its impact on the black community. While progress has been made, systemic racism persists and impedes the advancement of African Americans. This point is contentious, as some argue that the historical legacy of racism continues to affect socioeconomic opportunities and outcomes for marginalized communities.

The discussion of the Black Lives Matter movement and its impact on the black community introduces a nuanced perspective. While there are criticisms of the movement, including its stance on the nuclear family and the political affiliations of its founders, it's crucial to recognize that the movement's goals extend to addressing systemic racism and police brutality. Disagreement exists even within the black community regarding the movement's effectiveness and direction. Addressing systemic issues requires a comprehensive approach that considers historical context, economic factors, cultural influences, and policy-related considerations. While emphasizing the role of family structure in shaping outcomes is valid, it's equally vital to consider broader societal factors contributing to disparities.

In conclusion, the absence of fathers in households is a multifaceted issue with profound consequences. While it's legitimate to stress the significance of family structures and individual responsibility, it's essential to balance this perspective with an understanding of systemic factors, including historical context, economic opportunities, and racial disparities. Engaging in open and empathetic dialogues about these issues is critical to finding solutions that can uplift families and communities for generations to come. We must unite as a community, including our schools, to set a positive example for the rest of the nation and the world, steering away from the cycle of gang violence and mass shootings that harm our students and our community. It is imperative in my mind that preventing gang violence and mass shootings starts in the home with fathers being an integral part of the family. With that said I end with the following poem that will hopefully shape policies at the local, state, and federal levels that support this most critical component sorely lacking in our society:

A FATHER'S VALUE

In a world of change, where shadows drift and lift, one truth remains, a constant, like a gift. Children, in their innocence, so tender, Yearn for fathers' love, pure and warm and tender.

Research speaks, its voice, unwavering, clear, Father absence breeds troubles, we must fear. A public health challenge, it stands today, an issue we must face without delay.

In the intricate web, consequences weave, from father absence, darkness seeks to thieve. Children suffer, their hearts and minds in strife, without their fathers, they seek for light in life.

Bob Griffin's words, a clarion call to heed, "The father deficit," it's time we pay heed. A staggering count, 18.4 million souls growing without fathers, their stories take their toll.

Research, a tapestry of wisdom grand, Fatherhood's role, we must understand. Children thrive when fathers are engaged, they say, in their presence, love and strength hold sway.

Father absence isn't mere data on a chart, It's a wound in the soul, a pain, a heavy heart. Mental anguish, substance's cruel embrace, A cycle of despair, a never-ending race.

Mothers, too, bear burdens not their own, with father gone, they face the unknown. Stress and strain, their weary hearts do bear, while seeking to provide love, solace, and care.

A present father, a beacon shining bright, Guiding through the storms, the darkest night. Teaching justice, fairness, duty's call, in their presence, children stand tall.

Interwoven threads, a tapestry of time, Father absence casts a shadow, a somber rhyme. Identity and bonds, they may not find, Loneliness and isolation, a heavy bind.

Yet, in the face of darkness, let us not despair, for fathers' love can lighten burdens, make us dare. Together we must strive, our purpose clear, to heal the wounds of father absence, draw near.

In the symphony of life, let's change the key, Support fathers, break the chains and set them free. For in their presence, futures can be bright, A world where love and hope take flight.

Society, too, bears the heavy cost, of father absence, a battle often lost. Risky paths, academic woes untold, the price we pay is more than gold.

Different fathers, different lives they lead, Economic woes or choices, diverse indeed. Tailored strategies, support that's just, to help them be the fathers they can trust.

Predictors of absence, pathways intertwined, Socioeconomic status, culture combined. We must create a world where fathers stand, with tools and love, to hold their children's hand.

So let us heed this call, both far and wide, in father's love, let our children's hearts confide. For in the presence of fathers, we shall find, A brighter future for all of humankind.

African American History Assembly

Awards Assembly

Compton Court House Judges working with Compton High Students and Staff and Principal Edward Gilliam

Compton Court House Judges working with Compton High Students and Staff and Principal Edward Gilliam

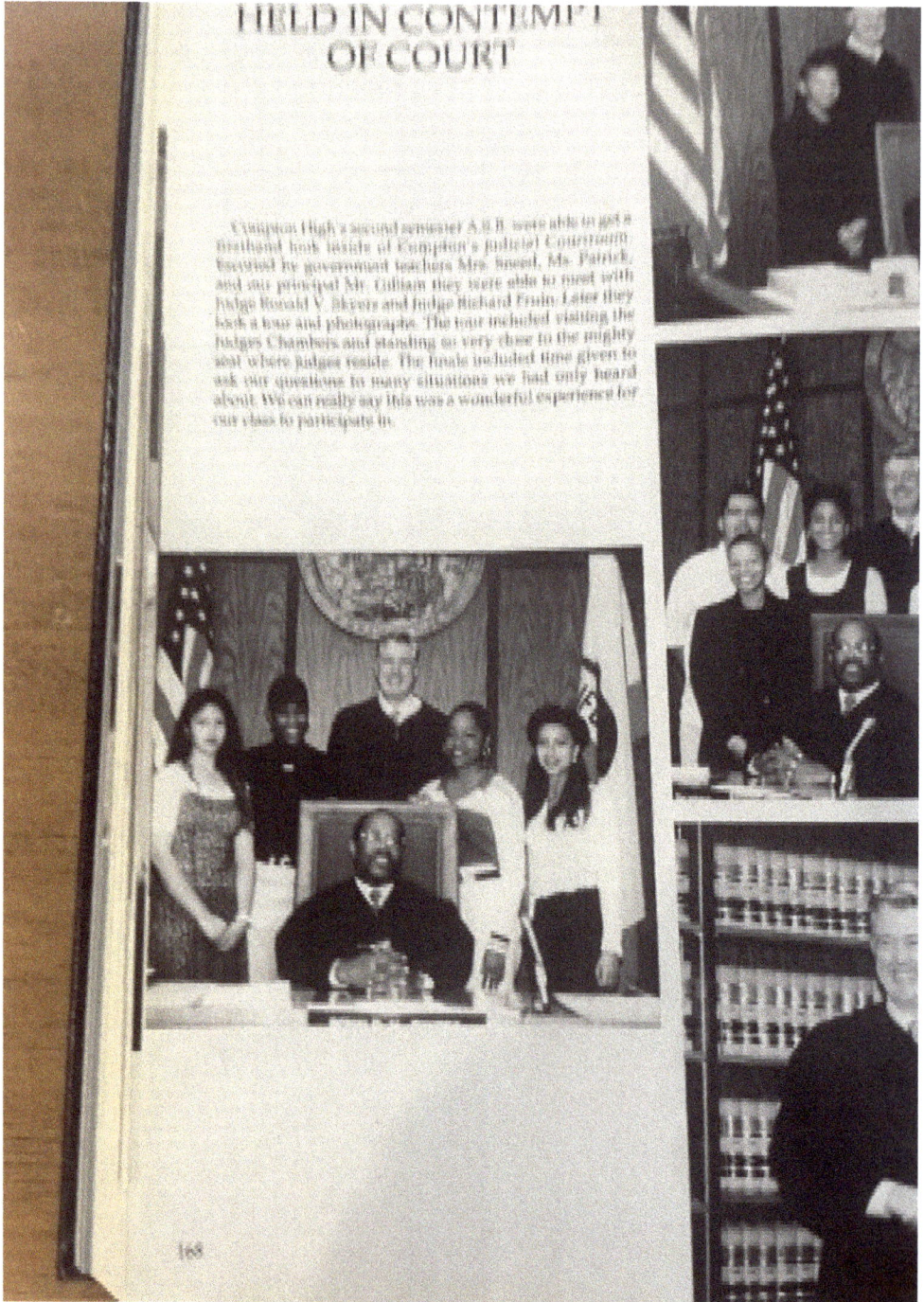

Compton Court House Judges working with Compton High Students and Staff and Principal Edward Gilliam

COMPTON HIGH

148

CENTENNIAL HIGH

SPIRIT OF CENTENNIAL

Who are the driving forces behind our great Apache Spirit? Why are the Pep assemblies filled with such high energy? Give credit to the Apache Band, the Centennettes, the choir, the DJ Crew, and the Cheerleaders for they keep the good times rollin'.

Although we watch them perform and see how much spirit they have, it's not easy and takes a lot of hard work, practice, and dedication to fill our school with harmony and rhythm.

Not only do they fill Centennial with spirit, but they are so outstanding that they were asked to march in the Rose Bowl Parade and the openings of several businesses. Let the Apache Spirit continue to be #1 in Compton and in the world!

Cheerleaders Juakisha Turner, Tiana McDowell and Latisia Ma...

Band in Action

ADMINISTRATORS

Principal's Message

This year (1992-93) has been a very exciting school year. I'm very proud of you. You have demonstrated again that Centennial High School certainly is a school which has excelled in a number of areas. Our goals this year were to continue to reduce the drop out rate, improve attendance, improve on our standardized test scores, graduate more seniors, to teach you a sense about being responsible citizens and to expand your knowledge about our global society.

We produced a School Accountability Report Card that showed, for the second year in a row, that Centennial has the highest attendance rate compared to the other high schools in the district.

You have shown the community, teachers, and the entire district that the Apaches are certainly a group of students who will be able to compete successfully in the world market. Competition makes people perform. Throughout this year, I have challenged you to accomplish and overcome many difficult goals. You have performed and you've chosen the difficult and your efforts have been very successful.

The Apache tradition is characterized by a multitude of people and alumni who have achieved greatness. Some of your alumni include judges, politicians, brain surgeons, doctors, lawyers, Olympic gold medalists, humanitarians, writers, reporters, entertainers, actors, actresses, and successful athletes who are not only rich and famous in America, but who have made their mark all over this world.

I hope you will always continue to compete. Never give up. Strive for high and higher goals and always use your time wisely. Keep the faith and stay alive with it. Apaches, go forth and continue the rich tradition of your Apaches forever.

Mr Gilliam talks with Mr Calvin during lunch.

279

PSAC

The Principals Student Advisory Council (PSAC) mirrors our campus. It consists of students from different ethnic groups and various organizations—from class officers to gang members.

The purpose of PSAC is to prevent campus disruptions before they happen. PSAC members meet with Mr Gilliam often because they have found the problem before it happens often cuts down on a lot of disturbances on campus" said Davon Fowler, a PSAC member.

Mr Gilliam and Mr O Montgomery are the PSAC advisors. Mr Gilliam emphasizes to Apaches that are in the PSAC and also to those that are not, to always come to him if you know of a problem in the making.

Marco Contreras designs wall.

Miguel Padilla, Daniel Lopez—teamwork

Artists at Work

ese photos reflect different pro-
s that Apaches have been creating
ing the school year under the di-
ion of Mr. Flynn. Apaches contin-
take pride in our school as they
te murals that dazzle our eyes. We
you for your artistic excellence.

Vincent Miller "What's flying on my back?"

www.ingramcontent.com/pod-product-compliance
Lightning Source LLC
Chambersburg PA
CBHW041602260326
41914CB00011B/1351